THE ATHEIST SYNDROME

John P. Koster, Jr.

Wolgemuth & Hyatt, Publishers, Inc.
Brentwood, Tennessee

The mission of Wolgemuth & Hyatt, Publishers, Inc., is to publish and distribute books that lead individuals toward:

- A personal faith in the one true God: Father, Son, and Holy Spirit;

- A lifestyle of practical discipleship; and

- A worldview that is consistent with the historic, Christian faith.

Moreover, the company endeavors to accomplish this mission at a reasonable profit and in a manner which glorifies God and serves His Kingdom.

Unless otherwise noted, all Scripture quotations are from the New King James Version of the Bible, copyrighted 1984 by Thomas Nelson, Inc., Nashville, Tennessee.

Wolgemuth & Hyatt, Publishers, Inc.
P.O. Box 1941, Brentwood, Tennessee 37027
Printed in the United States of America

Library of Congress Cataloging-in-Publication Data

Koster, John P., 1945–
    The atheist syndrome / John P. Koster, Jr. — 1st ed.
        p. c.m.
    Bibliography: p.194
    ISBN 0-943497-33-7
        1. Atheism — Controversial literature. 2. Materialism — Controversial literature.
I. Title.

BL2747.3.K675   1988   88-27469
211'.8 — dc19   CIP

Ψυχη—
Νυνι δε μενει πιστις, ελπις, αγαπη,
τα τρια ταυτα· μειζων δε τουτων η
αγαπη.

1 Corinthians 13:13

CONTENTS

ACKNOWLEDGMENTS

M y father taught me a love of reading—and of argument. My mother taught me an affection for people. My wife taught me that even sane and normal people can incorporate intuitive and spiritual experiences into their everyday lives without being unbalanced. All these lessons played a primary role in shaping this book.

Beyond these three primary influences, it is necessary, for the sake of space, to limit my acknowledgments to the people who actually helped in the production of the manuscript itself. Before going on to this list though, I have to remember many friends, especially Dorothy Allison and the late Jean May, whose lives are and were a dynamic refutation of atheistic materialism.

Dr. Ian Stevenson, M.D., whom I believe will one day be remembered as the greatest psychiatrist and perhaps the greatest scientist of our era, took time out from an incredibly busy schedule to correspond with me several times. Dr. Stevenson's clinically documented and statistically evaluated work forms the solid base of a pyramid for my own theorizing, though I don't expect him to accept one shred of the blame for any mistakes I may have made. His comments, particularly on Darwin and on Freud, helped sharpen my chapters on both men.

Dr. Norman Vincent Peale, the dean of mainstream Protestant evangelists, also took time from a busy schedule to encourage me in the early stages of this project and to endorse the concept for the book. I was greatly heartened by his interest, impressed by his graciousness, and thoroughly impressed that a gentleman then eighty-eight years old would so easily assimilate such a seemingly radical idea and comment on it so astutely—and on such short notice.

John Lofton encouraged my work and put me in touch with Dr. Magnus Verbrugge, M.D., whose works and personal correspondence provided significant information for two of the chapters in the book. Dr.

Verbrugge's book *Alive: An Enquiry into the Origin and Meaning of Life,* while somewhat demanding for the layman in biochemistry and physiology, is a masterpiece and should be more widely read—and its implications better understood.

Ron Stepneski broke into a hectic newspaper publication schedule to send me information so I could complete a chapter on my own self-imposed deadline. He also encouraged me to think of myself as a serious writer when we were both starting our careers in journalism together. We've bailed one another out more times than either of us can remember. His professional but favorable criticism of the pamphlet that first expressed the ideas in this book was astute and immensely encouraging.

Schuyler Grant, who also provided an extremely valuable constructive criticism of the original pamphlet, provided me with rare insights into the lifestyles of Victorian women and the influence this had on their behavior. She also jogged my memory about the evidence provided by embryonic development for interspecies development, and reminded me to concentrate on explaining that spiritual events can be viewed in the context of cross-cultural and empiric facts as well as reinforcements for specific theologies. She also inspired me to believe that the ideas in this book may be taken to heart by a generation of college and senior high school students who often "see through" materialist dogma much more easily than my generation did.

Michael Hyatt and George Grant of Wolgemuth & Hyatt, Publishers literally made this book possible, through encouragement, advice, and editing which turned ideas into reality. The fact that this book exists at all is due largely to their trust in my probity. To them, to all the others listed above, and to my children, Emily and Johnny, who gave me the huge slabs of free time I needed to write this book by running interference for me and taking over my share of the household chores, my sincere thanks.

PART ONE

THE SYNDROME'S SYMPTOMS

ONE

AN IDEA WHOSE TIME IS GONE

Since men and women first began to think, they have always asked themselves three questions more important than all others.

Is the universe ruled by law or by chance?

What is the right way to live?

Where do we go when we die?

In Greek and Roman times, men and women who believed in a universe ruled by law, the brotherhood of humanity, and a life after death were known as *Stoics*. Those who believed in a universe of blind cosmic chance, avoidance of pain and cultivation of pleasure as the good life, and the extinction of the soul at death were known as *Epicureans*. The debate between those two opposing philosophies has marked the history of ideas being found in Judaism, in medieval Islam, and in the religions of the Hindus and Buddhists.

However, for most people in the Western world, Christianity settled the debate. Christians, the spiritual and philosophical heirs of the Jews — and to some extent, of the Greek and Roman Stoics — believed in a universe created and ruled by God, in an ethical system based on the Ten Commandments handed down by God to Moses on Mount Sinai, in the teachings of Jesus of Nazareth, and in a life after death in which the good would be rewarded and evil-doers punished.

Christianity — and the Christian spiritual and philosophical system — reigned supreme in the West, setting the cultural and societal agenda for nearly two millennia.

But in the middle of the nineteenth century, a new force rose up to challenge Christianity for the possession of the souls of men and women in the Western world. This force denied that there was a divine purpose

3

to the universe, regarded Moses and Jesus as mythical figures who may not have existed at all, and certainly couldn't have done the things Christians believed they did, and absolutely refused to believe in a life after death.

The new rival to Christianity has variously been called materialism, rationalism, secular humanism, or scientific atheism.

In ancient times, the Stoics and the Epicureans each sustained their beliefs on the basis of abstract logic and of choice. People who preferred to believe in an order to the universe and an immortal soul became Stoics. People who preferred a cosmos of blind chance and found the idea of peaceful extinction at death to be attractive became Epicureans. The two philosophies were rivals rather than enemies; the debate between them, honorable.

Christianity and scientific atheism, however, are both rivals *and* enemies, and the debate between them has been anything *but* honorable. Christianity is, or has been, the prevailing religion of most countries which permit free elections and attempt to guarantee basic human rights. Scientific atheism, on the other hand, is or has been the "religion" of those nations in which people have been "liquidated" on the basis of race or social class "for the good of the state." Individual guilt or innocence—important to Christians and those whose outlook has been shaped by Christianity—is irrelevant in scientific atheism because "good" and "evil" are meaningless without some concept of God. In Stalinist Russia in the 1920s through the 1950s, in Nazi Germany in the 1930s through the 1940s, and in Pol Pot's Cambodia in the 1970s through the 1980s, to list three of the worst examples, millions of people, including children, were murdered because their race or social class made them "undesirables." In Christianity, murder is an aberration. In political atheism, it is the norm.

Scientific atheism sustains itself as a "religion" by claiming to be based on factual evidence. Unlike most religions, which require the believer to accept some matters on faith, scientific atheism states flatly that faith is irrelevant and only facts matter. Atheism tolerates no rivals. You either believe in the "facts" of scientific atheism, or you are "wrong."

Even so, in countries where atheism is the official creed, a significant number of people—and in some cases a majority—continue to believe in God and to practice their faith despite economic and political discrimination against believers. Where fear and force are available, atheists have never been reluctant to use them.

In those Christian countries where the law guarantees political tolerance of religious beliefs, partisans of atheism employ more subtle methods of intolerance. The favored method is to claim that atheism is "scientific," that science makes atheism the only acceptable philosophy, and that anyone who isn't an atheist is a superstitious fool.

Religions have their prophets. Atheism also has its prophets. Beginning in the middle of the nineteenth century and into the first few decades of the twentieth century, several of the most important scientists in England and in the German-speaking world were prominent advocates of scientific atheism. Atheists and agnostics of our own era have cloaked these men in imaginary robes of sanctity and of the kind of infallibility that the pope could only envy. The history of human thought, according to atheist and agnostic writers, has been a steady negative progression from the worship of many gods, to the worship of one God, then to disbelief in any God. To support this picture of a steady slide away from belief, the atheists cite the importance of Charles Darwin who first popularized the theory of evolution; of Thomas Henry Huxley, who was known as "Darwin's Bulldog" for his work in advancing Darwin's theories and in attempting to demonstrate that the human brain and the human mind are one and the same thing; of Friedrich Nietzsche, the man who first claimed that "God is dead" and who attempted to banish God and Jesus from philosophy; and of Sigmund Freud who tried to prove that religious experiences, like those described in the Bible or in more recent times, were actually examples of "mental illness," if they weren't outright lies.

A number of atheists who followed the Big Four added to their work, or at least brought it to the attention of a wider public. Some of these were Robert Ingersoll, Clarence Darrow, Bertrand Russell, Albert Camus, and Jean-Paul Sartre. The comparatively large number of irreligious people in the academic and publishing industries has compelled high school and college students to take these people very seriously. The general impression is that religious faith can be maintained only in an atmosphere of near-total ignorance and that "scientific facts" support atheism and refute Christianity.

This is not true.

In the days when Darwin, Huxley, Nietzsche, and Freud walked the earth, they shared the limelight with many other scientists and thinkers of equal or greater importance. Atheist and agnostic writers usually describe Charles Darwin as the most important scientist of the nineteenth century because Darwin's theory of evolution drove or appeared to drive a wedge between science and religion. They tend to overlook, however, a more important and more constructive scientist: Louis Pasteur. While Darwin was working out his still unsubstantiated theory, Pasteur was able to prove that diseases were caused by tiny living organisms. Pasteur called them microbes. Today we call them germs. In his lifetime, Pasteur discovered the cures for a number of diseases of men and animals. His research ultimately reduced infant mortality so dramatically that he is said to have "slammed the nursery door in death's face." Readers who have walked through a nineteenth-century graveyard may have been struck by the number of children who died before reaching adulthood. The discoveries of Pasteur changed all this within a single generation. Yet atheist writers insist that Darwin, not Pasteur, was the most important scientist of his era. Why? One reason might be that Louis Pasteur never lost his faith.

Darwin's theory was championed and expanded by Thomas Henry Huxley, the man who invented the term *agnostic* to describe someone who claimed to have no knowledge of God or the supernatural. Huxley, too, is described by atheist and agnostic writers as a "hero of science." Pasteur's discoveries, on the other hand, were expanded by Joseph Lister, an English physician who used Pasteur's microbe theory of disease to pioneer antiseptic surgery, sterile wound dressing, and hospital sanitation—which again greatly reduced mortality. Joseph Lister, certainly a greater benefactor of mankind than either Darwin or Huxley, is today practically forgotten, unmentioned in schools or scientific literature. Could that be because throughout his life Lister remained a Christian gentleman both publicly and privately?

Friedrich Nietzsche used Darwin's and Huxley's theories to concoct the philosophy of the "superman." According to Nietzsche, the strong not only have a right but they have a duty to trample on the weak. His philosophy—the inspiration for Hitler, Mussolini, Ho Chi Minh, Idi Amin, Fidel Castro, and Daniel Ortega—remains so wildly popular that many anthologies describe him as the "last great philosopher in the tradition that began with Descartes and Kant." On the other hand, those philosophers who saw the Creation as the handiwork of God and taught that people have a moral responsibility to other people—great Christian thinkers like Abraham Kuyper, G. K. Chesterton, and Cornelius Van Til—have oddly yet to receive "equal time."

Sigmund Freud is considered the founder of psychoanalysis. If the average educated person were asked what Freud's most important discovery was, the answer would probably be the subconscious. This means that we sometimes do things without knowing why we're doing them. Freud, however, did not discover the subconscious. The subconscious was actually discovered by F. W. H. Myers, an Englishman doing research on various psychic phenomena. Myers not only believed in God, but believed that he had found convincing scientific evidence of life after death. Freud was repelled by the idea of an afterlife and didn't believe in God, but he thought enough of Myers's ideas about the subconscious to use them as the basis of his own career.

Freud had a brilliant follower named Carl Gustav Jung. While Freud was a fanatical atheist, Jung believed in God and believed that he had had personal experiences that might be evidence for life after death. Thus, despite Jung's obvious abilities and growing stature, Freud dumped him.

Atheists, who argue that their case is "scientific," have yet to explain why so many of these ground-breaking scientists disagree with them, and they have yet to explain why they blackball these scientists when they do disagree. Propaganda, rather than evidence, has in fact created a prejudice favorable to atheism among many modern scientists, and among many writers about science — including those who write the texts and curricula for our schools.

But in the lab, the case for atheism has begun to collapse.

When the atheist scientists first began their attacks on Christianity, science was still in its infancy, and, in particular, scientific instrumentation was still simple and rather crude. Large amounts of information could not be obtained. This created a sort of "free market" in which atheists and believers could both advance their philosophies based on a narrow basis of facts. In this climate — and because most of the atheists were people with training in the natural sciences, and most of their opponents were clergymen with training in theology and languages — the atheists scored a number of media victories.

However, with the development of more sophisticated measuring devices in the twentieth century, something completely unexpected happened. Science itself, as a practice rather than as a philosophy, began to discover and record evidence in favor of belief rather than atheism. Scientific findings began to show not only that scientific atheism isn't scientific, but that it *never was*.

Modern atheists, whose creed at this point has become not a response to genuine scientific evidence but a sort of God-less religion, now maintain their dogma by slippery explanations of "scientific" myths which don't stand up to analysis, by crude attempts to portray honest

Christians as fakirs and mountebanks, and pro-Christian scientists as snake-oil merchants, and, above all, by thumping the works of Darwin, Huxley, Nietzsche, and Freud in exactly the same way that TV and tent-show revivalists thump the Holy Bible—without really reading the words. If we examine the actual writings of the four atheist "prophets" with a knowledge of modern scientific *facts*, we can see how very wrong they actually were. We can also see that each man deliberately ignored or concealed information available even in his own era to fabricate a sort of atheist model of the universe—a model that left out anything which might prove destructive to atheism or supportive of Christian belief.

Darwin, Huxley, Nietzsche, and Freud are dead. To those people who can look facts in the face, many of their ideas are also dead. But the four atheist "prophets" still exert a death-grip which has not only maintained a fictitious breach between science and faith, but has actually prevented progress in science in many fields that could benefit suffering humanity.

The purpose of this book will be to show *why* Darwin, Huxley, Nietzsche, Freud, and their followers twisted science into an attack on religion; why they concocted the theory of scientific atheism to begin with; why they ignored all available evidence that contradicted their dead-end materialism in their own era; and why their worshipers continue to ignore this information today. The person who reads *The Atheist Syndrome* with an open mind may find himself drawn back from skepticism and doubt to an acceptance of traditional Christianity. He or she will, in any case, have to acknowledge that the atheists have not had the last word on the subject of science and faith.

T W O

THE ROOTS OF
A MADNESS

Darwinism has been all but abandoned. The old master's essential theories simply cannot be corroborated by modern biological or geological evidences.

Freudianism has been utterly abandoned. Modern psychology has discovered too many inconsistencies in the work of their "founding father" to take it seriously any longer.

Nietzsche and Huxley have been discarded by academia as little more than arcane and anachronistic footnotes to modern philosophy and science. Their ideas are given little if any credence anymore.

The men and women who work day after day in the clinics, laboratories, research centers, and classrooms know that the *materialism* of Darwin, Freud, Huxley, and Nietzsche is no longer a workable theory of human consciousness and personality. This may not force the entire literate world to accept Christianity. However, it certainly means that materialistic atheism is no longer valid as a "religion," because materialistic atheism was purported to be a religion based on facts. And the "facts" it was purportedly based on turned out to be glaring mistakes and miscalculations, if not out-and-out lies.

Still, one question remains to be answered: How was scientific atheism ever launched into supremacy? How was this false "religion" fabricated out of whole cloth and then billed as the only creed worthy of any man or any woman who wasn't a sentimental fool or a peasant idiot?

That's a very good question.

Unfortunately, the answer is not particularly satisfying. But the fact is that scientific atheism grew out of the social, cultural, and political vices of a few upper-class libertines.

There were several short-term social, cultural, and political advantages to repudiating Biblical Christianity for them. Christianity is a faith that comes packaged with very precise and demanding laws — laws that center on the Ten Commandments: Thou shalt not kill, thou shalt not steal, thou shalt not commit adultery, thou shalt not bear false witness, and the others.

During the so-called Enlightenment of the eighteenth century — when it was virtually impossible for upper-class Englishmen and Frenchmen to maintain an active social life if they didn't commit adultery almost routinely and kill people in duels if their "honor" was ever called into question — the upper classes used what little they knew about the physical sciences to invent a religion called deism. Enlightened people believed in God but ignored any of the Ten Commandments they happened to find inconvenient. They needed a faith that justified their sin, or at least ignored it. Deists believed in a God revealed through "Nature and Nature's Laws," or in some cases through pure "logic" or the "laws of mathematics," which were then just being formulated. They usually preserved a certain "regard" for Jesus as a "philosopher" but didn't believe that He was their personal Savior or even, as a rule, a divinely inspired Prophet.

But besides being a social, cultural, and political convenience in a society where adultery was rampant and refusal to kill your best friend in a duel was considered vulgar and cowardly, belief in deism was also encouraged by the unfortunate but genuine fact that the Church had, in many cases, become a sort of "no-show employer" for hypocrites, libertines, and upper-class ne'er-do-wells who couldn't find "real jobs." As a result the clergy was riddled with corruption. The malevolent churchmen described by Voltaire, the most famous and representative deist writer who is still widely read today, were not entirely conjured up by Voltaire's vivid and malicious imagination.

This movement of deism in the eighteenth century has been widely regarded by some Christians as the first great defection from belief in Scripture and divine revelation. This isn't strictly true. There have been a number of departures from traditional orthodoxy, usually brought on when the Church itself moved away from Scriptural beliefs and became brittle, brutal, or hypocritical. There have been dozens of deistic movements throughout church history. Scientific atheism, however, *was* something new: the first attempt to create a factually based, uncompromising, and completely comprehensive system of absolute disbelief. Many deists became utterly livid when the handful of genuine eighteenth-century atheists actually denied the existence of any God at all. What the deists were rejecting was either the uncompromising strictness of Scriptural morality, or the degree of hypocrisy, and in some cases cruelty, that they found in the churches of their own time. They were hostile to institutions — not, as the scientific atheists were, to the concept of God.

The Victorian Legacy

The era that shaped the thinking of the founders of scientific atheism came with the end of the Enlightenment: The society of the deists collapsed with the French Revolution and the Napoleonic Wars that followed. Romanticism, a literary movement that emphasized *feeling* over *intellect*, became popular among the upper-class intellectuals who had once been deists or extremely lackluster Christians. And formal religion underwent a tremendous resurgence, particularly after the ascension of Queen Victoria to the British throne in 1837. Idealistic and conventionally pious, Victoria married Prince Albert of Saxe-Coburg-Gotha, a German prince who imported the intensely Romantic spirit of nineteenth-century Germany to England, where it took hold and created the Victorian era.

During the Enlightenment, upper-class people hadn't had much time for children. The customary eighteenth-century marriage of convenience: Wife raised in seclusion marries rakehell husband, bears one child of unquestioned legitimacy to inherit the estate, and then does what she feels like provided she isn't too obvious about it. Children, other than the first-born, were of no particular importance and were usually raised by servants.

During the Victorian era, however, the fashion changed. The customary nineteenth-century marriage: Wife raised in seclusion marries circumspect husband, who may well be as inexperienced as she is, and they have eight children, four or five of whom may live; parents supervise every aspect of the child's development, often including private religious services or Bible readings at home, as well as religious and academic training.

The change in lifestyles meant an enormous change for children. In the eighteenth century, children who had frivolous or bad-tempered parents could ride out their childhoods without too much trouble because their parents were so busy with their social lives that the children were basically raised by servants. In the Victorian era, the kid who got a couple of ogres for parents was really stuck. Leaving the children home most of the time was no longer socially acceptable. Her Majesty took an active part in raising her own children and the upper classes and upper-middle classes were expected to do likewise.

Each era shapes its own styles in belief and in disbelief. Thus, the rather cool, detached family life of the upper classes in the eighteenth century is reflected in the cool, logical creed of deism, in which one was urged to believe in God on purely logical grounds — and then do whatever one wanted to, free of fear or retribution. However, in the closer, more intense family life of the Victorian era in the nineteenth century, believers were impassioned Scriptural Christians while disbelievers were impassioned God-hating atheists.

Of course that simplistic analysis doesn't tell the whole story. The "founding fathers" of scientific atheism didn't merely decide to despisingly ignore the God of Nature as well as the God of Scripture. No, their reaction was far more radical than that. They twisted the facts of science itself in an attempt to make belief of any kind impossible, not just for themselves but for anyone. This they portrayed as a "search for truth." But it wasn't a search for truth at all. It was a subjective and deliberate denial of God based on an inadequate framework of facts, and originating in an era when most people were religious, either in a naturalistic or Scriptural way.

When we come to the question of why it happened — why brilliant and privileged men deliberately distorted facts, denied evidence, and conjured fantasies simply to debunk the cherished faith of others — we have to consider the possibility of mental illness.

Materialists and atheists will, of course, be offended if we suggest that their heroes were actually insane, and that their attack on God, Jesus, and human immortality was a deranged fantasy and not an expansion of scientific knowledge. But, as we shall see, each of the Big Four of materialistic atheism — Charles Darwin, Thomas Henry Huxley, Friedrich Nietzsche, and Sigmund Freud — had many of the hallmarks of mental illness stamped on his personality. In point of fact, a careful study of their biographies in the light of improved scientific knowledge may reveal not only that each man was mentally ill, but that each man suffered from the same form of mental illness. It was this mental illness that led each of them to pervert science into an attack on God. And it was this same illness that led each man to suffer from a nearly identical set of psychosomatic illnesses in his mature life and to share similar obsessions outside the sphere of science-versus-religion.

The pattern that caused Darwin, Huxley, Nietzsche, and Freud to develop their antireligious obsessions can, for want of a better name, be called *The Atheist Syndrome*. The atheist syndrome was by no means limited to the Big Four. It was probably fairly common in Victorian society, most particularly in Victorian England and in the German-speaking world of the same era, where the social mores and culture were similar in most ways to those of England.

So then, what was it about Victorian culture that spawned such radical madness? What was it about the Victorian legacy that produced such demented perversion?

Lovelessness.

The Victorian home was all too often marked by a severe lack of demonstrative love.

It is interesting to note that love is one facet of human personality that radical atheists simply have no use for. In the materialistic scheme of things, *love*, as either the Christian or the pure Romantic sentimentalist understands it, is flatly impossible. Such reaction or emotion is passed off by materialists as a conditioned reflex. Since a relatively small percentage of the population has been exposed to "behaviorism" in psychology, this rather remarkable concept hasn't yet been treated with the mass contempt it deserves. The absence of *love* in any genuine spiritual sense, however, is as much a part of scientific atheism as the absence of faith. Amazingly it was grafted into atheism by the culture of Victorianism.

It's a well-known fact that children who receive an inadequate amount of love from their parents either die in infancy or grow up to be mentally and spiritually stunted adults. Stories about the absence of love are frequently found in literature beginning in the earliest days of history. In Herodotus, a Greek historian who wrote about 400 B.C., we find a narrative concerning Croesus, a fabulously rich king of Lydia, who performed an experiment in which he hoped to find out what the world's oldest language was.[1] Croesus rounded up some unwanted babies, isolated them from all human contact, and had them suckled by female sheep until they learned to talk so that he could hear what language first came out of their mouths. According to Herodotus, though the children failed to thrive, they did survive, and they first uttered the word *bekos*. The king's courtiers couldn't agree whether this was an actual word or an imitation of the sheep. More than a thousand years later, according to a papal historian, the strange and mysterious German Emperor Frederick II decided to carry out the same experiment, but this time the infants all died before they were old enough to speak because they had been deprived of human affection expressed through the stroking and cooing of their nurses.

At the end of the eighteenth century, when the once formidable but fast-fading Iroquois Indians of upstate New York were experiencing a tragic mortality among newborn infants, the Indians asked Handsome Lake, an Iroquois social reformer, what they could do about the epidemic of what we would call crib deaths. Handsome Lake told them that the babies were coming into the world as fresh and tender spirits, but when they looked around them and saw the chronic family strife — much of it engendered by alcohol abuse — they decided not to live. It's fascinating to observe that this Iroquois temperance advocate understood the basic principle that unwanted children often fail to thrive and even die from time to time.[2]

These stories, and dozens of others like them throughout the annals of time corroborate modern science's affirmation of man's biological need for maternal or maternal-surrogate love and affection.

So, what does all this have to do with Victorianism?

The fact is, the Victorian era produced a great number of unwanted children even in prudish settings. People had many children in England and Germany in the 1800s, more children, in many cases, than they really wanted or had any idea of how to properly raise. Large broods were fashionable. But the arbiters of fashion didn't tell people how to cope with big families. Under the pressure of large families and of the new fashion for strictness, "discipline" became a watchword in Victorian homes. This discipline all too often took the form of abusive punishment administered with rod, switch, hairbrush, or anything else that came to hand. And — note this — while the Victorian father administered this harsh discipline, he usually invoked the specter of an angry Old Testament God of Wrath, who not only permitted but *ordered* him to inflict harsh punishment for this child's own good. Children were told to "honor their father and mother," and then beaten. "Spare the rod and spoil the child" was an ever popular maxim, justifying an exaggerated and distorted perspective of the Bible's balanced teaching of correction, reproof, and rebuke (Proverbs 13:24; 22:6, 15; 23:13-14). Thus, the message that Victorian children received was clear enough: I'm abusing you because God wants me to.

The Victorian child imbibed this message early. God and his father were viciously stern disciplinarians. And in cases where the father was actually a sadist who used "discipline" as an excuse to enjoy beating his son, the son imbibed the message that his father's God was also a sadist.

It would be hard for us to realize the amount of beating and verbal abuse that many Victorian children absorbed without acknowledging that something very sick was going on. Beating a seven-year-old until he bleeds for failure to memorize the conjugations of Greek and Latin verbs or a hundred lines of dull poetry is not what we would normally expect from a normal mind. Justifying the abuse with Scripture certainly doesn't make it any healthier. The evident pathology of some of the documented cases is almost overwhelming. In one heart-breaking account an orphaned boy was sent to live with a spinster aunt who cloaked an almost hysterical cruelty behind a pious facade. The boy's only consolation was his pet cat. The spinster aunt decided that the cat was "interfering with his devotion to God" — so one day while he was out playing she hanged it and left the body dangling in his room. Sadly, the hapless boy developed a deep subconscious aversion to God as well as to his sadistic aunt.

Having endured all sorts of abuse from his ruthlessly brutal parents or guardians, much of it done in the name of God and backed by a misbegotten application of the Bible, the hapless Victorian child would be bundled off to public school. British public schools were, of course, actually private schools for "public men." They were schools in which men were trained for public life, not at all schools which were open to the general public. At the public schools, the children studied intensive courses which would make them proper public servants: huge amounts of Latin and Greek, English, history, mathematics, and some extremely rough athletics. The atmosphere of brutality at public schools was taken for granted. Headmasters and instructors browbeat the students regularly, usually in the name of God, while the bigger children terrorized and robbed the smaller ones and sometimes sodomized them, usually in the name of Jolly Good Fun. This was said to build character.

From the days of Percy Bysshe Shelley at the end of the eighteenth century through the days of young Winston Churchill at the end of the nineteenth century, the story of the British public schools is a chronicle of sensitive children beaten and tormented until they rebelled, inwardly or outwardly, in a variety of ways. Shelley, tormented and beaten in a religiously oriented school, reacted by writing a pamphlet called "The Necessity of Atheism." That a sensitive child would blame God for his predicament was fairly predictable. Churchill's reaction was different. He seems to have subconsciously contrived to fail virtually every course except English and history as a rebellion against the brutality of his early education and the indifference of his father and cold aloofness of his mother.

There are children, however, who had other ways of dealing with chronic child abuse systematized as "discipline" and supposedly backed by Scripture. These sons of feared and hated fathers did not act out their rebellion in a visible way. Their wounds were too deep and their fear too great. Perhaps their high intelligence and greater sensitivity encouraged a deeper, much more subtle form of rebellion against a hostile father they identified with a hostile God.

The hurt son of the abusive father all too often organized a subconscious plan of attack. Direct confrontation with the hostile father, or his God, was too dangerous. The son knuckled under, temporarily, but nurtured a deep resentment both against his father and against God.

Subconsciously, he decided to make his life's work the destruction of his father and the destruction of the God who had come to symbolize his father: angry, cruel, hostile, or at very best totally indifferent to suffering.

The son tried to do this in a subtle way. He could not attack his father or God openly, because Victorian familial piety forbade him to say to his father, "You're a brute and I hate you for it!" Instead, he struck at his father by denying God. The emerging "science" of the mid-nineteenth century provided a good avenue of attack because many of the old truths and assumed facts were being questioned. If the "facts" could be reinterpreted to shut God out, the victimized son would have acted out an attack without a direct confrontation against the father he feared.

The subtle manipulation of "scientific facts" into an attack on God as a symbolic father is the core of the atheist syndrome.

It should be emphasized that this all took place on a subconscious level. The son-victim didn't hop out of bed one fine Victorian morning and say to himself, Well then, today I'm going to get back at the old man at home by blasting the Old Man upstairs out of the sky! His subconscious urge for revenge on God took the conscious form of denying the existence of God. The best way to neutralize a powerful (assumed) enemy is to will or wish Him out of existence. It's also much safer to deny that a Person one fears actually exists than it is to risk a confrontation which experience has shown to be painful and dangerous.

This then was the Victorian legacy: a stern, and in some cases brutally, loveless culture, producing a reactionary and genuinely mad generation of psychotic God-haters. The uniquely pious aberrations of the Victorian times actually generated the atheist syndrome. What an irony!

The Three Phases of the Syndrome

The son-victim suffering from the atheist syndrome generally went through three recognizable phases.

As a child and student, he tended to be weak, submissive, an under-achiever, and unsure of his goals and desires. The physical and verbal abuse he had absorbed, coupled with his parent's lack of respect for him, never allowed him to develop any genuine self-respect, and the facade he presented to the world was one of confusion and apathy.

As an adolescent and a young adult, the picture of the son-victim changed dramatically. As soon as an opportunity arose, he attempted to flee, to put as much distance as possible between himself and the family he hated and wanted to escape from. For British subjects, whose second home was the sea, the flight often took place by ship. For Europeans, the flight was more likely to be by land, to a foreign country where their parent's language and religion were outlandish and foreign. Children and teenagers run away from home all the time. In the case of the son-victim in the atheist syndrome, however, the flight took place after the son-victim had already become an educated adult and after the poison of faulty parenting had had a chance to sink deep into his personality.

During the escape phase of the atheist syndrome, the son-victim shook off his weakness, his apathy, and his confusion. Freed from the oppression and fear of his father's roof, he found himself stronger, smarter, more resourceful than he ever dreamed possible. At this phase, during the escape, he usually began the actual work that ultimately made him famous and important.

The third phase was the inevitable conclusion of the son-victim's tragedy. Around the age of thirty-five to forty, the son-victim looked into the mirror and made a terrible discovery. He had begun to turn into a copy of his own father as the son-victim remembered him. At this point, the father-hatred, which had led to apathy in youth and rebellion in adolescence and early maturity, spilled over into something even deadlier: self-hatred. The son-victim began to realize that he was turning out to be just like his father. But he, of course, didn't want to be just like his father. He hated his father more than anything on earth. And so his mind sent a message to his body: self-destruct! Destroy yourself rather than turn into a copy of the hated original. In this phase, the self-rejection phase, the son-victim suffering from the atheist syndrome began to be afflicted by a set of psychosomatic illnesses which virtually paralyzed him. These were diseases, as a rule, with no organic or physical cause. The most typical were chronic headaches, chronic indigestion, extreme lassitude, nervous phobias, and an inability to concentrate on anything other than a few pet obsessions or to appreciate the kind of higher cultural things — literature, art, classical music — that usually appeal to people of high intelligence and education. In other words, they were beset by chronic clinical depression. Their minds had unconsciously turned against their bodies and were attempting to destroy the body. Their minds, of course, had also turned against themselves.

The idea that this chronic clinical depression originated in the mind, rather than in the body, can readily be seen in the lives of scientific atheism's Big Four. First, each of these son-victims survived for many years, even decades after the onset of the breakdowns of their health. Their illnesses went on for half a lifetime in three out of four cases. And second, particularly in the case of Huxley and of Freud, the son-victims were actually able to relieve their symptoms of depression by one sure-fire method: raving against Christianity. Huxley called his rage "crib-biting" and noted that his spirits and his digestion both improved when he was dipping his pen in vitriol for another attack on Scripture. Freud lived longer than either his friends or his enemies thought humanly possible, his flesh so rotten with disease that even his beloved chow dog wouldn't go near him because of the stench. Yet he hammered away on his final book, *Moses and Monotheism,* an attack on the common roots of Judaism and Christianity. The year was 1938, and Freud, in exile from Nazi-dominated Vienna, had chosen this time to attack his father's religion even while the Nazis were gearing up to exile or destroy his own relatives. It was more than a Freudian slip.

The sort of parenting that produced son-victims of the atheist syndrome, thankfully, no longer predominates. Except among the poor and the drug-ravaged, fathers today don't usually resent their children as the unwanted by-products of sexual activities they regard as shameful or use them as punching bags and scapegoats. Today we rightly recognize obsessive child-beating as vile and pathological and tend to forget that it was a staple of middle-class parenting gone just slightly off-beam a century ago.

The upshot of all this Victorian domestic violence has been world embracing, and we still feel its repercussions. By giving the stamp of scientific respectability to scientific atheism, the prophets of atheism have fueled most of the irrational and dangerous cultural and political movements of the twentieth century. In the next chapters, we will examine how the atheist syndrome and its anti-God obsession led each man to build a monument of twisted "science" as a form of subconscious revenge against the father he hated and feared.

PART TWO

THE SYNDROME'S BIG FOUR

THREE

CHARLES DARWIN: HIS ORIGIN AND DESCENT

To most atheists and agnostics, Charles Darwin is a figure of reverential awe. To many Bible-believing Christians, Darwin is Satan's ambassador to planet Earth. Atheists love Darwin and Christians disdain him because he's constantly cited as the man who "discovered" the theory of evolution, "proved" that the world wasn't really created in six days, and thus "invalidated" the Bible.

Devout atheists would go even further. They would say that, after Darwin, God became unnecessary.

Darwin did *not* invent the theory of evolution. The belief that higher types of animals arose from lower types of animals has existed since Greek and Roman times, in the days before the New Testament. Years before Darwin was born, his own grandfather suggested that animals might be struggling upward from simpler to more advanced forms of life. The same idea can be found in the writings of Johann Wolfgang von Goethe and of Jean Baptiste Lamarck.

Darwin's theory of evolution is called *natural selection*. Its only real contribution was that it devised a scheme which got around the principal objection to the earlier theories, in particular the theories of Lamarck. Lamarck, an archmaterialist who admitted that his goal was to "destroy religion," had said that all life could be explained by "motion working on matter." In other words, nothing is really "alive" in either a spiritual sense or in any physical sense. It merely acts and reacts mechanically. He also believed that an animal could pass on *acquired* physical changes to its offspring. The first belief is, for want of a better word, ridiculous. Scientists can now easily distinguish between what is alive and what is not alive by purely chemical means. And no one has ever seen a case of an acquired physical change being passed on by genetic means in the sense that Lamarck predicted. Darwin tried to distance himself from these aspects of Lamarck's theory, which is the reason that evolutionists today are called Darwinians instead of Lamarckians. Lamarckianism is simply out of touch with all reality. In fact, when the Stalinists in the Soviet Union tried to treat Lamarck's theory as a legitimate science rather than a mistake, they undermined not only their understanding of biology but many of their agricultural programs.

Even so, Lamarck's work formed the foundation upon which Darwin built. Darwin knew that full well, and so did the other prominent scientists who worked in the field.

There were, in fact, four men who played important roles in cosmetically remaking Lamarck's fallacious theory of evolution into the widely accepted Darwinian theory of evolution by natural selection. Charles Lyell wrote the book which convinced Darwin that changes in the earth's surface had been "gradual" rather than "catastrophic" and that the earth was far more than six thousand years old. Lyell didn't believe in the literal truth of the Old Testament, but he did appear to hold onto some form of the Christian faith. Louis Agassiz observed that embryonic animals go through a miniature evolution-like transformation from simpler to more complicated forms while still in their unborn, fetal stages. This "recapitulation" provided what he felt was the strongest possible confirmation for the development from lower to higher species. Agassiz also investigated the ice ages which he felt explained changes in the earth's crust that had always before been regarded as the aftermath of catastrophes like Noah's Flood. But despite this wide-ranging theorizing, Louis Agassiz remained a pious Christian of some sort. Last but not least, Alfred Russel Wallace developed a theory of evolution independently from Darwin, using the same sources and reaching many of the same conclusions Darwin did separately and at the same time. It was, in fact, under pressure of the knowledge that Alfred Russel Wallace might be first to publish the theory of evolution through natural selection that Darwin finally buckled down and wrote his famous book *Origin of Species*. Amazingly, Alfred Russel Wallace was an occultic spiritualist and believed he had encountered plausible scientific evidence of life after death.

If a rafter had broken free from Darwin's roof and conked him on the head with fatal consequences, the theory of evolution by natural selection would have almost certainly been propounded by someone else.

Interestingly, of the four men most responsible for the development of the theory of evolution by natural selection, only Darwin was an atheist or agnostic. The other three proponents were all believers of one sort or another. Evolution — as far off the Biblical standard as it is — was not originally developed as an inherently atheistic system. Only Darwin perceived it in that light.

When only one out of the four people most responsible for a theory turns the theory into a direct and rabid attack on God, we have to wonder if the atheism resides in the theory or the theorist.

Darwin turned the discussion of evolution into a crusade, and, as a result, the scientific data were never properly taken into consideration. Taken out of the context of Darwin's scientific atheism, Lyell, Agassiz, and Wallace's notions of evolution would have been judged on the dispassionate scales of truth — and been found wanting. But because the issue became a "cause," objectivity was tossed to the winds and, sadly, in that context Darwin and his faithless friends were able to prevail.

Charles Darwin was a decent man who hated slavery — and said so at the risk of controversy. He was a devoted husband and father. He was also a keen observer of animal life — when he limited his perspective to the lower animals. His defects lay in a strong and subjective antireligious bias which seems to have been rooted in his childhood but became increasingly powerful as he grew older. This bias destroyed his objectivity, his ability to make fair judgments based on facts. Prejudice injected an overwhelming negative inclination against religion into his scientific work, causing him to make serious mistakes later discovered by improved technology.

Darwin was, in short, perhaps the single most important victim of the atheist syndrome. The atheist syndrome colored his legitimate observations with a subconscious bias against God. The syndrome ruined his health through an agonizing and otherwise unexplained collection of psychosomatic illnesses that turned him into an invalid for the second half of his life. Ultimately, the atheist syndrome destroyed not God, but Darwin.

Darwin's Childhood: Phase One

Our primary source for the early life of Charles Darwin is his autobiography. Darwin began writing it in 1876 when he was sixty-seven years old and already locked in deep depression with an endless roster of maladies of no obvious physical cause. He said, in fact, that he felt as if he were writing from another world and that he had only another few years, at most, to live. He actually lived another six years. But his depressive symptoms may have made him believe he was literally dying for most of that time.

His grandfather was Erasmus Darwin, physician, botanist, zoologist, poet, inventor, philosopher, and successful businessman. Erasmus wrote a book called *Zoonomia*, (Greek for "law of life"), in which he proposed some evolutionary ideas more than half a century before Charles electrified England with *Origin of Species*.

Erasmus's first wife, Charles Darwin's grandmother, appears to have died young due to some disease which the medicine of the time was unable to explain. To young Darwin this must have been a terrifying experience. In fact, years later, Charles's father, Dr. Robert Darwin, exchanged letters with Erasmus, in which he probed that awful episode in an attempt to find out if there was a history of insanity in the family.

"I now know many families, who had insanity in one side, and the children now old people have no symptom of it," Erasmus wrote back to his worried son Robert. "If it was otherwise, there would not be a family in the kingdom without epileptic, gouty or insane people in it. . . . I well remember when your mother fainted away in these hysteric fits (which she often did) that she told me, you who was [sic] not then two or two and a half years old, run into the kitchen to call the maid-servant to her assistance."[1]

In the same letter, Erasmus told Robert that his wife's father, "the late Mr. Howard was never to my knowledge in the least insane, though he was a drunkard both in public and in private — and when he went to London he became connected with a woman and lived a debauched life in respect to drink, hence he always had the Gout of which he died but without any the least symptom of insanity or epilepsy, but from the debility of digestion and Gout as other drunkards die."[2] Despite Erasmus's denial, it isn't hard to see that mental illness, or at least the fear of mental illness, preyed on the Darwins.

Robert — Erasmus's son and Charles's father — married into the Wedgwood family, another locally prominent clan whose Etruria Works, Ltd., produced the classically inspired pottery prized by the royal family and many other upper-class Britons. The family members were considered part of England's gentry, with money, education, and opinions. The Darwins and the Wedgwoods were fully men and women of their times. They believed in unrestricted human progress. They believed in science and industry. And many of them were religious freethinkers who doubted the accuracy of the Bible both in historical and ethical terms. They baptized their children in the Church of England out of family tradition, but most of them were actually Unitarians if they were anything at all. Some were outright atheists. People who believe Charles Darwin discovered atheism when he discovered evolution will probably be surprised to learn that it actually ran in his family, possibly side by side with insanity. He himself tells us in his autobiography that his father, his brother, and his father's sister-in-law, Kitty Wedgwood, were all skeptics.

Robert, Charles's father, stood six feet, two inches tall in an era when most men topped out at five-feet-six. He weighed 345 pounds. Darwin as an old man claimed that he loved his father, but Darwin was notoriously unctuous where his family was concerned and may have been trying to shield posterity from unhappy family secrets. Outsiders reported that one of the staples of Darwin's childhood was being lined up with his brother and four sisters and made to stand and listen for *two hours* while his father lectured the small children about their defects of character. Anyone who knows small children knows how difficult it is to get them to stand still for five minutes. The kind of "discipline" that would make a six-year-old stand rigid for two hours at a stretch is better imagined than witnessed.

Whatever annoyed or pained him did so to an extreme degree, Darwin admitted. Emma Wedgwood, who was to marry Charles and to be his closest confidante, wrote after his death that Darwin's father didn't "understand or sympathize with him as a boy."

Robert was a physician who hated medicine. He often complained, even to his children, that his own father, Erasmus, hadn't provided for him adequately, and he openly resented the fact that he had to work to support himself. But he was good at what he did. Darwin tells us for four pages in his autobiography of how his father, "the largest man I ever saw," used what almost sounds like some sort of psychic power to make "snap diagnoses" and to "pull names out of the air" during polite conversations. He wrote:

The Earl of _____ brought his nephew, who was insane but quite gentle, to my father. And the young man's insanity led him to accuse himself of all the crimes under heaven. When my father afterwards talked about the case with the uncle, he said "I am sure that your nephew is guilty of. . . . a heinous crime." Whereupon the Earl of _____ exclaimed, "Good God, Dr. Darwin, who told you; we thought that no human being knew the fact but ourselves!" My Father told me the story many years after the event, and I asked him how he distinguished the true from the false self-accusations; and it was very characteristic of my Father that he said he could not explain how it was.[3]

Darwin flatly calls this predicting power of his father's "almost supernatural." He cites many other instances. It also may be revealing that, in writing down the story about the earl's nephew and his father's discovery of which of "all the crimes under heaven" the young man had actually committed, Charles Darwin capitalizes the word *father* in the last two references — as if he were writing about God.

"He had the art of making everyone obey him to the letter," Darwin added. "Many persons were much afraid of him."[4]

It's not merely due to the fashion of a cynical age that most modern biographers refuse to take at face value Darwin's statements that he loved his father. Making children stand at attention for two hours doesn't sound like the act of a man who overflowed with the milk of human kindness. Emma Darwin was a patently honest woman, and she seems to have picked up on the hostility quite clearly. And from what Darwin himself tells us, he was always much happier roaming the fields and woods observing animals — or killing them — than he was in the bosom of his prototypical Victorian family. When a person of any age shows such a marked preference for animals over people, we suspect a failure of human love.

Darwin's home life was actually pre-Victorian rather than Victorian. He was born on February 12, 1809, (the same day as Abraham Lincoln) and Victoria didn't become Queen of England until 1837. Many of the other people we think of as Victorians were, of course, born before Victoria's reign actually began.

In the homelife of pre-Victorian and Victorian England, almost all children were much closer to their mothers than to their fathers. Darwin, however, says he remembers almost nothing of his mother. "My mother died in July 1817, when I was a little over eight years old, and it is odd that I can remember hardly anything about her except her death-bed, her black velvet gown, and her curiously constructed worktable," Darwin wrote when he was sixty-seven. "I believe that my forgetfulness is partly due to my sisters, owing to their great grief, never being able to speak about her or mention her name; and partly to her previous invalid state. In the spring of that same year I was sent to a day-school in Shrewsbury, where I stayed a year."[5]

This is very strange. Darwin remembers sea bathing at Abergele when he was four years old; he remembers clearly the funeral of a British dragoon who was buried the same year his mother died. However, he can't remember his mother at all.

There's a name for this kind of psychological pattern. It's called *repression*. When an event is so painful that the mind can't handle it, repression — total forgetfulness — is said to take place. Darwin was clearly a first-rate observer and far above average intelligence, and the inability of a child who lost his mother at eight years of age to remember anything at all about her is undoubtedly a severe case of repression, particularly considering the intense grief he mentions on the part of his sisters.

Since Darwin's father — a huge, powerful, brilliant man and a physician who saved the lives of many people, especially, as Darwin tells us, many women — had tremendous diagnostic powers described as "almost supernatural," the impact of his mother's tragic death seems to have been something like this: *My God-like father who knows everything didn't save my mother. He took her away from me.*

Now all this may sound a bit too pat. Most modern psychiatric research holds that young children tend to blame surviving parents for the deaths of deceased parents, particularly when the all-powerful males are the survivors. At the back of Charles Darwin's mind one thought must have taken root every time he thought about his father: *You killed my mother.*

Father-hatred and a subconscious confusion of the father with God, the heavenly Father, is part of the atheist syndrome. On the surface, Darwin *claimed* to love his father because, quite simply, he was afraid of him. His father, after all, "knew everything" by a power that was "almost supernatural." He was a giant of a man, a physician who held the power of life and death in his hands. Darwin, shy, sensitive, and motherless, was terribly vulnerable to such an omniscient monster. He didn't dare to rebel or to express his rage at the death of his mother. He buried his fear and hatred beneath a facade of filial piety and obedience.

This analysis is by no means novel. In the 1940s and 1950s, long after Darwin had died, his granddaughter, Nora Barlow, compiled some papers to flesh out his autobiography and included the opinions of four physicians with extensive experience in treating psychosomatic disorders, which are diseases in which the mind "tells" the body to be sick. Dr.

Walter Alvarez said that Darwin's digestive and nervous disorders were due to "poor nervous heredity on both sides." He wrote this after examining the records of psychological instability among Darwin's ancestors.[6] Dr. Rankine Good, writing in *Lancet*, the British medical journal, said that Darwin's chronic illness during his later life "was compounded of depressive, obsessional, anxiety and hysterical symptoms . . . (a) Distorted expression of the aggression, hate, resentment, felt at an unconscious level, by Darwin towards his tyrannical father." In Dr. Good's opinion, Darwin's forty years of ill-health were the punishment for his revolt.[7] Dr. Douglas Hubble, also writing in *Lancet*, said: "Charles Darwin's illness, then, arose from the suppression and nonrecognition of a painful emotion. Such an emotion is always compounded of fear, guilt, or hate . . . in Charles Darwin this emotion arose from his relationship with his father."[8] Earlier in 1921, Dr. E. J. Kempf stated that Darwin's health problems were due to the loss of his mother, who died when Darwin was eight, and to his father's authoritarian attitude toward his family.[9]

Open revolt against a giant father whose power was "almost supernatural" was out of the question. Charles Darwin rebelled against his father in another way: constant failure. Son of a respected physician, grandson of two brilliant inventors, he should have found school easy. However, his school work was marked by mediocrity and inability to focus his attention.

Instead of applying himself to his studies, he discovered a love of killing: "How well I remember killing my first snipe, and my excitement was so great that I had much difficulty in reloading my gun from the trembling of my hands. This taste long continued and I became a very good shot."[10] Snap diagnosis: displaced aggression. Darwin probably would have loved to use his gun on his father on a subconscious level, and the very least we can surmise is that his oppressed and repressed personality derived some sort of catharsis from killing small animals. Yet as much as he loved killing birds with his gun, he couldn't stick a hook into a worm. He tells us he used to salt the worms to kill them before using them for bait. The killing of birds with his gun was an explosive outlet for his pent-up explosive anger. But with small, helpless animals, he identified with the *victim*. And since he saw himself as a victim of his father, it isn't hard to see why he would.

So, while Darwin enjoyed his shooting episodes, he had a great deal of trouble concentrating on his studies. Even those subjects which later fascinated him, like geology and botany, were boring when he was living near his father and within his father's sphere of influence. He studied medicine at Edinburgh for two years; but medicine was his father's profession, and, predictably, he didn't want to be a physician. Besides, the realities of human suffering had little appeal for him.

"I . . . attended on two occasions the operating theatre in the hospital at Edinburgh, and saw two very bad operations, one on a child, but I rushed away before they were completed," Darwin wrote. "Nor did I ever attend again, for hardly any inducement would have been strong enough to make me do so; this being long before the blessed days of chloroform. The two cases fairly haunted me for many a long year."[11]

The sight of a *physician* "torturing" a *child* by operating without anesthetics would horrify any normal person. But the effect on Darwin was cathartic. He had built up a small practice of patients among the village people in Shrewsbury, with his father serving as a senior consulting physician. He dropped the practice.

Darwin's Flight: Phase Two

Father and son, still in uneasy cooperation, began to cast around for something else for Charles Darwin to do. Robert decided that Charles should be a clergyman. It was a strange-sounding decision for a freethinker who had no religious beliefs of his own. But the father may have reasoned as follows: Clergymen are of no particular use; Charles is of no particular use; therefore Charles is ideally suited to be a clergyman.

"From what little I had thought and heard on the subject I had scruples about declaring my belief in all the dogmas of the Church of England," said Charles, whose relatives were mostly Unitarians or atheists. "Though otherwise I liked the thought of being a country parson."[12]

More from convenience than faith, Charles decided to study to be a clergyman. It seems to us rather bizarre that a man of no particular faith would want to be a clergyman. But in England of this era a clergyman's job was a frequent sinecure for gentlemen's sons who weren't cut out for medicine, law, or the army or navy. There were few other alternatives in the caste-conscious society of pre-Victorian England.

Darwin studied for the ministry for two years. He says that he convinced himself for a time of the literal truth of the Bible. He was much happier, however, when he was roaming in countryside shooting birds or collecting beetles. The majesties of Scripture were less impressive to the would-be clergyman than the natural sciences.

"No poet ever felt more delight at seeing his first poem published than I did in seeing in Stephen's *Illustrations of British Insects* the magic words 'captured by C. Darwin, Esq.'" Darwin wrote.[13]

While studying at Cambridge Darwin met Professor John Stevens Henslow and became such a close disciple of the professor that other students called Darwin "the man who walks with Henslow." Henslow was an expert in botany, chemistry, mineralogy, geology, and, of course, entomology, the study of insects, which was Darwin's real interest. Henslow was also "deeply religious, and so orthodox . . . his moral qualities were in every way admirable. He was free from every tinge of vanity or other petty feeling; and I never saw a man who thought so little about himself or his own concerns. His temper was imperturbably good, and with the most winning and courteous manners."[14] Darwin all but worshiped this devout Christian scientist and seems to have regarded him as a sort of idealized version of the kind of father he would have liked to have.

Henslow realized that Darwin wasn't cut out for the ministry. He advised him to study geology, a subject Darwin had disliked when he first approached it. Under Henslow's guidance, however, Darwin soon became an expert.

It was through Henslow that Darwin was offered an opportunity that was to change his life and the history of the world. HMS *Beagle*, a British warship, was going on a surveying journey anticipated to last for several years. Having read the works of Baron von Humboldt on his travels in South America, one of the *Beagle's* destinations, Darwin was eager to go. He asked his father's permission, but his father was dead set against the idea of Charles becoming the ship's naturalist.

"If you can find any man of common sense, who advises you to go, I will give my consent," Robert Darwin said. Charles' uncle interceded on his behalf and he received his father's grudging permission. In December 1831 Darwin set out on a voyage of discovery.

It's fascinating to observe Darwin as he prepared to set out. He was twenty-two years old and had already practiced medicine, but he wouldn't leave unless he could obtain his father's permission — this in an era when even boys from upper-class families sometimes went to sea on warships in their early teens and lower-class children shipped before the mast at ten or eleven. He tells us he agonized over the prospect of parting from his beloved family, but he was so excited at the prospect of *escaping* from his father that he began to suffer palpitations of the heart. With the foretaste of the hypochondria that would turn the second half of his life into a torment, Darwin half-convinced himself that he had heart disease. But he was so eager to escape from England — and his father's influence — that he avoided seeing a physician for fear that he might be correct in his diagnosis.

Just before Darwin set out, his friend Henslow had given him the first volume of *Principles of Geology* by Charles Lyell. Lyell, the materialist prognosticator of evolutionary theories, was a "uniformitarian." This means that Lyell thought the geological features of the natural world — mountains, valleys, continents, islands — had been created by processes which were still in action in the workaday world. The opponents of the uniformitarians were called catastrophists. They believed that the mountains, valleys, islands, and continents had been formed by cosmic catastrophes, gigantic disasters, in the remote past. When miners or souvenir hunters found the bones of extinct animals like mammoths or mastodons, or the fossils of dinosaurs, they argued that these beasts were extinct because they'd been wiped out in an ancient catastrophe, most probably in Noah's Flood. Darwin read Lyell's book and gradually became a uniformitarian or "gradualist" himself.

The captain of HMS *Beagle* was Robert Fitzroy, somewhat of a scientist himself and a man of great courage and irascible temper. Fitzroy believed that every word of the Bible was literally true. He also believed that the Bible justified slavery. Darwin had been raised to hate slavery in theory, and what he saw of the practice in Brazil, where slavery was still widely practiced in the 1830s, outraged him. The fact that Fitzroy rather obtusely used the Bible to defend slavery may well have reignited Darwin's childhood prejudice against the Bible and against unquestioning Christians.

But the linkage between Christianity and slavery, if indeed it was established in Darwin's mind, was not a logical one. While Darwin and Fitzroy were cruising around arguing aboard HMS *Beagle,* Britain outlawed the export of slaves from Africa under the prodding of William Wilberforce, a devout Christian who literally worked himself to death fighting to end slavery throughout the world. In the United States, liberals like Elijah Lovejoy and armed radicals like John Brown and his sons supported their antislavery sentiments with Biblical quotes and Biblical faith. While the atheistic Darwin of the later years cringed under his shawl, suffering an endless catalogue of psychosomatic ailments, fearless Christians like Dr. David Livingstone and General Charles Gordon roamed Africa to stamp out slave trading and slave raiding by Arab traders and by the Africans themselves. Livingstone, in particular, was a man of such intense Christian conscience that even the Arabs he was struggling to put out of business respected him for his integrity. Indeed, it was Christianity that put an end to slavery around the globe.

Darwin argued with Fitzroy as he never would have dared to argue with his father. Once he almost moved his gear out of the cabin they shared, and another time he almost abandoned the whole voyage and considered booking passage home separately. At the last moment the two men patched up their relationship. Something had happened to Darwin almost as soon as *Beagle* lost sight of England. Charles Darwin stopped being the shy ne'er-do-well of his boyhood and became a strong and self-reliant young man. Even the weather-hardened British sailors were sometimes amazed by his strength and toughness.

The story of the voyage of the *Beagle* is a saga of adventure. Darwin wandered the jungles of Brazil. He rode across the pampas of Argentina, side by side with gauchos. He marched through the middle of an Indian war in which neither side took prisoners. He climbed the mighty Andes, undeterred in his search for fossil shells by the *puna*, a shortness of breath caused by altitude, which would have had a drastic effect on anyone with a bad heart. His health was robust. Five young men in the prime of life died on the *Beagle* expedition, but the once-sickly Darwin was not one of them. Instead, he had the time of his life.

"I always look back to our boat cruises, and my land journeys, when through unfrequented countries, with an extreme delight which no scenes of civilization would have created," Darwin wrote in his *Voyage of the* Beagle. "I do not doubt that every traveler must remember the glowing sense of happiness which he experienced when he first breathed in a foreign clime where the civilized man had seldom or never trod."

Interestingly, at this point, Darwin the voyager still possessed a sense of religious awe:

> Among the scenes which are deeply impressed on my mind, none exceeded in sublimity the primeval forests, undefaced by the hand of man, whether those of Brazil, where the powers of life are predominant, or those of Tierra Del Fuego, where death and decay prevail. Both are temples filled with the various productions of the God of Nature. No one can stand unmoved in these solitudes, without feeling that there is more in man than the mere breath of his body.[15]

Standing in a Brazilian rain forest surrounded by killer wasps and poisonous spiders, Darwin exulted in his belief in Nature's God and in the immortal soul. What changed him into an atheist — and an invalid?

The *Beagle* touched a number of landfalls on the voyage. In Tierra del Fuego, Captain Fitzroy stopped over to establish a mission and to drop off three Indians that Fitzroy and another British captain had picked up as hostages on a previous voyage. Reading Darwin's descriptions of the three Indians, two men nicknamed York Minster and Jemmy Button and a young girl called Fuegia Basket, it's hard to avoid an impression that he regarded them as less than fully human. His descriptions of their knack for mimicry and their "affectionate" nature sound as if he were talking about monkeys rather than of two men and a girl. He was particularly horrified when Jemmy Button told him that, in the wintertime, the Indians ate their wives when food ran out. Darwin believed Jemmy's story of cannibalism to be factual. Later, when missionaries had studied the Fuegans for years, they failed to authenticate a single case of cannibalism among them. But Darwin seems to have assumed that the Indians were too stupid to have a sense of humor, or to indulge it at the expense of an educated English gentleman. Actually though, Indians constantly joke and tease when among friends, and delight in putting on outsiders with all kinds of absurd stories. Fuegan cannibalism was a figment of Jemmy Button's sense of humor, but Darwin believed it. Perhaps "barbarians" eating wives is the kind of thing one could expect, especially when your own behemoth father had *killed your mother*. Could it be that to the subconscious fear and hatred of his father, Darwin added an utter contempt for the idea of "primitive" man?

The early stages of the voyage of the *Beagle* reveal Darwin as a young man full of energy, self-confidence, and even of intuitive religious feelings. "I never experienced such delight," he wrote to his mentor, Professor Henslow, of his first weeks in the Brazilian rain forest. The reason for his delight? He had escaped from his father and his father's influence. He was finally free. Neither the brutality of the slavery he saw in Brazil nor the genocidal massacre of the last free Indians of the pampas in Argentina destroyed his sense of vitality and his zest for life, though he deplored both the slavery and the genocide. Only the primitive Fuegans with their cock-and-bull stories of wife-eating cast a dark mood over Darwin. After the ship left Tierra del Fuego and sailed up the west coast of South America, his vitality and ebullience returned.

In Chile Darwin experienced a severe earthquake and later visited the town of Concepción, which had been massively damaged. From this, and from finding fossilized sea shells high in the Andes Mountains, Darwin realized the power of the natural forces which had shaped the Earth's crust. This, and Lyell's geology, moved him away from catastrophism and into the gradualist camp, believing that the forces which shaped the Earth and its living creatures were still in operation.

The Galápagos Islands proved to be the forcing-bed in which Darwin brought forth his theory of evolution by natural selection. Darwin observed that many of the creatures on different islands seemed to be variations of the same ancestral creature. He asked himself if these creatures could each have been created separately by divine intervention, or if they had developed for earthly, practical reasons into slightly different but distinct breeds of animals.

There were, for instance, fourteen separate breeds of finches in the Galápagos Islands. Each breed of finch had a beak ideally suited for gathering the kind of food most abundant on its own particular island. Finches on islands where insects lived in cracks in the trees had long beaks ideal for snagging insects. Finches on islands where there were abundant seeds had thick beaks ideally suited to cracking seeds.

Captain Fitzroy said the different beaks of the fourteen types of finches posed no problem for his own belief in the literal truth of the Bible: "This appears to be one of those admirable provisions of Infinite Wisdom by which each created thing is adapted to the place for which it was intended."

Darwin wasn't sure. Some years later, after reading *An Essay on the Principle of Population* by Thomas Malthus, an English clergyman of the previous generation, he worked out a different theory. Malthus said that populations tend to increase *geometrically*: Two parents have eight children, and eight children produce thirty-two grandchildren, and one hundred twenty eight great-grandchildren. Because of this, all life sooner or later becomes a struggle for food, which only increases *arithmetically*. The successful strugglers for food live; the failures die before they can reproduce. Life becomes a simple struggle for food and sex.

Though Malthus's thesis had already been thoroughly discredited by undeniable scientific evidence, Darwin used it to imagine what might have happened on the Galápagos: The finches, having arrived in small numbers due to some storm which carried them to the isolated islands, continued to breed until there was a struggle for food. At this point, the islands were filled with finches of basically the same type, but the struggle for food favored those finches which were best adapted. Long-beaked finches flourished on islands where there were plenty of insects to be snagged out of cracks in trees; heavy-beaked finches flourished on islands where there were plenty of seeds to be cracked. The finches that ate the best survived the best, living to breed the most. Their descendants had the same features — long beaks or thick beaks — that had made the parents successful competitors. Gradually, very gradually, some types of finches developed very long beaks and others developed very thick beaks, depending on what kind of food was available on their own particular island. By the time Darwin and the *Beagle* arrived, the separate species had all developed.

Although the scenario was hardly original, Darwin worked out the details for twenty years before he actually published it in *Origin of Species* in 1859. The fact is, he was motivated to publish because of a paper written and printed by Alfred Russel Wallace, who had observed similar phenomena and drawn similar conclusions in Malaya. Wallace's paper was published *before* Darwin's book. Under the house rules of science, Alfred Russel Wallace should be carried on the books as the actual developer of the theory of evolution by natural selection. But because Darwin's book was more thoroughly researched, it was regarded as having *supported* the theory of evolution by natural selection. Wallace and Darwin, in fact, read a joint paper on natural selection before the Linnaean Society in 1858, before *Origin of Species* was published. Wallace, a gentleman as well as a scientist, was more interested in pursuing truth than in pursuing credit. He admitted in a chivalrous letter to Darwin that Darwin's mustering of facts had been more convincing than his own theoretical approach to the problem of the origin of various species. Darwin, for his part, admitted that Wallace had played an important role in "his" theory of evolution. On the other hand, he totally discounted any influence on the part of his own grandfather, Erasmus Darwin, who had cogently stated some of the same ideas more than half a century before in *Zoonomia*. When someone asked him, Darwin replied that he had read *Zoonomia* once, but that it hadn't made much of an impression on him. Similarly, he admitted to having had an excited discussion of the works of Jean Baptiste Lamarck, the Frenchman who had promulgated a crude but somewhat similar theory of evolution around 1800. But Darwin felt that Lamarck didn't deserve much credit either. Evolution by natural selection was *his* theory.

The people of Victorian England seized on *Origin of Species* for a variety of reasons. It seemed to be an idea whose time had come. Clearly, if Darwin hadn't brought it forth in *Origin of Species*, Alfred Russel Wallace would have mustered his own arguments for evolution and received full and solitary credit. And the recapitulation theory of the Swiss naturalist Louis Agassiz, that embryonic animals seem to go through a miniature evolution of their own from simpler to more complex forms of life, indicates that someone, within the same generation, would have produced "Darwin's" theory without Darwin. And the Victorians would have accepted it as "gospel" just as readily.

But why?

Was evolution by natural selection indeed an idea whose time had come?

The Origin of the Universe

Atheists and believers have each always had a theory of the origin of the universe that served as a keystone to their beliefs. Believers hold that God created the universe beginning at a specific point in time. "In the beginning, God created heaven and earth . . ." as the book of Genesis says. Atheists, on the other hand, hold that the universe has always been here. They say that it was never created at all, but has always existed. This is called the steady state theory.

The scientific theories of the creation of the universe existed in a sort of free market during Darwin's lifetime. Scientific instruments hadn't become advanced enough to provide proof for either Creation or the steady state theory. Anybody could pick a favorite solution based on subjective preferences and defend it adequately if he were bright enough.

The free market of ideas about Creation started to close down in 1913 when Vesto Melvin Slipher, an American astronomer, made observations that convinced him that the universe was expanding. Meanwhile, unaware of Slipher's discoveries, Albert Einstein published his equations of general relativity in 1917. Working with Einstein's equations, a Dutch astronomer named Willem de Sitter found a solution predicting an expanding, in fact an exploding universe. Independently Alexander Friedmann, a Russian mathematician, found a glitch in Einstein's calculations which also showed that the universe was expanding rapidly in the aftermath of an explosion — the first day of Creation. Because World War I was raging and because Einstein tried to fudge before he admitted the loophole, it took a full decade before the importance of Slipher's observations and Einstein's mathematics were brought into harmony to show that they pointed to the same thing: the creation of the universe at a specific moment in time.

Scientific atheists the world over were horrified. Their steady state theory was a horrendous mistake, a scientifically demonstrated mistake. And what is more, even a person with no traditional or intuitive religious beliefs could see that Creation pointed to the existence of a Creator. Many formerly agnostic astronomers said so. Even Einstein, who believed in a God of logic and order all his life but was not traditionally religious, found the created universe unsettling. As a result some astronomers who were formal atheists virtually frothed at the mouth.

The atheists hoped that the Creation nightmare would go away. It didn't. It got stronger all the time. In 1948, Ralph Alpher and Robert Herman predicted that a faint glow of radiation from the cosmic explosion of the first day of Creation would some day be found by sensitive astronomical instruments. In 1965, while shooing stray pigeons out of their equipment, Arno Penzias and Robert Wilson of Bell Laboratories actually discovered the radiation. The theory was now confirmed beyond any reasonable doubt. The universe had been created. The steady state theory of the atheists was dead.

"At the present time, the Big Bang theory has no competitors," Robert Jastrow wrote in *God and the Astronomers* in 1978. "Theologians generally are delighted with the proof that the Universe had a beginning, but astronomers are curiously upset. . . . For the scientist who has lived by his faith in the power of reason, the story ends like a bad dream. He has scaled the mountains of ignorance; He is about to conquer the highest peak; as he pulls himself over the final rock, he is greeted by a band of theologians who have been sitting there for centuries."[16]

The collapse of the steady state theory of the atheists has reached the point where a speculative scientist like Edward Fredkin can at one breath disown any "specific religious belief" and still say he sees "evidence of intelligent planning" in the cosmos, which would seem to most people to imply belief in a Creator. Fredkin's comparison of the physical universe to a computer may seem a bit too chic or cute to be believable by some of his colleagues. But it illustrates the point that the steady state theory of atheistic materialism is as dead as a door nail as far as modern scientists are concerned. If the propagandists of scientific atheism were really interested in facts, the confirmation of Creation would have blown the atheism out of the atheists. But they aren't, so it didn't.

The Origin of Life

Since the days of the Epicureans in ancient Greece and ancient Rome, materialists have believed that life arose by itself from sterile, nonliving matter. This made it possible for the materialists to explain how there would be a Creation without a Creator. Aristotle, for instance, believed that whole species of animals, ranging from eels to fleas, were generated by dust or mud, not by parents of the same species. Today we know that the eels which live in European rivers migrate to the middle of the Atlantic Ocean to lay their eggs, which is why Aristotle never saw an eel egg. For centuries the idea that living organisms arose from dead sterile matter was accepted by almost everyone. In the Middle Ages, Emperor Frederick II sent voyagers to discover if a species of European waterfowl called barnacle geese were descended from barnacles or geese. Any farmer knows that geese came from eggs, but Frederick had read Aristotle.

The definitive experiment about the origin of life in sterile matter took place in what might be called the "second Renaissance" of Italian civilization during the 1700s. This was the era in which Galvani and Volta made major advances in physiology, the study of how the body functions physically and chemically. The problem of how life arose became an open one as scientists lost their faith in Aristotle.

In 1765, the Italian priest-scientist Abbé Lazzaro Spallanzani, who had already made some remarkable contributions to the world's expanding knowledge, set out to find out whether "spontaneous generation" (life arising from sterile matter) actually took place. Abbé Spallanzani knew that meat was notorious for incubating all kinds of life forms, from maggots to mold, if the meat were left exposed to air. In careful experiments, he sealed meat in flasks after subjecting the meat and the air in the flasks to great heat. The meat in those flasks which remained tightly sealed failed to generate any life forms at all. The meat in the flasks which were subsequently cracked open and left to stand developed life forms. Abbé Spallanzani had shown that the meat didn't generate any life forms so long as it remained sterile. Life came only from life, not from sterile matter. Spontaneous generation was disproved.

Abbé Spallanzani corresponded regularly with his English and French colleagues in science, and some of them repeated his experiment with sealed flasks, finding that they obtained the same results: Spontaneous generation proved to be about as "scientific" as the "monster report" of ship-eating krakens in the Atlantic. Life did not arise from sterile matter, and belief in noncreated life forms no longer had any currency with the educated masses.

Except, of course, among the scientific atheists. Scientific atheists needed spontaneous generation because, without it, they couldn't explain the origin of life on earth without invoking God. Since they didn't believe in God—or perhaps subconsciously *did* believe in God, but hated their idea of Him—they had to come up with some other explanation. So they invoked spontaneous generation with a ferocious sort of don't-confuse-me-with-the-facts determination. Somehow this bit of intellectual dishonesty brought spurious comfort to godless scientists. Sadly though, it also prevented an understanding of the actual nature of infectious diseases and infected wounds that probably doomed millions of people to extremely painful and prolonged deaths. Most of the physicians practicing before the 1860s didn't know enough science to realize that spontaneous generation was but a myth. They regarded infections as inevitable, thus taking no measures to prevent them. Infections usually followed surgery, and death often followed the infections. A belief in spontaneous generation went on killing people long after the theory itself was "dead" in scientific terms.

Any theory such as Darwin's, which discounts a divine Providence operating through or behind physical creation, can only fall back on some sort of spontaneous generation or on the "accidental" creation of life: abiogenesis. The difference between the two is that in spontaneous generation, fairly sophisticated creatures like eels and fleas—and barnacle geese—arise from sterile mud or dust, while in abiogenesis (which means "birth without life") sterile, lifeless chemicals somehow come to life through a chance combination of just the right chemicals by pure accident.

While Darwin was writing *Origin of Species* and preparing a jolt for churchmen, another scientist with a strong practical and humanitarian bent that Darwin lacked was doing the work that would ultimately prepare a jolt for the materialists. Louis Pasteur, son of a peasant tanner and veteran of Napoleon's armies, originally trained as an artist and working as a chemist, began to investigate the problem of how wine and food became contaminated. Having forgotten Abbé Lazzaro Spallanzani, most scientists of Pasteur's day believed that the materials themselves contained some form of innate corruption. Pasteur, however, hadn't forgotten Abbé Spallanzani and admired him so much that he kept Spallanzani's portrait in his laboratory.

Pasteur began his work on spontaneous generation in 1860. Two years before, an influential French scientist had written: "Animals and plants could be generated in a medium absolutely free from atmospheric air, and in which, therefore, no germ of organic bodies could have been brought by air." Under this theory, Darwin's *Origin* would have worked. Pasteur, however, was unconvinced. "In experimental science it is always a mistake not to doubt when facts do not compel affirmation — in my opinion the question is not decisively proved. What is there in the air that gives rise to these creatures? Are they germs? Is it a solid? Is it a gas? Is it a fluid? . . . All this is unknown and we have to experiment to find the answers."[17]

Pasteur experimented. He filled flasks with a suspension of yeast in water, boiled the water, and closed the flasks while steam was still rolling up out of the flasks. After the flasks had cooled, he opened some flasks and left others sealed. Inspection of the flasks which had been opened produced living molds. The sealed flasks remained sterile and lifeless. Pasteur had proved once again that spontaneous generation did not occur. He had also provoked the wrath of the materialists who needed spontaneous generation to explain the origin of life. One elderly scientist actually challenged Pasteur to a duel for daring to contradict spontaneous generation. But repeated experiments proved that Pasteur and Spallanzani had been right: sterile matter does *not* generate life. Spontaneous generation remained dead. Except to the scientific atheists.

Pasteur used his experimentally proven conclusions to revolutionize food processing and the treatment of disease. His French, German, and English continuators used his knowledge to find treatments for the most dreaded diseases of the nineteenth century. But meanwhile, the propagandists of scientific atheism used the lie that spontaneous generation was a fact to go on concocting absurd theories about the accidental origins of life.

In his superb book *Alive: An Enquiry into the Origin and Meaning of Life*, Dr. Magnus Verbrugge, M.D., a physician and scientist, examines the twentieth-century attempts to explain the origins of life through abiogenesis. Dr. Verbrugge's staunch Christianity has offended some who insist that scientists remain agnostic, at least in terms of research; but his scientific sifting of facts is beyond any reproach. His conclusion is that abiogenesis is a fraud perpetrated consciously or subconsciously, by "scientists" for whom materialism is actually a sort of godless religion. Another of the many important insights in his book is that mass-media showmen have convinced the public that abiogenesis is a fact, while the atheist scientists can't even show that it's a workable theory.

The biochemical details of even the simplest cells make it virtually impossible that life could ever have arisen by accident from sterile matter. It is in any case a matter of uncontested fact that no laboratory has ever been able to generate living tissue from sterile chemicals. Materialists, however, profess to know that this happened completely by accident and without intelligent guidance in the sterile, lifeless seas of a barren, lifeless world. They have absolutely no evidence. They have a "faith" that this must have happened because they need to believe in spontaneous generation or in abiogenesis as an antidote to God.

And it was as an antidote to belief in God that Darwin tacitly accepted spontaneous generation as the origin of life even though it had been disproved by Abbé Spallanzani before Darwin was born and was disproved conclusively by Louis Pasteur during Darwin's own lifetime.

The Timetable of Species Development

If you ask the average intelligent layman exactly what Charles Darwin accomplished, he will probably say that Darwin discovered the theory of evolution. This, as we have seen, is not true. Ideas about evolution had been described from the days of ancient Greece and Rome. What Darwin actually did was to concoct a theory by which evolution might work without the intervention of God or Providence. And it was for this that he became the flag-bearer for atheists, materialists, and "progressive" anti-religionists, later to include the Marxists and the Nazis.

Darwin dealt with the first two problems of imagining evolution in a godless universe by the time-honored method of ignoring them. He supplied no explanation either for the origin of the universe or the origin of life. Darwin's dealing with the third great problem shows far more energy and imagination. His description of how simple creatures develop into more complicated animals and plants through natural selection and the survival of the fittest is a brilliant solution to the problem of progress without a plan.

Unfortunately, Darwin forgot one factor: time. In dealing with the fourteen types of finches, he showed that he had a fertile imagination. How did the birds adapt different shaped beaks? Darwin suggested: through success in feeding, allowing those birds who fed best to breed most, or avoiding starvation long enough to breed at all. So far, so good.

But what Darwin overlooked was that the fourteen species of finches were all relatively similar. Today, even evolutionists — including atheists and agnostics who regard Darwin as their hero — are forced to admit that his scheme of evolutionary gradualism didn't and doesn't leave enough time for the full development of living species from simple one-celled animals to modern athletes and astronauts. Among serious students of evolution, this point isn't even debatable. The problem arose, after Darwin's time, for two reasons.[18] First, new evidence for a created universe and improved techniques of dating showed that the amount of time available for species development was much shorter than Darwin thought it was. Remember that the early evolutionists pinned their hope on the steady state theory, which blew up in their faces after the turn of the twentieth century.

The second problem is that, with some exceptions, the fossil record after a hundred years of digging, often with evolution in mind, seems to show that transition from one species to another, if it occurred at all, must have taken place rather abruptly, because most transitional fossils are missing. Creationist scientists, who take every word of the Bible to be literally true, argue that the transitional fossils haven't been found because they don't exist and never did exist. They believe the evidence overwhelmingly demonstrates that each major phylum of animal or plant life was created separately and that whatever evolution takes place takes place only within the species — like Darwin's fourteen Galápagos finches. Of course, evolutionists will have none of this. They offer a strident rebuttal claiming that in some cases, there *are* transitional fossils. One example they say is the archaeopteryx, a winged creature which probably looked like a cross between a reptile and a bird. Further, they argue that many of the soft-bodied animals on the lower rungs of the evolutionary ladder would not have made very good fossil material in any case. Fossils are not actual bones, but impressions of bones left in mud and subsequently filled by mineral seepings which harden into stone. A jellyfish or a tubeworm obviously wouldn't offer enough resistance to the pressure of the mud to leave the necessary hole to be filled by seepage. So they argue on the basis of "the one that got away."

In any case, the absence of transitional fossils is a good bet for endless argument among specialists. The bottom line is that the time factor permits no serious argument. Even an inflamed partisan of atheist materialism must admit that Darwin blew it where time was concerned. There simply never was enough time to permit evolution across the broad spectrum of plant and animal life under Darwin's scheme of sexual selection or natural selection.

What then? Is scientific atheism to sacrifice its greatest and most impressive theory simply because the evidence is weighed against it and the experts admit it doesn't work?

No! Faced with the fact that Darwin didn't calculate enough time for his scheme of godless, non-Providential evolution to work properly, the evolutionists have seized on a substitute for gradualism: peripetic speciation.

Peripetic speciation is a great theory for those who like their science laced with science fiction. Peripetic speciation has to sacrifice some of the "joy of sex," but it more than makes up for it with cosmic disasters right out of disaster comics, or out of the kid-vid ghetto of violent cartoons.

Peripetic speciation is the theory that evolution is speeded up by fits and starts through natural disasters so violent that they wipe out most existing species but allow certain species to survive. The handful of surviving creatures, freed from competition with the creatures that are not going anywhere interesting but just roaming around taking up space, can now multiply faster and fill up all the available space until the next catastrophe. It is a kind of evolution with hiccups! For it to work right, there would have to have been somewhere between six and a dozen catastrophes, each timed to wipe out the dead wood and allow those creatures with a future to breed their way up to Shakespeare and Beethoven. Note that each catastrophe would have to be sufficiently lethal to kill off most forms of animal life, but none could be bad enough to wipe out *all* life on earth, or none of us would be here—unless the catastrophe was somehow bad enough to revive spontaneous generation.

Evolutionists have always believed that life began in the sea. To move from the sea to the land, living creatures had to develop lungs, they have argued, because fish live in water and breathe dissolved oxygen through gills. Fish have no use of lungs. Land animals, on the other hand, breathe oxygen from the air and have no use for gills. Fish taken out of water die quickly because their gills can't accept oxygen directly from the air. Fish also move by swimming with winglike fins and fanlike tails. They have no more use for limbs with feet and toes than a bird would for a pair of humanlike arms instead of wings. So fish are not land animals.

Thus, according to the evolutionary scheme, fish must at one point have become amphibians. Peripetic speciation gives us this imaginary description of how they did it:

Once upon a time there were two fish living in a prehistoric lake. One day a cosmic ray from outer space operating by blind chance zapped these fish and hit two of their chromosomes. The zapped chromosomes caused the fish to have deformed offspring—mutants! The mutant fish had little pouches behind their nostrils that had to be filled with air: lungs. They also had stumpy fins with yucky things called toes growing out of them. The other fish thought they were disgusting and didn't want to go out with them. So they married each other. Despite the fact that they couldn't submerge without drowning and couldn't swim as fast as the other fish to catch their food or escape their enemies, the yucky mutant fish survived until the fortuitous arrival of the Death Star.

The Death Star is a necessary feature of the atheistic-catastrophist universe. Nobody has ever seen the Death Star through a telescope or has any solid evidence that it exists. With factual science it enjoys the same position as spontaneous generation or abiogenesis—as a myth. The atheists, however, believe in it because they can't get along without it, because the Death Star is a comet that causes catastrophic upheavals in the earth's crust. Whoosh! Look out, fish, here comes the Death Star, just in the nick of time, because the yucky mutant fish are having a hard time competing for food with these stupid lungs and legs instead of gills and fins. But now the mutant fish have the last laugh. The Death Star zooms through the earth's atmosphere, scores another very fortunate near miss, and departs for the next sixty million years. Meanwhile, the gravitational disturbance causes an earthquake and the bottom of the pond cracks.

"Laugh now, all you finny fiends!" the mutant fish think to themselves. As the pond grows progressively muddier, the gill-equipped fish choke and the mutants eat them. The food supply causes the mutants to reproduce like crazy, and in a few generations they have become lung-fish. The lung-fish are in such good shape that when the pond finally dries up completely, they can *walk* to safety on their once-clumsy legs. And a new subphylum of animals, the amphibians, have come into existence through the blind, purposeless, statistically random cooperation of a comet nobody has ever seen, a cosmic ray that hit the right two chromosomes without being aimed, and a pond that took just the right amount of time to dry up.

Believe it? Darwin wouldn't have. He had serious problems with father-rejection, chronic depression, and the cultural and racial prejudices of his nation and his age, but he wasn't gullible or stupid.

There are two things seriously wrong with peripetic speciation. The first is that in this kind of system, we are forced to blithely accept a run of fortunate coincidences which are statistically as improbable as finding out that the earth is really flat and the moon is made of green cheese. Blind cosmic chance might have pulled off *one* catastrophe bad enough to wipe out the larger life forms but spare the smaller and smarter ones. The odds against having it happen six to twelve times in a row are a little staggering. The second trouble with a reliance on peripetic speciation is that it involves a rather unseemly opportunism on the part of the evolutionists: A hundred years ago, Darwin devised his theories and made his reputation by fighting against catastrophism. His admirers now find themselves stuck with an odd variation of it as the only available alternative to Providence. How ironic! Catastrophism was the preference of the people who took the opposite side of the debate from Darwin when he was alive. Atheistic evolution now abandons atheistic gradualism and latches onto catastrophism to avoid drowning in a sea of religious acceptance.

It must take a powerful prejudice against any notion of a Creator to make the peripetic speciation theory more attractive to atheists than the simple admission that *something* operating behind or outside Nature has directed the progressive improvement of living creatures. This would, of course, make them theists or at least hopeful agnostics. And subjective prejudice against religion forbids many scientists to be open-minded enough to face facts fairly. So instead of the outmoded but reasonably plausible theory that Darwin proposed in 1859, we get science fiction served up as science by atheist propagandists posing as scientists.

Instinct and Intuition

Darwin's theory of gradualism and natural selection has failed the test of time. Fair enough. In Darwin's day, the instrumentation didn't exist to measure fossil diversity, to gauge the actual age of the universe, or to realize the extreme complexity of the living cell. The actual methods by which heredity functioned, in fact, weren't worked out until 1868 by Gregor Mendel, an Austrian monk who conducted genetic experiments with peas. And Mendel's findings weren't widely known or understood until around 1900. Creation of the universe, creation of life, and development within a realistic time frame were all failures of Darwin's gradualist theory that he couldn't have expected. The failure he *did* expect came from instinct.

Darwin devoted a whole chapter of *Origin of Species* to instinct. He began by predicting that instinct would prove the Achilles' heel of his whole theory.

"Many instincts are so wonderful that their development will probably appear to the reader a difficulty sufficient to overthrow my whole theory," Darwin wrote at the beginning of chapter 8 of *Origin of Species*. "I may here premise that I have nothing to do with the origin of the mental powers, any more than I have with that of life itself. We are concerned only with the diversities of instinct and of other mental faculties in animals of the same class."[19]

Darwin then proceeds to fudge through an entire chapter on instinct by explaining how the instinctive behavior that every naturalist has noticed in a variety of wild animals *might* have originated by accident or evolution. His arguments are very weak in this chapter, as he well knew, and the fact that he bothered to deal with such a potentially threatening topic shows that he was actually a more honest scientist than many of his modern admirers.

Hunting dogs point at game birds without being taught. Tumbler pigeons flip over in flight without being taught. Some species of ants keep other ants as slaves. Cuckoo birds lay their eggs in other birds' nests. Darwin notes all these instincts and points out that they are, or at one time were, necessary to the survival of the creatures, or later became so. The argument is that if creatures do zany and unexplained things which help them survive and reproduce, their descendants will do the same zany and unexplained things.

This begs the central point. How do you explain instinct in materialist terms? What brain process tells a hunting dog to point or a pigeon to tumble or ants to raid other ants for slaves? The materialist theory asserts that the brain controls all actions. The materialist theory also asserts that the brain of a newborn creature is a *tabula rasa*, a blank slate. All behavior is learned. Period. So, the blank slate theory is completely at a loss to explain why pointers point and pigeons tumble and ants raid other ants for slaves.

The blank slate theory can explain breathing and eating and drinking and the sex drive as functions triggered by sensory stimulation. But the blank slate can't explain instinct, even in such simple cases as the ones Darwin mentions. And the blank slate can't explain more complicated instincts at all.

Remember the eels that Aristotle believed were spontaneously generated in river mud? No one had even seen eel eggs, and since eels lived in muddy rivers it made a certain amount of sense to believe they were born in mud. The problem was that no matter how much the mud was strained and sifted, no one ever found an eel egg. The ancients decided that the eels were born not just *in* mud, but *from* mud, by spontaneous generation.

Truth isn't stranger than fiction. It's just more miraculous. The fact is that European river eels are born in the Sargasso Sea, a floating mass of seaweed in the middle of the Atlantic Ocean. Every eight or nine years, the mature eels living in European rivers are stirred with a powerful urge to breed. The eels take off and head downstream, down the river, out into the Baltic or the North Sea, and then through the trackless Atlantic Ocean headed back to the Sargasso Sea where they were born. How do they find the Sargasso Sea? By instinct. The reproductive instinct can be explained in purely sexual terms. Materialism works here. But how does materialism explain the navigation?

Salmon do the same thing in reverse. Salmon are born in rivers, migrate to the sea to live, and swim back up the river to spawn and to die. How do they find their way? Why don't they spawn right where they are? Nobody knows.

Tests of animals conducted after Darwin's time confirmed anecdotes that had existed for hundreds of years: Animals appear not only to have instinct but intuition. In other words, they seem to be endowed with prescience. Statistics seem to indicate that animals can make choices guided by instinct or intuition which show a greater accuracy in anticipating situations and circumstances than what would be expected from probability. Victorians regularly told stories about dogs or horses reacting drastically at the moment their owner died, hundreds of miles away and unexpectedly. People today talk about how animals seem to predict earthquakes. Whether they detect seismic vibrations that can't be registered by machine, or whether they are actually prescient, remains to be determined. The fact remains that the reactions, if not the explanations, were common enough in Darwin's own era to have played a part in his discussion of instinct, if he hadn't been uneasy about considering it.

Intuition stories in animals are, however, a mere sprinkling compared to the flood of evidences and anecdotes about spiritual and intuitive experiences in human beings. Stories about prophetic dreams occur in the Bible, which Darwin of course knew, and in the Greek and Roman classics, which he must have read, however badly, during his unhappy school days. And he was aware, as he later wrote in *The Descent of Man*, that "the belief in unseen or spiritual agencies . . . seems to be universal with the less civilized races."

Darwin, remember, never considered "the less civilized races" to be authentically human. For all his decent hatred of slavery, his writings reek with all kinds of comtempt for "primitive" people. Racism was culturally conditioned into educated Victorians by such "scientific" parlor tricks as Morton's measuring of brainpans with BB shot to prove that Africans and Indians had small brains, and hence had deficient minds and intellects. Meeting the simple Indians of Tierra del Fuego, Darwin wrote: "I could not have believed how wide was the difference between savage and civilized man; it is greater than between a wild and domesticated animal. . . . Viewing such man, one can hardly make oneself believe that they are fellow creatures and inhabitants of the same world."[20]

Darwin believed that the Fuegans, whom he describes as closely resembling "the devils which come on the stage in plays like *Der Freischutz*, spoke a language of grunts with a tiny vocabulary." However, an English missionary who later compiled a dictionary of Jahgan, the Fuegan language, recorded a vocabulary of 32,000 words, including more than 50 names that described family relationships alone. Darwin also believed that the Fuegans were cannibals, though closer investigation by people who lived with them for many years failed to disclose a single case of cannibalism. It's hard to believe that Darwin, a keen observer of animals and fossils, could make such glaring mistakes about human beings, whatever the color of their skin or the amount of their clothing. But his contempt for their intelligence and humanity isn't pointless. The Fuegans, primitive as they looked, believed in a spiritual world and in intuition; and Darwin had to discount the all-but-universal belief in life after death among native and natural people by assuming that they were apelike and subhuman. To credit tribal people with authentic humanity would have required him to consider their beliefs seriously.

Darwin encountered the belief in a spiritual realm when Jemmy Button, one of the captive Fuegans, told Darwin that he had learned that his father had died while Jemmy was a hostage in England. "He had already heard that his father was dead, but as he had had a 'dream in his head' to that effect, he did not seem to care much about it, and repeatedly comforted himself with the very natural reflection, 'Me no help it,'" Darwin wrote in his account of the voyage of the HMS *Beagle*. If Darwin hadn't already decided that Jemmy was a "sub-human," to use the parlance of the "neo-Darwinians," he might have tried to ask the same questions that F. W. H. Myers asked when investigating dreams. Instead, Darwin bought the materialistic explanation that prophetic dreams and spirituality were tricks people played on themselves. This was a *theory*. The fact was, and is, that statistical investigation of many forms of intuition shows a greater-than-chance accuracy. Like Freud a generation after him, Darwin used the materialist theory, that brain and mind are the same thing and that the soul dies with the body, to stifle the evidence provided by the widespread belief in the human soul even among people who had never read a Bible or, for that matter, spoken with a Christian.

"No one will dispute that instincts are of the highest importance to each animal," Darwin says near the end of the chapter on instinct in *Origin of Species*. "I do not pretend that the facts given in this chapter strengthen in any great degree my theory; but none of the cases of difficulty, to the best of my judgment, annihilate it."[21]

He was at least half-wrong even as far as he went. But he was completely wrong with regard to the role that instinct plays in devastating the materialist theory of consciousness, which is intimately bound up with scientific atheism. Darwin showed no scheme by which the physical brains of ants had been imprinted with instructions for slave-raiding the burrows of other ants. He also ignored the fact that most native and natural people believe in spirits and prophetic dreams that are actually quite familiar to any literate Englishman from the Bible and the classics. Were Darwin's flaws in his theory and his oversights in spiritual matters due to his deficiencies as a scientist? Or were they due to a problem with his mental health?

Darwin's Collapse: Phase Three

In October 1836, the *Beagle* returned to England and Darwin returned to his family and his father's roof. The imposing Robert Darwin, now growing obese, was startled at his son Charles' change in appearance. "Why, the shape of his head is quite altered," the old diagnostician told his daughters.

The Charles Darwin who had left England in December 1831 was a rather handsome young man with rust-blond hair and somewhat delicate features. The Charles Darwin who walked through the door and back under his father's roof in October 1836 was a coarser-looking man with a sharply receding hairline showing through his much darker hair and with a beetling brow. He actually did look almost like a different person.

He looked a lot more like his father.

Darwin's famous breakdown in health began almost as soon as he set foot under the family roof again. His vitality, once the envy of hearty British sailors, was barely able to deal with the life of a rich Victorian household with servants to do the harder work.

In 1839, he was still strong enough to marry his cousin, Emma Wedgwood, who became a loyal and devoted wife. But by 1842, when he was barely past thirty, he had become a semi-invalid — with no organic disease ever diagnosed which would explain his chronic health problems. "For nearly forty years he never knew one day of the health of ordinary man, and thus his life was one long struggle against the weariness and strain of sickness," his son Francis wrote in remembering his father.

Darwin didn't live with his father after he married, but he never left England again, and within a few years he was virtually confined to his own house and yard. His health and energy were so poor that he could only engage in scientific work for three hours a day of actual work: 8 A.M. to 9:30 followed by an hour's rest, and then on from 10:30 to 12 noon. He spent ten full years just working over the notes he had taken during the voyage of the *Beagle*. And there were times when he was so ill, or in such distress from headaches and indigestion, that he couldn't work at all for months on end.

As a young man, Darwin had loved reading Shakespeare, Milton, and Sir Walter Scott. He was so fond of music that he often hired groups of choirboys to sing in his rooms at college, and he regularly attended concerts. His wife, Emma, had been musical as well, and this had formed a mutual bond between them. He had also enjoyed art, even religious art. These tastes vanished with his unexplained illness of forty years' duration. "Up to the age of thirty, or beyond it, poetry of many kinds, such as the works of Milton, Gray, Byron, Wordsworth, Coleridge, and Shelley, gave me great pleasure, and even as a schoolboy

I took intense delight in Shakespeare, especially in the historical plays. I have also said that formerly pictures gave me considerable delight, and music very great delight," Darwin wrote in his autobiography. "But now for many years I cannot endure to read a line of poetry: I have tried lately to read Shakespeare and found it so intolerably dull that it nauseated me. I have also almost lost any taste for pictures or music."[22]

What Darwin is describing here are the unmistakable physical and mental symptoms of clinical depression.

Darwin himself didn't understand this, any more than he understood that his forty years of ill health were psychosomatic, produced by his own mind: "If I had my life to live over again I would have made a rule to read some poetry and listen to some music at least once every week; for perhaps the part of my brain now atrophied could thus have been kept active through use. The loss of these tastes is a loss of *happiness*, and may possibly be injurious to the intellect, and more probably to the moral character, by enfeebling the emotional part of our nature."[23]

Darwin was by this time wedded to the mechanistic/materialistic theory of consciousness which sees mind and brain as the same thing and all thought and behavior as a function of the physical brain. His explanation for his loss of taste in literature, art, and music is that part of his brain had shriveled up. Even mechanists probably acknowledge today that this is medical nonsense. Only chronic clinical depression can explain the loss of aesthetic taste, just as only it can explain the headaches, the indigestion, and the lassitude.

The cause of this depressed state has puzzled Darwin's admirers for many years. One theory was that chronic seasickness from the voyage of the *Beagle* undermined Darwin's metabolism. This theory doesn't hold much water. Darwin was never healthier than when on his voyage of discovery — and of escape from his father. His energy and vitality was amazing in those days, and his intuitive religious faith was probably stronger than at any time before or after.

Another theory is that Darwin had contracted Chagas' disease, a tropical infection of microscopic parasites which dwell inside insects and enter human bodies when the insects suck their blood. Chagas' disease wasn't widely understood until long after Darwin's death, but some of the symptoms described match what Darwin had to suffer for forty years. The disease begins with a high fever. Darwin suffered two high fevers while in South America. Chagas' disease causes edematous swelling, especially near the spot where the insects bit the victim. This is, very frequently, around the eyelids where the skin is thin. Darwin's family noted his change in facial appearance when he first arrived back home in England. Chagas' disease also causes extreme lassitude; it is, in fact, a milder form of African sleeping sickness or *trypanosomiasis*. This could help explain Darwin's lack of energy and at least some of his digestive problems.

Chagas' disease, however, can't have been more than a secondary symptom at best. Darwin retained his great vitality while he was voyaging on the *Beagle* even after he was stricken with both fevers. He was still able to climb the Andes and clamber over the rocks of the Galápagos Islands. The breakdown didn't occur until his return to England, where the temperate climate should have palliated the symptoms of a tropical infection.

The root cause of Darwin's forty years of ill health and of the loss of his taste in music, art, and literature can only be explained by the atheist syndrome. Darwin came back to England not only to face his father again but to find out that he'd begun to look like him. Much as he struggled to emulate his father, even in marrying a Wedgwood, as his father had done, he subconsciously feared and hated the godlike giant. The mind signaled the body to self-destruct. And forty years of ill health fell on a man who had showed such energy and strength as a voyager on the *Beagle*.

While Darwin was unable to work more than three hours a day and was repeatedly bedridden for weeks on end, he somehow found the strength to sire ten children. Seven of them lived to become adults— perhaps better than average for Victorian times. Interestingly, Darwin was a devoted and kindly father. He never disciplined his children harshly and they never feared him. His sensitive nature obviously had suffered from his own motherless boyhood and he didn't want to inflict suffering on his own children. Also, I think, his kindliness as a father was his way of repudiating his own father for whatever he had suffered during his own childhood. Charles in particular made a great fuss over any academic honors that his children won. He himself had felt unappreciated and very much under his father's ponderous shadow as a child and this was his way of making up for it.

Darwin's development of the theory of evolution by natural selection stems from this era of ill health and clinical depression. His health began to collapse in 1838 and worsened through 1842, then more or less stabilized at a semi-invalid condition. He didn't finish the notes from the voyage of the *Beagle* until 1846, and then another ten years passed before, under pressure of similar theorizing by Alfred Russel Wallace, he published *Origin of Species*. By this time—after two decades of bad health and clinical depression—his antireligious bias had become fairly intense, but he still maintained in his writings some sort of belief in a providential order to nature. "Thus, from the war of nature, from famine and death, the most exalted object which we are capable of conceiving, namely, the production of the higher animals, directly follows," Darwin wrote at the conclusion of *Origin of Species*. "This is grandeur in this view of life, with its several powers, having been originally breathed by the Creator into a few forms or into one; and that, while this planet has gone cycling on according to the fixed laws of gravity, from so simple a beginning endless forms most beautiful and most wonderful have been, and are being evolved."[24]

At this point, at least for the purposes of the reading public, Darwin still accepted some form of Divinity. He was obviously a deist rather than a Christian, but he hadn't hardened his position into atheism, or even into committed agnosticism.

When *Origin* was published, however, it touched off a war of words between the churchmen and scientists who believed in a literal six-day Creation and those who believed that the first books of the Old Testament were contradicted by scientific evidence. Attacks on Darwin and on his beloved theory of natural selection crystallized positions on both sides. The creationists soon began to argue that evolution was complete fraud. The evolutionists often turned their theory into an attack on Scripture—and, in some cases, an attack on God.

Of course, this was not true in every case. Charles Lyell, the man whose book on geology had helped Darwin work out his theory, remained, as Darwin notes, "thoroughly liberal in his religious beliefs or rather disbeliefs; but he was a strong Theist." Alfred Russel Wallace, the man who first published a pamphlet on the theory of evolution by natural selection, flatly refused to believe that human intelligence and consciousness could be purely biological in origin. He investigated spiritualism and discovered what he believed to be plausible evidence of life after death. Louis Agassiz remained a Christian.

Darwin's devoted wife, Emma, also remained a Christian. She also worried not only about Darwin's health but about the effect that Darwin's increasing obsession with bolstering evolution at the expense of God might have on both his mind and his soul. In a personal letter written to Darwin she mentions "that dread fear which the feeling of doubting first gives and which I do not think an unreasonable or superstitious feeling." She also writes:

It seems to me also that the line of your pursuits may have led you to view chiefly the difficulties of one side and that you have not had time to consider and study the chain of difficulties on the other. . . . May not the habit in scientific pursuits of believing nothing till it is proved, influence your mind too much in other things which cannot be proved in the same way, and which if true are likely to be above our comprehension? I should say also there is a danger in giving up revelation which does not exist on the other side, that is the fear of ingratitude in casting off what has been done for your benefit as well as for that of all the world and which ought to make you still more careful, perhaps even fearful lest you should not have taken all the pains you could to judge truly.[25]

Emma Darwin may have lacked any formal training in science. But besides being a pious Christian she was a remarkably astute critic of her husband's work where it infringed on faith. She says — correctly, in her genteel and rather convoluted way — that Darwin wasn't interested in any arguments from the religious or spiritual side of the controversy. His obsession at this point was not in finding out the truth, but in refuting Christianity because it threatened "his" precious theory. The underlying factor that the God of the Bible reminded him of the earthly father he subconsciously hated and feared must have played a critical role in this obsession. His need to feel important can't be overlooked either.

In 1858, while Darwin and Wallace were in the last stages of preparing their separately formulated theory of evolution by natural selection, the events at Lourdes in France began to occur. Bernadette Soubirous, a French peasant girl, claimed to have visions of the Virgin Mary. English Protestants of the Victorian age had an ingrained distrust of "Catholic" miracles that went back to the controversies and animosities of the sixteenth-century Reformation and Counter-Reformation, and most of them shrugged the vision off as a hallucination or a fraud. But a number of French officials investigated, and what they discovered was astonishing. At one point, Bernadette fell into a rapture while holding a votive candle in her hands in the presence of a number of witnesses. The candle burned itself out in her grasp and left no burns or marks on her palms. Several unbelievers fell to their knees and pronounced their conversion on the spot. Shortly after, people who drank the water of the Lourdes grotto or bathed in it reported miraculous cures of genuine physical ailments. The stories of the events at Lourdes created a sensation in France.

Darwin paid no attention. Since the only evidence available from Lourdes would have been in favor of Christianity, or at least in favor of some nonmaterialistic explanation of the human mind and soul, it didn't fit his theory. Darwin dismissed the events without a second thought.

In the 1860s, while the controversy about *Origin of Species* was raging, a number of British scientists couldn't accept the idea that materialism explained human personality. Neither could they bring themselves to investigate orthodox Christianity, so they became interested in the scientific study of spiritualism. Even this failed to interest Darwin. Again, the supposedly open-minded Darwin was unwilling to investigate anything that might conflict with "his" theory of evolution.

By 1871, Darwin, having ignored orthodox Christianity, Lourdes, and spiritualism, and anything else that might provide contradictory or conflicting evidence, fired off his views on human evolution in *The Descent of Man*. Darwin had soft-peddled the notion that man had descended from apelike ancestors in *Origin of Species* in 1859. But neither creationists nor evolutionists had missed the implication that human beings had developed from "monkeys," as they were to put it. Besides advancing the "monkey" theory, *The Descent of Man* takes a few left-handed swipes at Christianity, spiritualism, and Lourdes-type miracles.

"It is . . . probable . . . that dreams may have first given rise to the notion of spirits," Darwin wrote in *The Descent of Man*. "When a savage dreams, the figures which appear before him are believed to have come from a distance, and to stand over him; or the soul of the dreamer goes out on its travels, and comes home with a remembrance of what it has seen."

Spiritual phenomena were undeniably attested human experiences. Darwin, however, would have none of it. Writing in England, a country noted for its spiritual sensitivity, the friend of serious scientists he respected who believed that spiritual phenomena were at least worth investigating, he absolutely refused to budge in his hide-bound conviction that there was "no such thing." Yet in *Voyage of the* Beagle, before his antireligious beliefs had hardened into a dogma, he described Jemmy Button, the Fuegan Indian, predicting the death of Jemmy's father in a prophetic dream. And in Darwin's own autobiography, he describes his father as having a "most remarkable power" for "reading characters" which was — key phrase — "almost supernatural." Darwin adds, "A young Doctor in Shrewsbury, who disliked my father, used to say that he was wholly unscientific, but owned that his power of predicting the end of an illness was unparalleled." For four pages of the autobiography, Darwin describes his own father's spiritual proclivities. He refused, however, to credit that psychic abilities actually exist. Was he subconsciously trying to wish or to reason his father out of existence?

Now listen to his description of our "ancestors" in *The Descent of Man*: "For my own part I would as soon be descended from that heroic little monkey . . . as from a savage who delights to torture his enemy, offers up bloody sacrifices, practices infanticide without remorse, treats his wives like slaves, knows no decency, and is haunted by the grossest superstitions."[26]

"Torture" and "infanticide" may be echoes of a harsher childhood than Darwin cared to tell us about in his autobiography. The "infanticide," of course, would refer to a frightened son's *fear* of being killed. "Offers up bloody sacrifices" is a good metaphor for medicine in the days before anesthetics, as is "torture." "Treats his wives like slaves" is a sort of Victorian libel on native and natural culture. Since the Victorians sentimentalized women beyond the point of realism, and since Victorian boys were usually much closer to their mothers than to their fathers, Victorians wanted women to be well treated. The idea that "primitive" people *generally* mistreat their wives is part of the myth of Anglo-Saxon superiority over all men in all things. In some tribal cultures, both among Africans and among Indians, women enjoyed greater freedom and greater property rights than they did in Victorian England. The English, of course, argued otherwise. Darwin not only bought this myth, but helped promulgate it.

The comment about "treats his wives like slaves" harkens back, perhaps, to early Roman times, when an unfaithful wife could be killed by her husband without a trial, and fathers had the power of life and death over the entire family. Darwin himself knew such a *paterfamilias* — "the largest man I ever saw," who held the power of life and death in his ponderous hands — and failed to let Darwin's mother live. And this giant father was not merely "haunted by the grossest superstitions," but supposedly used spiritual power in his medical practice.

It is hardly stretching things to suppose that the "savage" Darwin is talking about is his own father. This explains the vehemence of his dislike of this hypothetical "savage" he invents as a figure of rhetoric. It explains why he refused to put any stock at all in stories of spiritual phenomena and held firmly to a materialistic view of mind, even when he wrote about evidence for spiritual reality in two of his books. And it explains his absolute revulsion against the idea that man had human ancestors at all.

Darwin closes *The Descent of Man* with a negative verdict on any vestige of soul or spirit in man. "We are not here concerned with hopes or fears, only with the truth as far as our reason permits us to discover it," Darwin tells us. "And I have given the evidence to the best of my ability . . . with all these exalted powers — man still bears in his bodily frame the indelible stamp of his lowly origin."[27]

It's hard to stifle a laugh. Darwin tells us he's looked at all the evidence when in fact he's deliberately ignored the scientific investigation of spiritualism and of the events at Lourdes, two of the greatest controversies of the 1860s. His decision to defend natural selection at the price of objectivity, as well as of religious faith, looks at first glance like the blunder of an enormously warped ego. But there is another explanation rooted in the atheist syndrome.

Darwin may have disliked the idea of an afterlife so intensely that he consciously or subconsciously rejected any and all evidence in its favor. The afterlife implied, among other things, yet another reunion with his "beloved" father — like the first one which had destroyed his health and vitality. It implied belief in an omniscient God who can only have reminded him of his "almost supernatural" Father, spelled with a capital F.

A clinically depressed person typically wakes up frightened but goes to sleep relieved. His depression makes life such a miserable experience that he struggles to blot out conscious existence by sleeping as much as possible. Sleep to him becomes an aspiration, an aspiration of what he hopes will permanently happen at death. If death is sleep, the depressed person finds it a consummation devoutly to be wished. His depression makes him consciously wish himself out of existence. This, of course, is the reason that so many seriously depressed people kill themselves. It's also the reason that mildly depressed people sleep longer than non-depressed people, and why they choose to sleep during daylight hours to avoid contact with reality to the greatest possible degree.

To the Christian, the afterlife holds the promise of a reward for his earthly struggles. To the hopeful agnostic who hasn't made up his mind, it holds out the possibility — to a bold and self-confident spirit — of more adventures. But to the person suffering clinical depression, the idea of a life after death is far more frightening and upsetting than the prospect of blissful sleep.

And I think that's why Darwin and many of his followers willfully overlooked any possible evidence for a life after death, whether it came from "savages," spiritualists, French Catholics, or the New Testament.

What arguments, after all, did the depressed and enfeebled Darwin advance for his disbelief in God, Jesus, and the immortal soul? In his autobiography, begun in 1876 five years after *The Descent of Man* and with the strong suspicion of his own approaching death, he summarized his position. "At the present day the most usual argument for the existence of an intelligent God is drawn from the deep inward conviction and feelings which are experienced by most persons," Darwin wrote. "But it cannot be doubted that Hindoos, Mahomadans [*sic*], and others might argue in the same manner and with equal force in favor of the existence of one God, or of many Gods, or as with the Buddhists of no God. There are also many barbarian tribes who cannot be said with any truth to believe in what we call God: they believe indeed in spirits or ghosts."[28]

This is a garbled argument. Only Darwin's inability to recognize native and natural peoples, including "Hindoos" and Moslems and Buddhists, as authentically human comes through in this argument. Certainly his logic doesn't.

"Nor must we overlook the probability," he continued, "of the constant inculcation in a belief in God on the minds of children producing so strong and perhaps an inherited effect on their brains not yet fully developed, that it would be as difficult for them to throw off their belief in God, as for a monkey to throw off its instinctive fear and hatred of a snake."[29]

Emma Darwin wrote to her son Francis after Darwin's death and asked Darwin's son to delete this passage because she personally found it upsetting and because it would give pain to those of Darwin's friends who were religious, and even to the family servants.[30] That the faithful Christian Emma Darwin would want to preserve her husband's name is understandable, and the passage has been deleted in some versions. But I think it speaks abundantly of Darwin's own fear and hatred, not so much for a God he professed not to believe in as for his symbolic confusion of God with his own father. The logic is nonexistent. If people can't bear *not* to believe in God, why do they become atheists?

"There seems to be no more design," Darwin asserted, "in the variability of organic beings and in the action of natural selection, than in the course which the wind blows. Everything in nature is the result of fixed laws."[31]

Is this really the great Charles Darwin's last shot at denying Christianity? Surely not. It is fraught with problems. First problem: Who fixed the laws of nature? Second problem: If evolution is pointless why does it produce higher and higher species? Is man really no more impressive than the amoeba or the salt-water sponge? If you're wrapped in deep clinical depression, perhaps not. But most sane people would feel otherwise.

"But I was very unwilling to give up my belief," Darwin says. "I feel sure of this for I can well remember often and often inventing daydreams of old letters between distinguished Romans and manuscripts being discovered at Pompeii or elsewhere which confirmed in the most striking manner all that was written in the Gospels."

Darwin here advances the argument that the New Testament is not only unreliable but that it represents the only written evidence that Jesus ever lived. The Stalinists used this same argument in the 1920s when they were campaigning against Christianity in the Soviet Union, only to abandon it when it proved to be entirely untenable. In fact, the textual and historical viability of the Bible is unassailable, and Jesus and the Christians are mentioned by name by innumerable classical Roman authors. Tacitus, who corroborates the Gospel accounts of the life of Jesus, goes on to say he was executed by Pontius Pilate and documents the work of Christians in Rome in A.D. 62, about thirty-five years after the Crucifixion. Suetonius mentions Christ in his biography of the Roman Emperor Claudius and repeatedly observes, in his biographies of Caligula and Vespasian, that the Romans knew about a prophecy of a King rising in the East who would rule the world. Jesus is also mentioned as a worker of wonders by Flavius Josephus, a Jewish scholar writing in Greek who was actually a contemporary of Jesus and the disciples. Atheists have long argued that the Jesus passage in Josephus is a medieval forgery, added centuries later by a pious monk. But in 1972, a Jewish scholar found a copy of the same passage in a translation from Josephus's original Greek into Arabic. The original translator must have been a Moslem. Since neither medieval Jews nor medieval Moslems would have had any reason to authenticate the historic life of Jesus, the mention of Jesus in Josephus seems to be undeniably authentic. There are also a number of references about Jesus in early Christian writings that the Church later rejected as not being authentic. Jesus is even mentioned, albeit obliquely, in the Jewish Talmud. Even a thoroughgoing skeptic today has to accept Jesus as an authentic historical figure or jeopardize his own credibility. And this raises a further question. If Jesus hadn't been an utterly remarkable figure, why was His life so important to so many people?

Darwin's arguments against Christianity are utterly illogical. Most people will find them unconvincing, just as Lyell, Wallace, Agassiz, and Emma Darwin did. With only one exception — as we shall see in the next chapter — the people closest to Darwin seem to have regarded his antireligious bias not as a brilliant breakthrough, but as the great flaw in his work and his character.

But that one exception (Thomas Henry Huxley) was to fill his own emotional needs by becoming a full-time propagandist for Darwin's evolutionary theories and for his own antireligious outlook. And perhaps even more than Darwin, he revealed the workings of the atheist syndrome.

FOUR

THOMAS HENRY HUXLEY: THE FIRST AGNOSTIC

Thomas Henry Huxley is a far less familiar figure to modern readers than Charles Darwin. Regarded in Victorian times as "Darwin's Bulldog," he rose to fame by defending Darwin's theories of natural selection when Darwin himself was too depressed and sick to defend them himself.

Ronald W. Clark, an extremely sympathetic biographer of the Huxley family, summed it up succinctly. "The *Origin* made Darwin: Its defense made Huxley."

Of course, there was more to Huxley's passions and fame than that. Darwin, in his deep depression, drifted slowly away from religious belief and pulled a large number of people slowly away with him. Huxley was one of them. He attacked Christianity with vigor and verbal violence. In his own field of expertise, physiology (the study of how living organisms function internally) he "invented" a theory of consciousness which eliminated the need for anything like a human soul or will as far as he himself was concerned. He also coined the term *agnostic* to describe a person who professed "not to know" about religious beliefs.

Time has not dealt kindly with Huxley, and this may be one of the reasons that modern atheists don't tout him as much as they tout Darwin or Freud. He's become something of an embarrassment. His antisoul theory of human consciousness was considered a joke when he devised it and has only become more ridiculous with time. And his claim of "disinterested objectivity" on the subject of faith versus doubt was such an obvious fraud in his lifetime that even his most admiring biographers couldn't help but note his deep-seated hatred of anything concerning religion.

So what was it that really drove the man?

Huxley's Childhood: Phase One

Huxley was the son of an unsuccessful schoolmaster. He left only a few fragments of autobiographical information about his youth and wrote very little about his father, but he plainly disliked him. One of the few passages says: "Physically I am the son of my mother so completely — even down to peculiar movements of the hands, which made their appearance in me as I reached the age she had when I noticed them — that I can hardly find any trace of my father in myself except an inborn facility for drawing, which, unfortunately, in my case, has never been cultivated, a hot temper, and that amount of tenacity of purpose which unfriendly observers sometimes call obstinacy."[1]

Today, if a boy identified so thoroughly with his mother that he admitted to imitating "the peculiar movements of her hands," while dismissing a very real skill at drawing because it supposedly came from his father's side of the family, it would be considered very unhealthy, to say the least. There can't be much doubt that Huxley disliked his "hot-tempered" father, particularly after the father abandoned him to the miseries of Victorian school days.

Lovelessness was not just evidenced in Huxley's home; it marked every facet of his life.

"The people who were set over us cared about as much for our intellectual and moral welfare as if they were baby-farmers," Huxley wrote of his school days. "We were left to the operation of the struggle for existence among ourselves; bullying was the least of the ill practices current among us."[2]

Huxley apparently also came into contact with the lengthy and often intimidating sermons of English country parsons who delighted in threatening those who doubted the truths of the Gospel with lurid hell-fire and damnation.

"From dark allusions to skeptics and infidels," he wrote, "I became aware of the existence of people who trusted in carnal reason; who audaciously doubted that the world was made in six natural days, or that the deluge was universal; perhaps went even so far as to question the literal accuracy of the story of Eve's temptation, or of Balaam's ass; and, from the horror of the tone in which they were mentioned, I should have been justified in drawing the conclusion that these men belonged to the criminal classes. At the same time, those who were more directly responsible with providing me with the knowledge essential to the right guidance of life . . . imagined that they were discharging that most sacred duty by impressing on my childish mind the necessity, on pain of reprobation in this world and damnation in the next, of accepting in the strict and literal sense, every statement made in the Protestant Bible. I was told to believe, and I did believe, that doubt about any of them was a sin, and not less reprehensible than a moral derelict. I suppose that, out of a thousand of my contemporaries, nine hundred, at least, had their minds systematically warped, in the name of the God of truth, by like discipline."[3]

Huxley wrote this as a mature man, but his dislike of Christianity and Scripture apparently began quite early. One of the family memories was that he once attempted to preach a sermon to the household, in imitation of the parsons at church, and became upset when nobody took his efforts very seriously. By his teens in the 1830s—long before Darwin had had any impact on the world of science—Huxley had abandoned faith in anything and everything but the vaguest sort of Providence.

Beyond resentment against his "hot-tempered" and financially unsuccessful father and his dislike of long-winded and threatening sermons and school bullying, there was something more sinister and more shameful gnawing at the teenaged Huxley: fear of hereditary insanity in his family line. Most admiring biographers don't mention this, but the Huxleys produced an alarming number of mentally ill people. George Huxley, his father, became "sunk in worse than childish imbecility of mind" when he was barely into his fifties and died in an insane asylum.[4] One Huxley brother suffered from "extreme mental anxiety," probably what we today would term some form of extreme neurosis. Another Huxley brother was described as being "as near mad as a sane man can be."[5] One sister's unhappy husband became an opium addict. Another Huxley brother-in-law fled one of Huxley's sisters for a new life in the United States after their marriage proved miserable. One has to suspect that, in both cases, the Huxley sisters played some role in the addiction of one husband and the flight—rather shocking in Victorian eyes—of the other one. In any case, a precociously senile father and two crazy brothers was a very unfortunate legacy in Victorian times. The psychological impact can only have been increased by the mystery that surrounded insanity in the early nineteenth century. New ideas about deterioration of the physical brain due to health or heredity seemed to conflict with the New

Testament picture of certain kinds of insanity caused by unclean spirits and habitual sin. One has to wonder if his hatred of the New Testament wasn't somehow rooted in Huxley's fear that the sin and insanity in his family were indeed caused by "unclean spirits" and were perhaps contagious.

The confirmation of Huxley's instability came when he was fourteen and interested in medicine. Two of his brothers-in-law arranged for him to attend an autopsy. Faced with a dead body cut open for examination on the table, Huxley suffered such a psychological shock that it almost killed him. Most medical students fear their first autopsy, and some react with nausea or nightmares. But Huxley's reaction was a total collapse. He lost his appetite, his vitality, and his will to live. He also believed — for the rest of his life — that he had somehow been poisoned by "vapors" from that cadaver. "I did not cut myself, and none of the ordinary symptoms of dissection-poison supervened, but poisoned I was somehow, and I remember sinking into a strange state of apathy," Huxley wrote afterwards. "By way of a last chance, I was sent to the care of some good, kind people, friends of my father's who lived in a farmhouse in the heart of Warwickshire. I remember staggering from my bed to the window on a bright spring morning after my arrival and throwing open the casement. Life seemed to come back on the wings of the breeze, and to this day the faint odor of wood-smoke, like that which floated across the farm-yard in the early morning, is as good to me as 'the sweet south upon a bed of violets.' I soon recovered but for years I suffered from occasional paroxysms of internal pain, and from that time my constant friend, hypochondriacal dyspepsia, commenced his half-century of contenancy [sic] upon my fleshly tabernacle."[6]

This brief description of Huxley's psychological state of confusion is critical to understanding his personality. In the same paragraph, he says he was poisoned by vapors from the cadaver, and admits to "hypochondriacal" indigestions (dyspepsia means indigestion). Since hypochondria, then as now, means a state of illness induced by the imagination, Huxley must have known, at some level, that his illness was brought on by the psychological shock of the autopsy. Yet he continued to believe, fifty years after the event, that he had been physically poisoned by the horrible corpse on the table.

This is a rather strange mentality for a scientist. Huxley showed every evidence of an overwhelming terror of death. This prevented him from ever dealing with the question of a possible afterlife either as a Christian or on any other basis. It also temporarily ended his desire to become a physician. He attempted to shift from medicine to mechanical engineering, but, he says dryly, "the fates were against me." Possibly, like Darwin before him and Freud after him, he had trouble with mathematics. It's fascinating, though perhaps irrelevant, that mathematics is the most precise and objective of all the major educational disciplines and that virtually everyone who suffered from the atheist syndrome had a notable deficiency in mathematic skill. Huxley, for whatever reason, dropped engineering and returned to medicine. But he said that the only field of medicine he was seriously interested in was physiology, which he called "the mechanical engineering of living organisms." Before he was out of his teens, long before Darwin wrote *Origin of Species*, Huxley had already begun to think of human beings as purely mechanical products.

"I knew and cared very little about medicine as the art of healing," he wrote frankly. Nor was he good at it. Throughout his career, long after he won fame as an antireligious propagandist, he remained a notably poor diagnostician. He just couldn't face the facts of human life and death with any insight or objectivity. His progress through his medical studies was subject to the sort of indecisiveness and failure of the ability to concentrate that usually crops up in atheist syndrome cases.

"I worked extremely hard when it pleased me, and when it did not, which was a frequent case, I was extremely idle," Huxley wrote, "or else wasted my industries in wrong directions. I . . . took up all sorts of pursuits to drop them again quite as speedily."[7]

Huxley had troubles with medicine per se, but he won prizes in chemistry, anatomy, and physiology. His high intelligence and his diligence in obsessively pursuing subjects that attracted his interest were never in doubt.

Once he became a physician, Huxley seemed to have hit another dead end. He disliked dealing with sick people. A brief medical practice around the slummy London docks convinced him that he wasn't cut out for family practice. He quickly gave it up. Despite his purported concern for the poor and downtrodden, a fact that his biographers constantly cite as an example of his great humanity, Huxley passed up a chance to do a genuine service for humanity. He showed absolutely no interest in being a physician in a neighborhood where physicians were urgently needed. Those who don't admire him could point out that, like a good many other "humanists" who claim to love "humanity," Huxley didn't care much about people.

Huxley's Flight: Phase Two

Huxley's escape from England, human service, and his father's symbolic roof, like Darwin's, came about through the good offices of the Royal Navy, which, once again, needed a naturalist for an extended sea voyage. At twenty-one, Huxley signed up as assistant surgeon aboard HMS *Rattlesnake*, a frigate which was sailing for northern Australia and New Guinea.

Huxley reacted in the way we should expect. His intellect blossomed. Surrounded by officers and sailors he regarded as bores and boors, but free from the curse of his father's roof and the fear of contagious family insanity, he continued a self-imposed regimen of lessons, perfecting his self-taught German and learning Italian well enough to read Dante in the original. He also worked on a paper about mollusks which would win him a coveted fellowship in the Royal Society at the age of twenty-six and boost him from a complete unknown to a "name" in science.

Like Darwin, Huxley had his first contact with "primitive" man at this time. The Papuan and Australian natives he met on the extended voyage appalled him. Huxley came from a family which, before his time, could probably have been described as "shabby-genteel." They could trace their ancestry back to the days of Richard the Lion-Hearted, circa A.D. 1190, but a lack of money and the ever-daunting threat of insanity cast dark shadows over his emotional security. Faced with people who were "different" and "primitive," he instinctively disliked and feared them. It's fascinating that those Victorians who stood higher on the social pyramid than the penurious Huxleys often got along extremely well with native and natural people instead of despising them. Queen Victoria herself was enormously impressed with the American Indians from western tribes that George Catlin had recruited more or less in a state of nature and brought to England about this time. She not only admired their robust physiques and alert expressions, but spent a great deal of time in unaffected conversations, through an interpreter, talking to the Indian women about childrearing and other domestic matters. Victoria thought the "wild" Indians to be splendid. Charles Dickens, who grew up on the edge of poverty, met the same Indians — and loathed them at first sight.

The long sea voyage had a tonic effect on Huxley, because, one suspects, he was able to act out his desires to escape. There's at least a chance, however, that it had another effect on him, one that may explain some of the amazingly zany ideas he concocted in the years after his return to England. During the years that HMS *Rattlesnake* was sailing the seas, the English were trying out a new technology: canned food, or, as they sometimes called it, "tinned grub." Unfortunately, in the 1840s the technique of canning was still in its infancy and Victorian medicine still hadn't discovered the dangers of lead poisoning, a poisoning far more dangerous than the imaginary "vapors" from the cadaver which Huxley blamed for his fifty years of indigestion. Early Victorian "tin" cans were sealed with lead solder which contaminated the preserved food. Canned food wasn't used much in English households because it was expensive and usually not very tasty. Butchers and greengrocers might call in person at the better homes and other people went to market or raised some of their own vegetables and fruit. But by the 1840s, canned food was widely employed on long sea voyages, where fresh greens and fruit and freshly killed meat might not be available.

In the 1840s, while Huxley and HMS *Rattlesnake* were headed south, another British expedition was headed north. Sir John Franklin and his men were sailing to find the Northwest Passage, the branch of the sea that they hoped would provide a water route from the north Atlantic to the north Pacific. Sir John Franklin's whole expedition, 149 men in two wooden ships, vanished for years and nothing was heard from them. Relief expeditions met Eskimos who told them of meeting Englishmen wandering the ice pack and dropping dead from hunger and exhaustion. Later searches found that the wooden ships had been trapped in the ice and the men had tried to walk out across the frozen seas and died of hunger and exhaustion. There were no survivors to report the incidents of heroism that may have punctuated an epic of tragedy and horror.

Three silent witnesses, however, remained behind in shallow graves in Greenland. Subsequent explorers found the neatly dug graves and wooden coffins of three Victorian explorers who didn't make the final trip north. A British sailor, a petty officer, and a Marine who had died during the course of the expedition had been buried in rocky graves. The icy waters had penetrated the wooden coffins and the three dead men were frozen stiff within hours of their deaths. They were uncovered in a near-perfect state of preservation in the 1980s, looking like men who had been dead a few days instead of 140 years.

Autopsies with modern technology revealed that the men had probably died of complications of pneumonia and tuberculosis. Both diseases were woefully common in Victorian times, especially among people who were malnourished. But the autopsy also found that each of the three men had near-toxic accumulations of lead in his system at the time of death, almost certainly from the canned food used on the voyage. Modern toxicologists said that lead in this sort of concentration could not only destroy the appetite, but could cause serious errors of judgment. Was lead poisoning a cause of the unexplained errors of judgment in the Franklin expedition to search for the Northwest Passage? Was it also perhaps a cause of some of the bizarre pronouncements and strange obsessions that characterized Huxley's career after the four-year sea voyage to Australia? The question deserves to be explored, because a whole host of the things that Huxley said and wrote and believed in his battle for science and against religion very simply border on madness.

Huxley's voyage of self-discovery and escape had one undoubted consequence. He met his future wife, Henrietta Heathorn, while in Australia. Blonde, blue-eyed, fond of German literature, and without any undue snobbery, Henrietta came from a family that had money and expected to have more money. Huxley spoke to her exactly four times before they became engaged. One shouldn't doubt that his affection for her was genuine and deep. The fact that her background and fortune were better than his can't have impeded his love. Huxley is described as being five-feet-eleven—quite tall for a Victorian—and darkly handsome. He was a romantic figure if ever there was one, and his hostility to religion was still held in check. This was important because Henrietta was quite pious and remained a believing Christian all her life.

Huxley and Henrietta pledged their love but he had to return to England to make some kind of fortune before he could marry. The voyage of HMS *Rattlesnake* was a rattling good adventure after the stopover. There were ambushes by bushmen. The captain grew sick and died in Huxley's arms. The ship returned to England in 1850.

But what now? Huxley's prospects of being able to marry in the near future seemed dim. But fortune, as he might have said, smiled on him. The paper he wrote on mollusks won him a fellowship in the Royal Society at the callow age of twenty-six, and this enabled him to secure various teaching and lecturing positions which provided an income.

Huxley sent for Henrietta. She arrived in England after a long voyage, worn down by the rigors of travel and a series of head colds and other maladies. Nervous physicians feared the onset of tuberculosis and gave her "six months to live." Huxley, a romantic for all his religious doubts, vowed to marry Henrietta and did—and they lived together in domestic devotion for the next forty years.

Henrietta not only recovered her health in a fairly short time but produced a son, Noel, so named because he was born during the Christmas season. Huxley was totally irreligious by this time, but he appeased his beloved wife with a church wedding and baptisms for all of their children, including the first-born, Noel. As is to be expected in a marriage of love and respect, Huxley doted on his son. In tracing the atheist syndrome, we can also see that, like Darwin, Huxley tried to make up for his own unhappy childhood, his hot-tempered father, and the bullying of his school days by treating Noel and his subsequent children with enormous love and fatherly concern. His writings about Noel are genuinely touching: "a lovely child with large blue eyes, golden curls, a clear firm skin, and regular features." Henrietta was fair-haired, while Huxley was dark-haired and dark-eyed. The fact that Noel resembled his cherished Henrietta instead of the spawn of Huxley's "hot-tempered" father, with their heritage of insanity and precocious senility, can only have been a tremendous relief. A more religious Victorian than Huxley might have called it a "blessing."

Once when Noel made a trip to the beach, Huxley penned a loving description: "My yellow-haired boy riots in the luxury of unlimited sand and a spade to dig withall." Clearly, Huxley loved Noel with deep sincerity and devotion, but he couldn't resist commenting on Noel's yellow hair, as if the blondness were proof that Huxley himself had managed to elude the feared insanity of his own dark-haired brothers and sisters. "He is a great comfort and solace in the troubles of this weary world and is my domestic chaplain, though he doesn't know it," Huxley also wrote.[8]

Toward the end of 1859, Huxley received proof copies of the as-yet-unpublished *Origin of Species* by Charles Darwin. He was electrified by the book, which bore on his own work. But even more than his direct professional interest, he was enamored by the book because he felt that it proved that the Bible was not literally correct and that species had evolved from earlier species instead of being specifically created. Huxley had ceased to believe in a personal God for personal reasons long before reading *Origin of Species*. Darwin's book didn't convince him of anything. It simply struck a responsive chord in his own mind. And he seized on it as if he'd thought of it himself.

Darwin's book, as we have seen, was the opening gun of the famous battle between science and religion. But the first major engagement was fought at Oxford, with science represented by Thomas Henry Huxley and religion by Samuel Wilberforce, Bishop of Oxford. This was the evolution-versus-creation version of the gunfight at the O.K. Corral, with each side seeing the other as the bad guys. Bishop Wilberforce, no scientist, was coached by some scientists who believed in creationism. Huxley was designated as a proxy hitter for Darwin, who was too ill with his usual collection of depressed maladies and shyness to show up. Huxley himself almost missed the debate, but when another scientist, Robert Chambers, jokingly accused him of cowardice, he felt irritated enough to attend the verbal shoot-out, officially called "The Intellectual Development of Europe Considered with Reference to the Views of Mr. Darwin" — not exactly a catchy title.

Bishop Wilberforce had come to be known as Soapy Sam, a title he shrugged off with whatever good humor he could muster. He joked that he was called "soapy" because he was always getting in hot water but always emerging with clean hands. Witty rather than profound, he owed his prominence in the church to his ability as a brilliant orator and to the fact that his famous father, William Wilberforce, had been a hero in the fight to have England outlaw slavery.

No actual dictation of the famous debate was taken and most of what the history books record is based on conflicting accounts from memory. Knowing little science, Wilberforce fell back on wit and gallantry. Noticing the number of elegant ladies who had attended, he paid a chivalrous compliment to womankind at the expense of mankind: "If anyone were to be willing to trace his descent through an ape as his *grandfather*, would he be willing to trace his descent through an ape on the side of his *grandmother*?"[9]

Huxley retaliated against this genial gallantry with a piece of nastiness that seems hard to believe. "If, then, the question is put to me, would I rather have a miserable ape for a grandfather, or a man highly endowed by nature and possessed of great means and influence, and yet who employs these faculties and that influence for the mere purpose of introducing ridicule into a grave scientific discussion — I unhesitatingly affirm my preference for the ape."[10]

The bishop's faction gasped. Huxley's faction went wild. One of the elegant ladies fainted. Nothing was resolved, and nobody on either side appears to have changed horses. But the level of the discussion was established. From now on, it was open warfare, at the verbal level, between churchmen who believed in Scripture and scientists who, in many cases, were openly hostile to Scripture and, for that matter, to any mention of God or Jesus or human immortality. Truth took a back seat to rhetorical swordsmanship.

The battle of Oxford took place in the summer of 1860. Huxley was now an established name. By defending Darwin's *Origin of Species*, he had ridden to fame on Darwin's coattails without actually making any major contributions of his own. During the rest of that summer, he basked in the esteem of Darwin and the Darwinians as the point man for the evolutionists and their battle against the creationists.

Huxley's Collapse: Phase Three

In September of that same year, Noel, Huxley's son, was stricken with scarlet fever. Two days later, he died.

The death of a child, especially a first-born son, is traumatic at best, even to people with religious convictions. The impact on Huxley was absolutely shattering. The autopsy he attended in his teens and the psychosomatic collapse of his health had shown his inability to deal with death. His avoidance of medicine as a career in preference to research, even when he had a family to support, confirms it. But Noel's death carried a double-barreled shock. As Huxley himself pointed out, the God he heard preached in his unhappy childhood was a "God of Vengeance" who punished doubters and blasphemers with disaster, death, and damnation. One can't escape the conclusion that Huxley took Noel's death as the gesture of retribution of an angry God, a God he himself had angered through his attack on Wilberforce and Scripture in defense of Darwin.

But there was no repentance. Instead, there was suppressed rage. Intellectually, Huxley simply moved away from a professed ignorance of any religious matters to a conviction that God, Jesus, and the afterlife didn't exist. But on the subconscious level, where people often make their most important life decisions, Huxley decided to not simply deny God but to become God's enemy. God had not only taken away his beloved son but also the visible yellow-haired sign that he'd be able to outdistance the hereditary Huxley taint of insanity and precocious senility. The death of Noel in 1860 finished Huxley as an objective scientist. At that point he became an obsessed antireligious propagandist.

For the rest of Huxley's career—he lived until 1895 and traveled and lectured widely—he defended Darwin's ideas, and the godless universe Darwin came to believe in during the forty-year bout of clinical depression, as the only worldview worthy of a free man and a scientist. To make the facts fit the theories, he sometimes had to mutate or mutilate the facts. He did this with all the power of a brilliant mind twisted by a flawed and fearful childhood and the shock of Noel's sudden death. He also followed the usual pattern of the atheist syndrome and throughout the second half of his life, his health was miserable. He suffered from the same collection of maladies that had afflicted Darwin: indigestion and headaches, lassitude, aches and pains that couldn't be explained. Huxley, however, found a temporary source of relief. He himself noted, more than once, that when he was making violent verbal or literary attacks on Christianity, his headaches went away, his appetite and digestion improved, and he felt cheerful and energetic. He seems never to have understood this, but he was never a good diagnostician even in his student days. Quite simply, raving against religion enabled him to dramatize his rejection of God. Symbolized by his father and the strict clergymen of his boyhood, God had stuck him in schools where he was bored and bullied; and the Old Testament God of Vengeance had killed Noel, his first-born and his bulwark against hereditary madness. Throw in a little lead poisoning, perhaps, from his four years at sea on HMS *Rattlesnake* and you have the explanation for some of the strangest theories ever to come out of an important scientist, theories which do and did become an accepted and vital part of scientific atheism and materialism.

The mistakes Huxley made and the violent ways in which he attacked religion and human spirituality could fill an entire book. To understand his role in scientific atheism, it's enough to look at just three aspects of his career after the Oxford debate and the death of Noel.

First is Huxley's theory of *epiphenomenalism.*

Epiphenomenalism, according to Huxley, was how human consciousness actually works. Huxley said that *no* action is planned in advance. The body does the action first and the mind, deluded by the body's previous action, *imagines* that the action had been planned when in fact it happened by sensory desire only, or by accident.

Let's follow an action. Under the normal understanding of human consciousness, I feel thirsty through my tongue or taste buds. These carry the message "thirst" to my brain, and either the brain or the brain/mind interaction consciously decides that it would be a good idea to get up and get a glass of water. The brain, or the mind/brain interaction, as you prefer, tells the body to get up and get a glass of water, and the body does so.

Under Huxley's theory of human consciousness, here's the same action. The taste buds tell the brain that the body is thirsty, and the body gets up and gets a glass of water. Meanwhile the brain, *which is just along for the ride*, is convinced that the decision to get up and get a glass of water was a conscious decision *after the body has already gotten up to get the glass of water*.

The layman in science will think that this makes absolutely no sense. He will be absolutely right. Epiphenomenalism is entirely unsupportable scientifically. It was a silly idea when Huxley thought of it and it's even sillier today. Huxley's invention of epiphenomenalism was an attempt to explain human consciousness in purely physical terms, avoiding any concept of the human soul or spirit or will, which has obvious religious overtones.

Epiphenomenalism had one great advantage. It enabled Huxley to get rid of free will and the Judeo-Christian concept of individual responsibility. But then it had one disadvantage. It didn't make any sense. The major scientific thinkers of Huxley's own day and age, at least those who didn't share his hidebound hatred of religion, ridiculed the idea. William James, who probably knew more about the physiology of the brain than anyone else in that generation, and far more about normal and abnormal psychology, said of epiphenomenalism: "If pleasures and pains have no efficacy, one does not see why the most noxious acts, such as burning, might not give thrills of delight, and the most necessary ones, such as breathing, cause agony."[11] What James meant was that by getting rid of will and choice, Huxley had gotten rid of common sense and self-preservation as well. The human being who was actually controlled by epiphenomenalism would lash around smashing into furniture and doors and then imagining that these bumps and crashes had originated through conscious, deliberate decisions. Viewed from the outside, an epiphenomenalist would bear an uncanny resemblance to the New Testament description of a hapless boy controlled by a "deaf-and-dumb spirit," which constantly tried to kill the boy it controlled by throwing him into fire or water. Try to imagine driving a car or writing a letter under epiphenomenal control. Now try to imagine an epiphenomenal Shakespeare or Mozart.

Epiphenomenalism was invented out of whole cloth to fill the scientific atheist need for a theory of consciousness that didn't involve a soul. The whole trend of research in the front lines of neurophysiology has been away from the strictly mechanical explanation. James and such Nobel laureates as Charles Sherrington, Wilder Penfield, and Sir John Carew Eccles all believed in some degree of mind-directed activity. And newer research evidence makes epiphenomenalism increasingly absurd.

Yet the behaviorists in psychology, who regard themselves as the most scientific of scientists, still believe in some form of epiphenomenalism, and so do the secular humanists and scientific atheists.

Even Houston Peterson, one of Huxley's earlier biographers and a believer in his greatness, wasn't impressed with the theory of epiphenomenalism and saw it as an oversimplification, if not a mistake. "It is a way of saving psychology from clergymen, and of keeping the immortal soul out of science, but it is hardly a complete answer to an abstruse philosophical problem . . . he made consciousness a pompous shadow in order to protect his beloved physiology and the law of conservation of energy. The brain, in functioning, gives off CO^2 as well as thoughts, hopes, and desires; but whereas the gas has its effect on the world, the so-called material phenomena are merely incompetent, irrelevant, and immaterial — they have no bearing on the course of events. The contradiction between this conception of consciousness and his belief in traditional moral conduct did not trouble Huxley, as it has troubled many of his readers and critics."[12]

Huxley claimed to believe in the scientific method: facts first; then theories; finally proof, if proof followed the facts. In a letter to Charles Kingsley, while he was heartbroken over the death of Noel, he wrote: "Sit down before fact as a little child, be prepared to give up every preconceived notion."

The same Huxley who wrote this was asked by Alfred Russel Wallace, a scientist he respected, to help other British men of learning investigate spiritualism. Instead of sitting down like a little child before the facts and giving up every preconceived notion, he penned this rather incredible reply: "It may all be true for anything I know to the contrary, but really I cannot get up any interest in the subject. I never cared for gossip in my life, and disembodied gossip such as these worthy ghosts supply their friends with, is not more interesting to me than any other. As for investigating the matter — I have half a dozen investigations of infinitely greater interest to me — to which any spare time I have will be devoted. I give it up for the same reason I abstain from chess — it's too amusing to be fair work, and too hard work to be amusing."[13]

Again and again, scientists and scholars asked Huxley to join their investigations. But Huxley always refused. After a single séance, which all present agreed to be fraudulent, he dropped out. "It was as gross an imposture as ever came under my notice," he wrote. "But supposing the phenomena to be genuine — they do not interest me."[14]

Supposing the phenomena to be genuine — they do not interest me? Can this possibly be the statement of a scientist whose creed was to examine facts objectively and fairly? Is it possible that anyone who had grown up in a religious atmosphere and lost his faith for factual reasons could be uninterested in possible evidence for life after death? Huxley, remember, was not refusing to investigate spiritual phenomena on the basis of any religious prohibition. He had, at this point, no religious beliefs whatsoever. Why was he so leery of such an investigation when so many other scientists of his era were at least willing to give the evidence a hearing before they made up their minds?

Huxley, his biographers admit, had absolutely no skill in diagnosis, and this was particularly true of matters concerning abnormal psychology. His coining of the word *agnostic* to describe a person with no proreligious or antireligious beliefs was a screen for his real feelings: on the surface, steadfast atheism and materialism; subconsciously, a belief that he was somehow under God's curse, as shown by the death of Noel and his own forty years of indigestion and headaches. He was also irrationally terrified of anything having to do with death. Huxley stayed away from spiritual things, because he was afraid of finding out that he might be wrong in his smug theory of epiphenomenalism.

As for having more important things to do, Huxley spent his last years attacking the New Testament, and one New Testament story in particular, the story of the Gadarene swine. This story is told in the Bible in two Gospels: Matthew 8:28-34 and Mark 5:1-20. A deranged man living in a tomb meets Jesus, who orders the unclean spirits to leave the man. The evil spirits leave the man and enter a herd of swine, which run into the lake and drown. The man is healed and goes on his way restored to sanity.

Huxley fixated on this story despite its relative obscurity in the Gospel accounts. He first said that the story showed cruelty to animals, and then claimed that Jewish farmers wouldn't have herded swine because pork isn't kosher — ignoring, of course, the fact that Gadarea was a gentile region. On and on went his irrational raging.

The ruckus soon involved William Ewart Gladstone, former prime minister of the British Empire under Queen Victoria, and a staunch Christian whose ministry involved helping to reform girls who had been forced into prostitution by teaching them handicrafts and householding at a little farm on his family estate, and then seeking out respectable positions for them in the community. Gladstone was a Greek scholar who loved Homer and read the Bible in the original, and the two aging

men spent their declining years battling over details of the Gadarene
swine story and over Gladstone's contention that the facts of Creation as
revealed by science matched the order of Creation described in the
Biblical book of Genesis.

Why did the story of the Gadarene Swine obsess Huxley? One guess
would be that it stirred his boyhood fear that insanity might be contagious. The unclean spirits which sprang from a madman to a herd of
swine might pose a very real subconscious threat to a man who had seen
so much insanity in his own family line, who wondered if he himself
might be susceptible to invasion.

Huxley's antireligious bias didn't mellow in his old age; it got worse.
Attacks on clergymen lifted his spirits and restored his digestion often
enough to keep him alive to the age of seventy. His obsessive hatred of
Christianity remained constant. When Robert Collier, an artist and future son-in-law, remarked to Huxley that Egyptian art had deteriorated
from the time of the pharaohs to the time of the Greco-Roman rule in
Egypt, Huxley smugly remarked: "My boy, it got into the hands of the
priests." He had, of course, no idea what he was talking about.
Pharaonic Egyptian art was in the hands of the priests from the very
beginning. But with Huxley, only opinions counted, facts were irrelevant.

In 1895, beset with influenza and kidney and heart trouble, Huxley
wrote to a friend that he was suffering nausea and vomiting but that he
expected his native toughness to pull him through. Once again, his diagnostic skills proved to be poor. He died three days later.

Huxley was buried beside Noel and his brother George. A clergyman
officiated at the private ceremony, and on his tomb were written three
lines composed by his long-suffering wife, Henrietta, who had remained
a Christian believer through forty years of marriage to the leading antireligious propagandist of the Victorian age:

> Be not afraid, ye waiting hearts that weep;
> For still He giveth His beloved sleep,
> And if an endless sleep He wills, so best.

The sterility of antireligious dogma and its lack of appeal to healthy
minds is illustrated by the fact that, after forty years, Huxley had failed
to convert his own wife to agnosticism. But the real irony of his life
would wait a generation before it surfaced.

Victorian critics, both Christian and agnostic, wondered about the fact that Huxley, the man who didn't believe in God or Jesus and tried to throw the human soul out of science, was preoccupied with preserving conventional morality.

"Morality, in Professor Huxley, I can well believe is strong enough to hold its own," wrote one critic in 1886. "But will it be strong enough in Professor Huxley's grandchildren?"

Professor Huxley's most famous grandchild was Aldous Huxley. Raised in a home where God was scarcely mentioned, a complete rationalist in his youth, Aldous Huxley became a believer of virtually everything from Hindu mysticism to medieval Catholic shrines, and a pioneer experimenter in hallucinogenic drugs. He wrote books which repudiated scientific materialism. His last request while dying was for a massive dose of LSD — apparently to help his soul to make a graceful exit from his body. The grandchild of Professor Huxley, the man who irrationally believed in nothing, had become a man who irrationally believed in *everything*.

FIVE

FRIEDRICH NIETZSCHE: SUPERMAN AND SYPHILITIC

Darwin and Huxley repudiated God, Jesus, and the immortal soul, but they never deviated from the mainstream of Victorian morality. Darwin, in fact, regularly contributed to Christian missionaries through the second half of his life, even while he tried to argue God out of existence by ignoring evidence that didn't fit the picture of an atheistic cosmos. Huxley nurtured an almost boyish hero worship for General Charles Gordon, the devoutly Christian soldier who broke up the slave trade in the Sudan. And one of his closest friends was Charles Kingsley, clergyman, Christian moralist, and author of *The Water Babies*.

This was, of course, patently ironic. Without some sort of belief in God, Jesus, and immortality, Christian ethics become a sort of social convention without any vitality or force, and, to the consistent atheist, without much logic either.

Darwin and Huxley, in the stodgy doldrums of their chronic clinical depression, never grasped the magnitude of what they professed to have discovered. To their stifled minds, the world was composed of Victorians and "savages." They actually believed that educated people would continue to accept monogamy, mercy, and charity even without faith and hope.

There was a man, however, who realized the real social and philosophical impact of what Darwin and Huxley had "proved" in biology and physiology. He understood, more clearly than the two Victorians, that if God and Jesus and the immortal soul had been "ruled out of order" in the court of ideas, all morality had been repealed at the same moment.

His name was Friedrich Nietzsche.

Nietzsche popularized the phrase "God is dead." He repudiated every religious system — Christian, Jewish, Islamic, and Buddhist. He sneered at traditional Judeo-Christian morality as tame, cowardly, and hypocritical. And running through his most popular and most famous book, *Thus Spake Zarathustra*, one encounters the "superman."

> *I teach you the Superman.* Man is something that is to be surpassed. What have ye done to surpass man?

> All beings hitherto have created something beyond themselves: And ye want to be the ebb of that great tide, and would rather go back to the beast than surpass man?

> What is the ape to man? A laughingstock, a thing of shame. And just the same shall man be to the Superman: A laughingstock, a thing of shame.

> Ye have made your way from the worm to man, and much within you is still worm. Once ye were apes, and even yet man is still more of an ape than any of the apes. . . .

> The Superman is the meaning of the earth. Let your will say: The Superman *shall* be the meaning of the earth!

> I conjure you, my brethren, *remain true to the earth*, and believe not those who speak unto you of superearthly hopes! Poisoners they are, whether they know it or not. . . .

> Once blasphemy against God was the greatest blasphemy; but God died, and therewith also those blasphemers. To blaspheme the earth is now the dreadfulest sin, and to rate the heart of the unknowable higher than the meaning of the earth![1]

Translated from Nietzsche's pseudo-Biblical language: Man himself is not the apex of evolution, but a missing link to a higher species — an idea he clearly derived from Darwin. Nietzsche also repudiates any idea of God or the supernatural. Earth is everything. Unlike Darwin and

Huxley, he maintains a consistent materialism mocking conventional morality. Darwin and Huxley loved and respected their wives, though Huxley, in particular, was a harsh critic of the nascent feminist movement. To Nietzsche, woman was "a plaything."

Man shall be trained for war, and woman for the recreation of the warrior: all else is folly.

The happiness of man is *I will*. The happiness of woman is *He will*.

Thou goest to women? Do not forget thy whip![2]

Of this last phrase, Nietzsche's fellow atheist, Bertrand Russell, noted that since nine out of ten women would have gotten the whip away from Nietzsche, and Nietzsche knew it, he didn't go to women.

Darwin and Huxley, as we have seen, each spent half a lifetime suffering from all sorts of headaches, nausea, depression, and obsessive fears, coupled with a complete loss of taste in the arts, and a marked personality change: extreme shyness in Darwin's case, extreme irritability in Huxley's case. Nobody at the time seems to have figured out what was wrong with either man. The obvious mistakes they made in their own fields were allowed to stand as brilliant discoveries.

Nietzsche's basic medical problem was easier to diagnose. Even a notably poor diagnostician like Huxley couldn't have missed spotting syphilitic paresis.

The symptoms are obvious, and, in the late nineteenth century, they were extremely common: gradual creeping paralysis, mental problems in which the mind was sometimes extremely excited, sometimes depressed and lethargic, failing eyesight, and, at the end, precocious drooling senility. Every physician in the nineteenth century knew what syphilitic paresis looked like. The roster of victims who had died of syphilis included dozens of celebrities, ranging from Franz Schubert to Charles Baudelaire to Lord Randolph Churchill, Winston's father. Jack London gave a terrifying description of the later stages of paresis in *The Sea Wolf*, in 1904. The rogue sea captain, Wolf Larson, keeps copies of Nietzsche's books in his cabin and spouts atheist philosophy to justify his cruelty and greed, even while his eyesight fails and his brother, "Death" Larson, hunts him relentlessly in another ship. Many critics have said that Wolf Larson is modeled after Nietzsche. Another character based on

Nietzsche was Sherlock Holmes's archenemy, Professor Moriarty, the "Napoleon of Crime" created by Sir Arthur Conan Doyle.

Nietzsche's influence on literature was clearly enormous. What's more surprising is that Europeans, and some Americans, regarded him as a hero and the greatest of all philosophers. H. L. Mencken, foe of Biblical Christianity and spokesman of the skeptics in early twentieth-century America, absolutely adored Nietzsche. He's a favorite among many university-level students of philosophy today, perhaps more for his lurid prose style than for the ideas he advanced, which found their logical culmination in Hitler's political and social programs to make the superman a reality.

Who was Nietzsche? His admirers, stuck with the fact that he went terminally mad at forty-four and lived the rest of his life as a vegetable, have to draw a sort of artificial wall around his insanity and prove that he was completely sane, in fact brilliant, when he wrote his ravings against God in *Thus Spake Zarathustra*. "The statement that his books were those of a madman is entirely without foundation," Willard Huntington Wright wrote in the introduction to his collected works published by the Modern Library. "His works were thought out in the most clarified manner . . . his insanity was sudden; it came without warning; and it is puerile to point to his state of mind during the last years of his life as a criticism of his philosophy. His books must stand or fall from internal evidence. Judged from that standpoint they are scrupulously sane."[3]

Wright dates Nietzsche's insanity from an attack of "apoplexy" in January 1889. Before this "apoplexy"—actually, it was probably a stroke brought on by syphilitic damage to the brain—Wright tells us that Nietzsche was completely sane.

Thus Spake Zarathustra was written in 1883, almost six years before Nietzsche's "sudden" madness. In 1888, also before the stroke, he described the mood he was in when he wrote it. "Has any one at the end of the nineteenth century any distinct notion of what poets of a stronger age understood by the word *inspiration*? If not, I will describe it. If one had the smallest vestige of superstition in one, it would hardly be to set aside completely the idea that one is the mere incarnation, mouthpiece, or *medium* of an *almighty power*. The idea of revelation in the sense that something becomes suddenly visible and audible with indescribably certainty and accuracy, which profoundly convulses and upsets one—describes simply the matter of fact. One hears—one does not seek; one takes—one does not ask who gives: A thought suddenly flashes up like lightning, it comes with necessity, unhesitatingly — I never have any choice in the matter. There is an ecstacy such that the immense strain of it is sometimes relaxed by a flood of tears, along with which one's steps either rush or involuntarily lag, alternately. There is the feeling *that one is completely out of hand.* . . . Everything happens quite involuntarily, as if in a tempestuous outburst of freedom, of absoluteness, or power and divinity. . . . This is *my* experience of inspiration. I do not doubt but that one would have to go back thousands of years in order to find some one who could say to me: It is mine also!"[4]

Problem: Nietzsche here describes what can only be either a religious experience or an attack of madness. The word *inspiration*[5] in fact means to have a "spirit" come "in." Yet Nietzsche was an atheist who didn't believe in spirits or souls. So we can only believe that Nietzsche was either lying about not believing in spirits or crazy when he wrote *Thus Spake Zarathustra.*

Some have considered the ravings in *Thus Spake Zarathustra* and assumed, not without some warrant, that the "inspiration" for the book was demonic. A more conservative explanation, however, is that Nietzsche was mad at least six years before his final breakdown and that the "inspiration" he describes was due to syphilitic paresis. In either case, it would seem to invalidate anything he said or wrote as a philosopher.

Some madmen become atheists, and some others become violent religious fanatics. If we trace the atheist syndrome through Nietzsche's early life, we can readily see why the syphilitic prophet of the superman became an atheist.

Nietzsche's Childhood: Phase One

In 1848, all Europe was aflame. In France, in Italy, in Austria, workers and the middle class, stirred up by radicals and revolutionaries, rose to demand popular participation in government. Even in authoritarian Prussia, mobs drove King Friedrich Wilhelm IV out of Berlin and he had to seek safety with his army.

In the small village of Röcken, Pastor Ludwig Nietzsche violently opposed the revolutionaries' demands. He hoped that King Friedrich Wilhelm IV — the namesake for his first-born son, Friedrich Wilhelm Nietzsche — would order the insurgents shot down like dogs. When the king instead put on the red-gold-and-black cockade of the protestors and granted them certain legal and human rights, Pastor Ludwig Nietzsche slumped into severe depression. One day, while depressed and distracted, he stumbled and fell on the steps of his own cellar, was injured, took to his bed, and died.

That, at least, was the story later told by Elisabeth Förster-Nietzsche, the pastor's daughter and the philosopher's sister and publicist. Pastor Nietzsche's wife, an honest, if naive, woman and the daughter of another Lutheran pastor, sometimes told a different story. Before his collapse, even before the king's condescending concessions to the Berlin rabble, Pastor Nietzsche had sometimes stopped speaking in midsentence and stared blindly into space. He had sudden losses of memory even when he wasn't being distracted or annoyed.

Elisabeth Förster-Nietzsche would have none of such stories. She warned her mother not to mention such things, either about her father or about members of the mother's own family, the Oehlers, because someone might suspect hereditary madness: "Uncle Edmund was also very odd, and Uncle Theobald, Gustav Knieling, and poor Lieschen. . . . Defend yourself against such tales! . . . And please don't talk such nonsense about poor Papa. If he had not fallen down those stone steps, he would probably still be alive today."[6]

Pastor Ludwig Nietzsche's death at the age of thirty-six sounds very much like a case of syphilis, or possibly epilepsy. Whatever it was that killed him, his children didn't want to talk about it. And they didn't want their mother talking about the traces of hereditary insanity that appear to have run through Nietzsche's ancestry just as they did through Darwin's and Huxley's.

Bereft of his father at the age of four, Friedrich Nietzsche was raised by his mother, his grandmother, two maiden aunts, and a family servant—all female. His closest companion was his younger sister, Elisabeth. Another boy had been born to Pastor Nietzsche and his wife but had died in infancy. From the time when his memories must have begun, Friedrich Nietzsche had no male role model of any importance in his life.

Modern psychologists and psychiatrists believe that they have devised a pattern which explains homosexuality.[7] The child who grows up with a hostile or abusive father, or with no father at all, often identifies so closely with his mother that she becomes a role model. In other cases, he develops an incestuous attachment to his mother and thinks of himself as her lover. When he learns that incest is taboo and forbidden, he develops a phobia against his sexual thoughts about his mother which extends to other women—in extreme cases, to all women. This fear and rejection of normal sexuality may make the victim impotent, or it may condition him to pervert his sex drive away from women and toward other men. There is also an emotional aspect to homosexuality that isn't always sexual: The boy who grows up without a father or father-substitute seems to have a lifelong need for the companionship and guidance of an older male "companion." In some cases this relationship is sexual; in other cases, chaste, more a form of hero-worship than sexual passion. This is not the only explanation of homosexuality, but it is tenable enough for most psychiatrists and psychologists to adopt it as a working theory.

The idea that Nietzsche was either secretly or latently homosexual has a lot to recommend it. Throughout his career, Nietzsche advocated immorality but—perhaps except for his student days—lived a chaste life. He appears to have had no normal adult experiences of sex, even though his religious scruples were nonexistent. He also spewed out torrents of hatred and contempt for women, despite the fact that many women had shown him considerable kindness during his frequent illnesses, and despite his lifelong attachment to his mother and his sister. His affected he-man heroics appear to have been a cover for the fact that he felt inadequate around women. The two simplest explanations for this: either Nietzsche was homosexual and knew it, or his syphilis was congenital, and by his early manhood the disease had already caused considerable physical as well as mental damage.

Nietzsche's first schooling came from his mother and his aunts. A year at public school, where some of the boys came from "the working class," convinced him that he wasn't suited to commune with ordinary mortals. The rest of his education was inflicted at a Spartan boarding school where upper-class boys as young as nine or ten were subjected to strict regulations like little Prussian soldiers. Nietzsche hated the school and was frequently sick, but he did very well academically. His family hoped that he would follow his deceased father and both grandfathers into the ministry.

But there was a slight problem with this, to say the least. By his late teens, Nietzsche had lost his faith in God, or at least in the God of the Bible. His loss of faith came not from an examination of the facts of science but from a study of the works of Schopenhauer, a philosopher of the previous generation who had abandoned Christianity and propounded a creed of his own based very closely on the darker, more pessimistic side of Buddhism or Hinduism. To Schopenhauer, as to those Buddhists and Hindus, the real world as we see it exists only as an illusion and is full of suffering and foolishness. Life after death may exist, but only for the unlucky. The real goal of life is to "drop out" of existence — nirvana. Nietzsche, the future advocate of violent action, found this negative view of the active life very congenial, perhaps as a revenge on the father-pastor who had "abandoned" him by dying.

Nietzsche dropped his plans for the clergy and decided on a career in philology, the study of the history and uses of language. He found his first "godfather" in Professor Friedrich Ritschl, who helped him secure a teaching position at the University of Basel in Switzerland when he was only twenty-four years old. While visiting Switzerland, Nietzsche met the next older man in his life, the one who was to wield the greatest influence.

As a teenager, Nietzsche had doted on the music of Richard Wagner, the controversial composer of *Tristan und Isolde* and *Lohengrin*. Wagner had been born in 1813 and was the same age as Nietzsche's deceased father, which may be important. He was also in temporary disgrace, having fled the Bavarian court at Munich with the wife of his friend, Hans Bülow. The love affair of Richard Wagner and Cosima Liszt von Bülow was the scandal of the age. Nietzsche's arrival on the scene took place just as Wagner's son Siegfried was born. His first visit to the Wagner-Liszt von Bülow household, in fact, took place on the day of Siegfried's birth. Nietzsche was an inveterate snob, even as a young man, and Wagner's fame and Cosima's aristocratic background overcame whatever reservations he may have had about the relationship between Cosima and Wagner — or Wagner and Nietzsche.

Nietzsche's attachment to Wagner was clearly of an emotional intensity unusual in friendships between healthy normal males. Later in life, when he criticized a student for constantly writing stories and poems based on the romantic love between men and women, the student replied that this was a natural topic for literature because of the intense emotions involved. What better topic, the student asked, could Nietzsche suggest?

"Why, friendship, for example!" Nietzsche replied. "Friendship has quite similar conflicts, but on a much higher plane. First there is the mutual attraction caused by sharing the same views of life, and then the happiness of *belonging to one another and forming mutual plans for the future.* Furthermore, there is the mutual admiration and glorification. A sudden distrust is awakened on one side, doubts arise as to the excellences of the friend and his viewpoints on the other side, and finally the consciousness is borne upon both that the parting of the ways has been reached, although neither one feels himself ready for this renunciation.

Does all this not represent unceasing conflicts, carrying with them suffering of the most intense character?"[8]

"The student looked dubious and it was evident that he had never dreamed that friendship could be so passionate," Nietzsche's sister tells us.

Probably because the student wasn't a homosexual.

Nietzsche's passionate emotional involvement doesn't appear to have been reciprocated. Wagner was one of the nineteenth-century's most pronounced and promiscuous heterosexuals. As a child, Wagner tells us, he used to feign sleep on the sofa so he could fondle the bosoms of the obliging ladies who toted him off to bed. His first wife, Minna Planer, had been an actress who had already borne a child out of wedlock by another man. Neither of the newlyweds was scrupulously faithful, though only Minna made an issue of it. People still argue about whether the great love of Wagner's life was Mathilde Wesendonck, or whether she was a passing fancy whose husband had money. When Wagner finally died of a heart attack at seventy, he was supposedly in literary pursuit of yet another woman, this one also married and in her early twenties. Courtiers had tried to create a scandal, just before Nietzsche's arrival on the Wagner scene, by charging that King Ludwig of Bavaria was in love with Wagner the man, as opposed to Wagner the musician, but nobody really seems to have believed it. Wagner's few comments on the subject indicate that he thought homosexuality was disgusting. The relentless pursuit of women took up all his time not set aside for music.

Wagner clearly didn't want Nietzsche as a lover. He wanted him as a publicist. Nietzsche, whatever the degree of his sanity then or later, was a gifted writer, and his dramatic, somewhat lurid style fitted Wagner's needs perfectly: for raising money. For the purposes of posterity, Wagner did his own writing. He was one of the few composers to write the texts for his own operas, and he also designed the costumes and sets. His step-father, and father-surrogate, Ludwig Geyer, had been an actor/playwright and minor composer and he knew his way around the theater as he knew the back of his hand.

Nietzsche's work as Wagner's full-time admirer and sometime publicist was interrupted by the Franco-Prussian War of 1870-71. Nietzsche was a Swiss citizen by now and didn't want to jeopardize his job by serving as a regular Prussian officer. He signed up as a medical orderly.

Nietzsche's war service has been heavily whitewashed by his admirers. His adoring sister tells us that "he often had to make his way from ambulance to ambulance and from hospital to hospital, under a rain of bullets, stopping as occasion demanded to receive the last words of dying men . . . under the very walls of Metz."[9]

Elisabeth Förster-Nietzsche makes the siege of Metz sound like a combination of Gettysburg and Custer's Last Stand. We're tempted to ask if there were any survivors on either side. In fact, the siege of Metz was such a lackluster defense that the French general in command, Achille Paul Bazaine, was later court-martialed and sentenced to death on the grounds that he committed treason by failing to attempt a breakout from Metz, or to conduct a more spirited resistance. During the siege of Paris, the French sent out sixty-five balloons over the heads of the Prussians, bearing letters, dispatches, diplomats, and homing pigeons to be sent back to besieged Paris with messages from outside. The defenders of Metz launched *one* balloon. They were slowly stitching a second one together when they discovered that all the available sulfuric acid needed to generate hydrogen for the balloon had been used to generate soda pop. No more balloons flew out of Metz. The French resistance there was so weak, in fact, that the Prussians kept transferring soldiers west to Paris or east to Belfort, where real fighting was still in progress.

Nietzsche's actual role in the "Soda Pop Siege" is thus problematical. His sister tried to imbue him with as much heroism as the warlike Prussians would concede to a noncombatant. More likely, he spent most of his military career emptying bedpans. His final military assignment was to keep watch over six wounded soldiers being transferred from France to Germany by railroad. These soldiers had been wounded during the encirclement battles like Gravelotte-St. Privat, which were, in fact, quite bloody but took place before Nietzsche arrived. One night in a boxcar with six hapless men who actually *had* seen combat finished the Franco-Prussian War for Nietzsche. When the transport arrived in Germany, Nietzsche went on the sick list and quickly received a medical discharge. The official version was that he had contracted diptheria and dysentery from the wounded men. Professor Walter Kaufmann, one of Nietzsche's most intense admirers, says that Nietzsche may also have contracted syphilis on his boxcar ride to glory. One hesitates to ask how.

Back in Germany, Wagner, having weathered some of the scandal of his flight with Cosima, had embarked on an ambitious plan. He wanted to build a special opera house for the first performance of his four-opera cycle, *The Ring of the Nibelungs.* Wagner was a rogue where women were concerned, but he was no fool. His "music of the future" had taken a pounding from critics in the days when French grand opera had dominated the stages of Europe. Prussia's upset victory over France in 1870-71 and the unification of Germany touched off a tidal wave of German nationalism, German economic expansion, and German pride and self-confidence. All over the world—even in the United States—regular armies threw away their French-style kepis and replaced them with Prussian-style spiked helmets. The Japanese went as far as to fire their French military advisers and replace them with Prussians. Even the Queen of Hawaii hired a German bandmaster for her royal brass band. Wagner, who had been a debt-ridden vagabond for a large part of his career, saw his moment. He made *The Ring of the Nibelungs,* which he'd been writing off and on for twenty years, into a touchstone of German nationalism. If you love Germany, Wagner told German aristocrats and millionaires, you'll love *The Ring of the Nibelungs.* And you'll send money or buy high-priced subscription tickets to help me stage it as it should be staged: in its own special opera house at Bayreuth.

Nietzsche participated in this scheme as much and as often as his health permitted. He himself had little money, but he lent his literary gifts to fund-raising for Bayreuth. From 1871 through 1876, he worked closely with Wagner and Cosima. But something was happening during these years. Siegfried Wagner, Wagner's son by Cosima, began to mature. Nietzsche may have realized that once Siegfried was a teenager, there would be no place for him as Wagner's "son." The symptoms of Nietzsche's disease were also getting worse. Periodically he would be seized with attacks of internal pain and prolonged bouts of vomiting, and headaches so intense he screamed out that he wished he could die. His eyesight began to fail, not permanently, but on and off. At times his eyesight shifted back to ordinary near-sightedness. At other times, he was all but blind. Nietzsche maintained the fantasy that he was suffering the strain of overwork, or of the diseases he had picked up in the boxcar during the "Soda Pop Siege."

In 1876—by coincidence, the centennial of the United States—the first complete performance of *The Ring of the Nibelungs* was ready at Bayreuth. But there were amusing last-minute disasters. Wagner knew the theater and knew that London had the best special-effects men in the business. He ordered a special giant-sized dragon for the second act of the opera *Siegfried,* based at least partly on a reconstructed dinosaur he had seen on a trip to England. The British dragon-dinosaur model was so big that it had to be shipped out of England in three boxes. The dragon's head and tail arrived in Bayreuth in Germany. The dragon's body showed up in Beirut, now Lebanon, where nobody knew what it was supposed to be or where it was supposed to go. The *Siegfried* dragon appeared on stage with a hastily improvised midriff.

The Bayreuth performance of the Ring Cycle was a huge success, but the friendship between Wagner and Nietzsche began to fall apart.

The collapse of this friendship is critical to any understanding of Nietzsche's major writings. The experts all have their own explanations. Elisabeth Förster-Nietzsche, who was a very subjective, and thus unreliable, witness to the proceedings, said that Nietzsche was revolted by the artistic compromises that Wagner made in catering to a wider public. She also claims that Wagner's vanity was wounded because Nietzsche became deathly sick in the middle of the performance cycle and couldn't stay for the whole ostentatious spectacle.

H. L. Mencken, the American journalist-skeptic who loved both Wagner's music and Nietzsche's philosophy, but hated Wagner's reversion to Christianity, came down heavily on Nietzsche's side when he discussed the Wagner-Nietzsche break-up. "Wagner's limitations were no less marked than his abilities," Mencken wrote in 1921, long after Wagner and Nietzsche were both dead.

> I believe that Wagner's music dramas are, by long odds, the most stupendous works of art ever contrived by man . . . but whoever enters the opera-house gets a smell of patchouli into his hair, and a dab of grease-paint on his nose. He may remain a genius, but he is a genius who is a bit of a mountebank—a genius who thinks of his audience as well as of his work, and is not forgetful of box-office statements. Actors make bad philosophers—and a man who writes operas, however gorgeous, becomes thereby partly an actor. . . . I believe that it is quite probable, as Frau Förster-Nietzsche says, that it is Wagner's snuffling gabble about Christianity that finished him. Put the thing on the best ground possible: say that Wagner was genuinely self-deluded, that his going to mass was honest, that the romantic mystery of the faith had at last found a weak spot in his armor and penetrated to his heart. In any case, the apostasy was incomprehensible to Nietzsche. He could no more imagine an intelligent man succumbing to all that ancient rubbish than he could imaging an honest man subscribing to it for worldly gain. The convert was as abhorrent to his tight and uncompromising mind as the hypocrite. In Wagner, I dare say, he saw parts of both.[10]

In Mencken, I dare say, we see the antireligious bigot who puts his hatred of Christianity above his taste in art. Wagner's operas have been steadily performed for the past century and rank second only to those of Giuseppi Verdi in popularity in the United States. Wagner's is perhaps first above all other operatic music in the respect it still receives from critics. Nietzsche, as we will see, is popular only with certain factions who find what they want to find in his works. But that limited reputation has suffered greatly since the 1920s. Mencken, however, responded emotionally to Nietzsche's violent atheism — and perhaps not a little to his latent homosexuality as well.

Walter Kaufmann, another Nietzsche admirer, attributes the break-up to Wagner's "jingoism and anti-Semitism" and adds that the breach spurred Nietzsche's ambition to rival and excel the composer and dramatist as a writer and philosopher.

Nietzsche spent the rest of his life alternatively yearning for Wagner to take him back and writing vicious attacks on his music and his religious beliefs — and most of all on Cosima, Wagner's wife and mother of Siegfried, a double rival for the "master's" affection. Cosima not only had Wagner's physical attentions, which Nietzsche may or may not have recognized that he wanted, but in providing Wagner with a male heir she had shut Nietzsche out both as lover and son. His initial hatred seems to have been directed far more against Cosima than against Wagner, and Cosima seems to have understood why.

Nietzsche's Flight: Phase Two

While Nietzsche was in seclusion, recovering from the syphilitic attack that had ruined the debut of the *Ring of the Nibelungs* for him, he wrote the first of his ultimately famous books, *Human, All Too Human*, a collection of aphorisms. Crude attacks on Christianity were mingled with flashes of genuine psychological insight and wit, childish attacks on other philosophers, and veiled potshots at Wagner and Cosima. The book was blasphemous, but it was also a curious mixture of talent and insanity, the pattern for most of Nietzsche's future work. And it was dripping with hatred for women.

Cosima seems to have been intuitively aware that Nietzsche hated her, and she found her confirmation in an aphorism in which Nietzsche remarked that the wives of great men were often like "lightning rods" and drew down abuse on their husbands. Cosima was doubly insulted. Her flight from Hans von Bülow to live with Wagner had affected her emotionally more than she was willing to admit. She was strongly attracted to Christianity and had gradually become more devout. And she was considerably taller than Wagner and took the "lightning rod" comparison as a slur on her height as well as her past immorality.

Cosima asked Elisabeth, Nietzsche's sister, whom he had had in mind when he wrote the lightning-rod aphorism. "I considered all possible men and finally asked myself: 'Should the author really have gained from his visits . . . no other than that malicious image?' "[11]

From this time on, Nietzsche's door back to Wagner's good graces was slammed in his face. Cosima probably realized when she married the composer of *Tristan* that she'd have to devote a great deal of her time "protecting" him from other women, but she wasn't about to tolerate Nietzsche as a rival. And his slurs on Christianity may also have been sincerely resented, especially since Cosima was working so diligently to turn Wagner back to a more traditional religious outlook.

Heartbroken, Nietzsche fled to Italy. This was his belated escape phase of the atheist syndrome. He was already over thirty; Darwin and Huxley had fled the paternal roof at twenty-one or twenty-two, but Nietzsche was remarkably immature in many ways. Italy appealed to him for many reasons. He believed that the climate might improve his precarious health, and, indeed, it seemed to work, off and on. The reasons for this are two-fold: Syphilitic paresis is notorious for the way in which the victim becomes first depressed and weak, then euphoric and energetic. But Italy had psychological advantages for Nietzsche, too. The father who had "abandoned" him by dying when he was four years old had been a Lutheran pastor. Italy was visibly, audibly Catholic, very much "enemy territory" as far as militant Lutherans were concerned. Luther himself had touched off the Reformation and founded the Lutheran Church after a pilgrimage to Rome, and the pope and Rome were Luther's greatest foes. Wagner and Cosima were also Lutherans. Departing for the sunny southland was a way to take revenge on their "coldness." Italy was also the homeland of Giuseppi Verdi, Wagner's only living rival for primacy on the opera stage. Verdi and Wagner, born the same year, disliked one another's music intensely, a mutual professional jealousy, since they were both superb composers. Their younger partisans sometimes celebrated debut performances by brawling in opera houses, throwing things, and writing scurrilous reviews in journals. The Paris debut of Wagner's revised *Tannhäuser* in 1861 had been a fisted festival with dozens of arrests and a massive police presence required to prevent the destruction of the opera house. Verdi's debut of *La Forza*

Del Destino in Moscow in 1877 had been disrupted by angry Wagnerites who criticized Verdi for not sounding more like Wagner. In deserting the frigid northland for the home of Verdi and the pope, Nietzsche was symbolically turning his back on his two "fathers," Pastor Ludwig and Richard Wagner, the recently returned Lutheran.

While roaming Italy, Nietzsche met a former student and sometime assistant, Dr. Paul Ree, who had helped him with the literary work on *Human, All Too Human*. Ree was somewhat surprised when Nietzsche introduced himself as the doge of Genoa and insisted on being treated as a dignitary. He was also astounded by Nietzsche's manic energy. This was the euphoric stage of the syphilis, coupled with the effect of the escape phase of the atheist syndrome. When he was in Italy, the "enemy territory" of his father's religion and Richard Wagner's musical genius, his mood and his appetite both improved and his weakness and despair gave way to creative energy and vitality, despite the gnawing of the syphilis.

Ree, who was five years younger than Nietzsche, told him about a remarkable young woman he had encountered in Rome. Her name, Ree said, was Louise Andreas-Salome, and she was not only extremely intelligent but notably free from the stifling conventions of the day. Nietzsche instantly decided that Louise Andreas-Salome would be his, and not Ree's. The two youthful swains—Nietzsche was now thirty-eight and Ree thirty-three—fell all over one another making plays for a twenty-one-year-old girl. Lou, as she preferred to be called, initially decided that the three of them should be "just good friends," though—to the horror of her mother and many other women—she agreed that the three of them should spend a year of study together while sharing an apartment suite. Warnings flew in from male and female friends that this was a disastrous idea and that a girl barely out of her teens couldn't cope with sophisticated older men like Nietzsche and Ree. In fact, she appears to have had little trouble making fools of both of them. The strange relationship capsized only when Lou Andreas-Salome arrived in Bayreuth, the new capital of Wagnerdom, for the debut of *Parsifal*, the most Christian of Wagner's later operas. The Wagnerites were delighted with her free spirit—one senses Cosima once again going into defensive maneuvers—but Nietzsche's sister Elisabeth, still clutching the rungs of the social ladder, hated Lou on sight. The two women got into a confrontation of immense verbal violence, in which Lou as much as told Elisabeth that she was an overgrown juvenile (Elisabeth was now thirty-six) and that her brother was a madman. The relationship splattered in three different directions: Nietzsche got the gate from Lou, and he was so furious with his sister that he terminated their own close friendship.

H. F. Peters, who has written excellent books on *Zarathustra's Sister* and on Lou Andreas-Salome, calls the Salome-Nietzsche-Ree triangle "a melodrama in four acts," and so it was. Those people who admire Nietzsche and cherish the notion that he was a heroic sinner and not merely an inept malcontent believe that Lou and Nietzsche were lovers. Peters doesn't seem to think so. The "affair," whatever it was, represents the sum total of Nietzsche's practical experience with romantic or physical love, other than a couple of conjectural trips to brothels as a student.

At any rate, the Great Man was now ready to proceed with his attack on God.

Nietzsche's Collapse: Phase Three

Nietzsche's first move after the dissolution of the Lou Andreas-Salome affair was to flee back to Italy. His next move — under, as he told us earlier, some sort of outside inspiration — was to write *Thus Spake Zarathustra*. Zarathustra (in English spelling, Zoroaster) was a Persian thinker of pre-Christian times who, Nietzsche says, first made the clear-cut distinction between "good" and "evil." Nietzsche, who had decided that he didn't believe in "good" and "evil," conjured up an imaginary Zarathustra to explain this important discovery to an eager public — which actually didn't exist. In vivid images and colorful, sometimes garish phraseology, Zarathustra wanders around telling people what's what, seemingly forever. From this "inspired" book came the phrase "God is dead" and Nietzsche's description of the superman, and some — but by no means all — of his ravings against women, against any concept of an afterlife, against Christian morality, and, in fact, against just about everything.

Nietzsche tells us that the last portion of *Zarathustra* was written "at that hallowed hour when Richard Wagner gave up the ghost in Venice." It's hard to tell whether he was being sanctimonious or sarcastic. When one is dealing with a person who refuses to believe in the supernatural and nevertheless claims to have supernatural experiences, one is not dealing with a mundane mortal. Richard Wagner, however, was not really dead as far as Nietzsche's subconscious was concerned. He continued to pour out hate mail to the dead composer for the rest of his life.

Nietzsche's sister Elisabeth, cut off from a relationship which must have bordered on platonic incest, took a revenge of her own by marrying

Bernhard Förster, a professional anti-Semite. Förster had gotten into legal trouble trading insults and blows with some Jewish passengers on a trolley car. He then began to circulate a petition to have the government limit immigration of persecuted Jews from the Russian Empire into Germany and to limit the civil rights of Jews born in Germany. Germany's chancellor, Otto von Bismarck, a convinced Christian with Jewish friends and advisers, treated this document with the scorn it deserved, which convinced Förster that the Jews were already in control of Germany. He fled to found a sort of master race colony in Paraguay. Elisabeth, not yet his wife but an intense admirer, pursued him by mail and wrote him letters of such muted but tormented passion that they agreed to marry. Elisabeth shortly thereafter took a ship for Paraguay. Nietzsche continued to roam restlessly around Italy scribbling out attacks on God, Wagner, and the Germans.

Nietzsche's admirers, some of them members of the secular Jewish community, constantly praise Nietzsche for *not* being an anti-Semite. This is a curious delusion. Nietzsche's admirers assume that he hated anti-Semitism. Actually, Nietzsche hated Bernhard Förster because Förster had deprived him of his one reliable worshiper, Elisabeth. He also hated — and feared — the sort of bullies and thugs who were attracted to organized anti-Semitism because they were vulgar and crude, and Nietzsche was nothing if not a snob. Nietzsche himself never took his anti-Semitism into the streets. He confined it to his writings. Vicious references to Jews dot his works like maggots on rotten meat. For instance, in *Twilight of the Idols*, a title chosen to attack one of Wagner's operas, he tells us: "Christianity, sprung from Jewish roots and comprehensible only as a growth on this soil, represents the counter-movement to any morality of breeding, of race, or privilege: it is the *anti*-Aryan religion par excellence. Christianity — the re-valuation of all Aryan values, the victory of *chandala*[12] values, the gospel preached to the poor and the base, the general revolt of all the downtrodden, the wretched, the failures, the less favored, against 'race'; the undying *chandala*[13] hatred as the religion of love."[14]

Or again, in *The Antichrist*: "The Jews are the most *catastrophic* people of world history: by their after-effect they have made mankind so thoroughly false that even today the Christian can feel anti-Jewish without realizing that he himself is *the ultimate Jewish consequence*."[15]

Also, in *The Antichrist*: "We would no more choose the first Christians to associate with than Polish Jews — not that one even required any objection to them: they both do not smell good."[16]

Nietzsche's admirers apparently can't recognize the language of Nazi-style anti-Semitism when they read it coupled with an attack on Christianity. Nietzsche's hatred of Christianity lifts them to such a peak of fervent excitement that they don't realize he's attacking Jews and Judaism at the same time, or they don't care, as long as he's anti-Christian. But what they really love are such lines as these, from the conclusion of *The Antichrist*: "I call Christianity the one great curse, the one great innermost corruption, the one great instinct of revenge. . . . I call it the one immortal blemish of mankind!"[17]

Why all this ritual? Because he blamed Christianity for taking his idealized Richard Wagner away from him? No. The fact is, Nietzsche's real problem with Wagner was not Christianity, but heterosexuality. Wagner just couldn't get up any enthusiasm for men or boys, either in his pagan or Christian phases. Women were Wagner's obsession, just as Wagner was Nietzsche's obsession. And thus it's no coincidence that Nietzsche's writings brim over with hatred and contempt for women. Despite the fact that various charitable women fed him and gave him shelter and money while he was sickly and unemployable, he could never forgive the female of the species for being more attractive to Wagner than he was, or for having produce ou Andreas-Salome, who jilted him, or his silly sister, who "left ʌim" for Bernhard Förster.

"Woman is by nature a snake, Heve," he says in *The Antichrist*, misusing the Hebrew name of Eve in a curious inversion because, since ancient times, the snake has usually been associated with the male reproductive organ. Freud, who also admired Nietzsche, could have had some real fun with that one.

Nietzsche's ravings were hailed by a handful of like-minded eccentrics as brilliant and illuminating. But most Germans of the 1880s found them blasphemous — and boring. Anyone who goes over the corpus of Nietzsche's work can't help but notice how much space he expends on plugging his previous books. The reason is easy to explain: they weren't selling. His later works were all printed privately. His money came from a Swiss pension and from well-meaning women who took pity (which, ironically, Nietzsche condemned) on the sickly, reclusive man with gracious, almost feminine manners.

While Nietzsche staggered between euphoria and depression, he continued to write: works on his hatred for Christianity; women; and Wagner — always Wagner. A single odd inconsistency turns up in his work. Nietzsche didn't hate the personality of Jesus, as he imagined Jesus to be. He portrayed Jesus as an admirable figure and saw Jesus' actual intention as a sort of "Buddhistic peace movement, for an actual, *not* merely promised happiness *on earth*."

"In truth, there was only one Christian, and he died on the cross," Nietzsche wrote in strophe 39 of *The Antichrist*. "Only Christian *practice*, a life such as he lived who died on the cross, is Christian."

After this one breakthrough, Nietzsche returned to belaboring Christians and Jews alike with more blasphemy. The believer who somehow finds something admirable in Nietzsche's writings will say, "See! He wasn't all bad! At least he didn't hate Jesus on a *personal* basis." In point of fact, Nietzsche probably had already begun to identify Jesus *as he fantasized Jesus* with *himself*. After all, a few strophes further on, he makes a line-by-line attack on some of Jesus' sayings as taken from the Gospels. In *The Antichrist*, Nietzsche created a sort of fatherless Jesus out of his own imagination because this was the only sort of figure he could identify with. He then portrayed this imaginary Jesus as the only real Christian, the better to attack other Christians, always including Wagner and Cosima.

On his forty-fourth birthday, Nietzsche rallied from his fits of euphoria and depression to crank out an incredible burst of writing. He titled his autobiographical outburst *Ecce Homo* ("Behold the Man"). This was the phrase Pontius Pilate used when he led Jesus out to be rejected by the Jerusalem mob and to be crucified. Nietzsche's admirers assume this was just another puerile blasphemy. But a student of abnormal psychology wouldn't have any trouble recognizing the onset of what is called delusions of grandeur (identification as Jesus Christ is probably the ultimate delusion of grandeur, and quite common among the seriously insane).

In the preface to *Ecce Homo*, Nietzsche virtually shrieks out this bizarre warning: "Verily, I advise you: depart from me, and guard yourselves against Zarathustra! And better still: be ashamed of him! Perhaps he hath deceived you. . . . Now do I bid you lose me and find yourselves; and only when ye have all denied me, will I return unto you!"[18]

Beyond the literary parody of the New Testament we can see more evidence of delusions of grandeur. And beyond the delusions, perhaps a warning: Did the intuition Nietzsche admitted to having, but refused to believe in, somehow warn him that his ravings would be used, or misused, after his departure from the stage of life?

Among the last of Nietzsche's writings was *Nietzsche contra Wagner*. After all his shrill railings against Wagner, akin to the rage of a vicious schoolgirl who couldn't get a date for the prom, Nietzsche capped his career with: "Wagner, . . . a decaying and despairing decadent, suddenly sank down, helpless and broken, before the Christian cross. . . . Not long after, I was sick, more than sick . . . for I had nobody except Richard Wagner."[19]

In January 1889, in Turin, Nietzsche saw a coachman beating a horse. He rushed into the street, embraced the horse, and collapsed. After his return to consciousness, he wrote short, euphoric letters — in one, he signed himself "The Crucified" — and then, no more. For the next twelve years, he wandered around the upstairs rooms of his mother's house, completely psychotic and unable to speak coherently, while his sister, now widowed, struggled to build his reputation. Nietzsche's big break as an author came only after his insanity: People bought books by "the mad philosopher" out of curiosity. His anti-Christian, antifeminist, antihumane rhetoric found few followers in the strong, self-confident Germany of the 1890s. Nietzsche himself had never liked the Germans much. He refers to them as "louts" and "Teutons and other buffalos" in his writings, and his first adherents were, in many cases, not Germans but Scandinavians and other foreigners. Later, when Germany was defeated in World War I, his ravings would attract a wider audience.

The prophet of the superman was in fact a syphilitic, a homosexual, and an incompetent as lover, friend, and author. Nietzsche told people to "be hard" and "live dangerously." Throughout his life he sponged off women and was drug-dependent for his syphilitic and depressive maladies. He was, in the current venacular, a wimp.

How did such a man get himself classified as the last of the great European philosophers?

Quite simply, Nietzsche was the necessary man. As his earnest admirer Walter Kaufmann points out, he was the only German, in fact the only continental philosopher of any importance, who was an avowed and consistent atheist. Descartes, Leibnitz, Kant, and other thinkers dropped out of traditional Christianity in search of unfettered truth, but each of them came to accept God and human immortality anyway. Johann Wolfgang von Goethe and Friedrich von Schiller, the two greatest German writers of the previous generation, also believed in God; and Goethe, a rebel against Scripture in his youth, came to accept the wisdom of the Bible in his lucid and vital old age. It seems impossible for the healthy and open mind to shut God out without intensive preconditioning. And this posed a real problem for atheistic academics of the twentieth century. They desperately needed an important European philosopher who was a consistent atheist.

So along came Nietzsche.

Nietzsche, of course, was not a "consistent" anything. People who think he was sane before January 1889 when he hugged the horse and hit the pavement, will have to reinvent the concept of sanity to prove it to the rest of us. He was, however, the best the academic atheists could come up with. And so the laurels of "philosophical greatness" are on Nietzsche's brow.

If Nietzsche had foreseen what was going to happen to his reputation after his madness, he might have written yet another chapter of *Zarathustra*:

At the end of day, Zarathustra, shambling and drooling, came to a fork in the road. If he turned right—to the University School of Medicine—he would be diagnosed as a case of syphilitic paresis, homosexual tendencies, and delusions of grandeur: Prognosis—insanity.

If he turned left—into the University School of Philosophy—he would be honored as the last great European philosopher: Prognosis—infamy.

SIGMUND FREUD: PSYCHOPATHOLOGY IN EVERYDAY LIFE

In the nineteenth century, cases of insanity like Nietzsche's were usually explained as brain disease. The materialism which had largely replaced Christianity in the scientific and medical community had rejected belief in demons or unclean spirits and saw insanity as purely physical in origin. Darwin, as we saw, believed that he had lost his taste in literature, music, and art because part of his physical brain had atrophied from lack of use. And Darwin and Huxley both tried to explain their headaches, indigestion, and lack of energy through imagining that they had contracted some sort of physical disease that had destroyed their vitality.

Sigmund Freud would have recognized that they were wrong. Freud was among the first wave of physicians to realize that a wide range of physical and mental illnesses were psychogenic: generated by the soul, or psyche. He did not invent the idea—which is at least as old as the New Testament. Freud, however, made the idea acceptable to his own era by putting the idea of soul-generated mental illness in a context which didn't require, or even allow, belief in a soul. For this, and for his belief that most forms of mental illness arise out of sexual conflicts and repressions, he won his laurels as the Father of Psychoanalysis. He was the last of the four great prophets of scientific atheism.

Freud's work was not free from inconsistencies. It's hard to see how a soul could generate mental and physical illnesses when it doesn't exist. The brain-is-mind epiphenomenalism propounded by Thomas Henry Huxley and adopted by the materialists makes human consciousness function rather like a photoelectric eye that opens the glass doors of supermarkets. Epiphenomenalism can explain simple reactions — like breathing. As Huxley described epiphenomenalism though, it has some problems explaining why we usually walk through a door instead of bashing into the wall next to the door — and then imagining that we had planned to do so all the time.

Freud, however, takes the simple mind-is-brain epiphenomenalism of Huxley and turns the photoelectric eye into a whole theater, with a cast of characters. As Freud explained personalities, there are three separate aspects of each individual personality: the id, which functions like an animal and knows only physical desires; the ego, which is conditioned by the demands of society and the hope of reward and fear of punishment; and the super-ego, which corresponds to what the Judeo-Christian world would call a mind or conscience by sorting out the demands of the id and the ego and choosing which ones to go with at any given moment. More than one critic has pointed out that there is no clinical or physical basis for any of this. Huxley cut people open, found no soul, and decided that men were machines and the brain explained everything. No neurosurgeon or neurophysiologist has ever yet cut open a human brain and found a theater and three dressing rooms for the id, ego, and super-ego. But Freudians believe that they exist. The "master" said so.

Freud, in fact, has been established as the secular deity of a recognizable cult. There is a doctrine which has to be accepted on his say-so, without evidence. All part of the Freudian cult, these include the concepts of the id, the ego, the super-ego, the death instinct; the idea that unrecognized sexual desires control most or all human actions; the non-existence of God and the immortal soul; and the natural inferiority and instability of women. His critics have observed — I think correctly — that Freud believed that a girl is a failed boy and a woman is a castrated man. He also believed that belief in God was a primitive belief in an archetypal father and that belief in human immortality was an attempt to compensate for man's earthly inadequacies. There is a cult shrine, the Freud archives, now located in England. There was a vestal virgin, his daughter Anna, who died just a few years ago. And there are the true believers, who have withstood every attempt to undermine Freud's doctrine by offering factual evidence to demonstrate the many mistakes he made.

Freud has taken a great deal of abuse, particularly in the past decade, from critics who have been able to penetrate the smoke screen of sanctified incense still offered by those who knew him personally or feel some sort of cult attachment to his name.

Freud's Jewishness has been a major complication in evaluating his life and work and separating his valuable contributions from his obsessions and errors. Anti-Semites assume that his attack on religion was limited to an attack on Christianity. They say his political-social hostility to Christianity explains his disbelief in God and the soul and his rejection of religious miracles as hallucinations or frauds. The more convinced anti-Semites, in fact, see Freud as the point-man of some arcane Jewish conspiracy to undermine Christianity. Nothing could be more far-fetched. Freud's followers, on the other hand, pass any criticism of his work off as just another example of ignorant anti-Semitism, even when the criticism is factual and plausible. This is equally absurd.

Actually, where Freud fell short was in his handling of the healthy mind. His understanding of psychopathology was deep and often sure, because in many cases he was describing his own troubles. But he himself never achieved true mental health. As a result his insights failed to extend beyond aberration. His whole outlook saw life as pathological.

This is reflected by the effect of the atheist syndrome on his life.

Freud's Childhood: Phase One

Nietzsche, whom Freud admired, said that all things love a mask. Freud was no exception. He found a mask-maker in Ernest Jones, a British physician and psychoanalyst who had been one of his most devoted — and uncritical — followers during the middle and later stages of his career. Jones's *The Life and Work of Sigmund Freud* was written with the cooperation and approval of Freud's survivors and for many years only Jones had access, through Freud's daughter Anna, the high priestess of the Freud cult, to the "great man's" papers.

In the 1970s, long after Jones had also died, a young Sanskrit scholar and psychoanalyst named Jeffrey Moussaieff Masson won the confidence of the aging Anna Freud and gained access of his own. What Masson found appalled him. He read papers which suggested that Freud had suppressed his own findings in some absolutely critical issues and that the suppression had been carried on after his death by what might be called "orthodox Freudians." Masson refused to continue the charade. The true believers in Freud were horrified. Masson was fired from his job as projects director of the Sigmund Freud archives in 1981 after a series of newspaper articles which reported some of his theories.

In 1984, however, Masson published *The Assault on Truth*, the most important book on Freud since Jones's sanctimonious triple-decker biography of the early 1950s. No one who wants to understand Freud as he really was, or may have been, should fail to read it.

From the works of Jones and Masson an amazing portrait of Freud emerges.

Most people think of Sigmund Freud as a Viennese. He was born, however, in Freiberg, Moravia, in 1856. His father, Jacob Freud, was a wool merchant, not particularly successful but far from poor. Jacob had married his first wife at seventeen, many years before. Some authorities believe that there was a second wife before Jacob married Sigmund's mother, though this hasn't been proven. At any rate, when Jacob married Amalie Nathansohn, he was over forty and she was not yet twenty. A vivacious woman of great vitality—she lived to be ninety-five—Sigmund's mother as a young wife appears to have exuded sensuality rather than sensibility. There's no doubt that Sigmund doted on his mother and she on him, in a way that wasn't particularly healthy.

The Austrian Empire, Freud's native land, was the remnant of Charlemagne's old Holy Roman Empire, ultimately of the Roman Empire, according to the rather revisionist version of history the Austrians themselves engaged in. Political unrest before Freud's birth, in 1848, and again in the 1860s, had shaped a state where two large minorities, German-speaking Austrians and Magyar-speaking Hungarians, were joint rulers over restless and dissatisfied Slavic, Italian, and Moslem minorities. The Jews of Austria-Hungary were put in a particularly awkward position. German-speaking and usually well-educated, they were outsiders to the official state religion of the Austro-Hungarian Empire. Multilingual Austria-Hungary was a palpably Roman Catholic state where religion and government were intimately associated. The Catholic Austrians often snubbed the Jews for their Jewishness, while the unhappy Slavic subjects of the Austrian emperor and the apostolic king of Hungary disliked and distrusted them both as reprobates and as Germans. During the Middle Ages, Jews had been denied the right to own land or bear arms because these rights involved the swearing of oaths as Christians. Because of this, and because of the high degree of literacy among them due to Scriptural study, Jews had usually become merchants. They were widely resented as nonproductive middlemen by the lower social classes, and anti-Semitic riots, which formed an excuse to loot Jewish homes, were deplorably common. The revolution of 1848, in fact, had featured extensive looting of Jewish homes and businesses in

Prague, the regional metropolis. Jacob Freud, concerned for his family and not particularly successful in Freiberg, decided to pack up and move from the city, which was 96 percent Roman Catholic. At the age of four, Sigmund Freud found himself on his way to Vienna.

It was while the Freud family was traveling to Vienna that Freud saw his mother naked and experienced a sexual arousal. This had such an impact on him that he wrote about it to Wilhelm Fliess, then his best friend, more than thirty years later. Freud was so fascinated that he became obsessed with incestuous conquest of his mother and rivalry with his father. At the age of seven or eight, he was caught urinating in his parents' bedroom and his father, intensely disgusted, predicted that he'd never amount to anything. The desire to have sex with his mother and to kill his father haunted Freud's dreams. He tells us so, repeatedly, in his writings. It was probably through his own obsession with incestuous conquest of his mother that Freud came to develop his theory of why some men become homosexual, one of the contributions he made to psychology that is still generally valued and highly regarded. Freud, however, believed that all little boys want to have sex with their mothers and to kill their fathers. He projected his own obsession onto the rest of the human race without any statistical evidence to back his claim. What probably happened was that Amalie Nathanson Freud, sensuous by nature, not very intellectual, and bored by a hard-working husband more than twenty years her senior, used her first-born son as a surrogate for her affectionate and subconsciously sexual outpourings; and the child Freud picked right up on it.

Freud's hostility to his father was probably formed in this crucible of incestuous desire for his mother. There was another reason for Freud's dislike of his father: rejection of the father's Jewish religion and heritage. Freud was intensely ambitious, intensely aggressive, and intensely preoccupied with the idea that every Christian he met was an anti-Semite. Jones tells us that Jacob Freud was a liberal and a freethinker, that is to say, irreligious. But then a few pages further on, he produces a Jewish Torah which Freud's father gave him, dedicated with an inscription in Hebrew:

> My dear Son: It was in the seventh year of your age that the spirit of God began to move you to learning. I would say the spirit of God speaketh to you: "Read in My Book; there will be opened to thee sources of knowledge and of the intellect." It is the Book of Books; it is the well that wise men have digged and from which lawgivers have drawn

the waters of their knowledge. Thou has seen in this Book the vision of the Almighty.[1]

Something is wrong here. Jones offers us this quote, obviously written by a religious Jew, only a few pages after he describes Jacob Freud as a freethinker. The man who wrote this dedication sounds like an orthodox Jew. We can only suspect that Freud, who never showed any interest in the practice of religious Judaism, was rejecting the father he secretly wanted to displace and kill as well as the religious heritage that restricted his social ambitions in Catholic Austria-Hungary.

So Freud's rejection of religion was not simply a Jewish hostility to a Christianity which had all too often treated Jews with cruelty. It was a hatred of Judaism as well. And in fact ultimately Freud's hatred for Judaism gained the upper hand over his sanity. This hatred of both Christianity and Judaism took the outward form of Freud's almost paranoid hostility to anything connected with evidence for the existence of spiritual phenomena. He was obsessive on this topic. The same mind that could accept son-to-mother incestuous desires as a normal part of growing up not only balked but panicked when faced with anything that could have pointed to life after death or spiritual reality.

Again, Freud did not reject the afterlife due to his Jewishness, but due to his rejection of his Jewishness. The Jews of the Old Testament clearly believed in an afterlife and this belief is featured in many Biblical passages. The Sadducees of Jesus' time did, admittedly, reject the afterlife, but they were a minority sect, influenced by the Greek Epicureans, and were criticized not only by Jesus but by the other Jews of their era. Medieval Judaism, like medieval Christianity, featured an extensive belief in mystical experiences and the spirit world, and among the Jews of eastern Europe there were pietist revivals which featured intense spiritual experiences. Freud's mother came from eastern Europe and had once lived in Odessa in Russia, where Jews tended to be oppressed far more than they were in Austria but also maintained a much more intense contact with spiritual Judaism.

Jones tells us how Freud lost most of his respect for his father. Jacob Freud, hoping to explain to him that things had gotten better for Jews since Jacob's own youth, told twelve-year-old Sigmund that a younger gentile had once knocked his new fur hat off and told him, "Get off the sidewalk, Jew!"

"And what did you do?" twelve-year-old Sigmund asked.

"I stepped into the gutter and picked up my hat," Jacob replied.[2]

Clearly, this kind of father wouldn't do for Sigmund Freud. He admits to having fantasized that his actual father was Emmanuel, his much older half brother by Jacob Freud's first wife. From here it would only be a short distance to rejecting God as the ultimate father symbol, and to systematically rejecting any evidence that might make God's reality plausible.

Freud's boyhood hero, in fact, was Hannibal, the Carthaginian warrior who had sworn his lifelong hatred of Rome (the Roman Catholic Church?) and had inflicted great defeats on the Romans before being defeated himself. Note that Hannibal was not only a Semite but also a pagan. The Carthaginians sacrificed infant boys to Baal, the same pagan idol that the prophets of Israel opposed so strongly in the Old Testament. Humanist historians used to deny that the stories of infant sacrifice were true, until excavations at Carthage in North Africa turned up the bones of sacrificed infants in the ruins of Baal's temple in Carthage. The God of Israel had defeated Baal in the Holy Land, and the Romans had leveled his temple in North Africa, plowed furrows, and sowed salt on the site of Carthage, and dedicated the site to their own "infernal gods." Freud, however, preferred Hannibal to any of the many Israelite heroes he might have admired.

Freud's Flight: Phase Two

Freud's inability to identify with his father is typical of the atheist syndrome. The result can be shown in his attitude toward his career. First he was attracted to literature, then to chemistry. The one thing he didn't want to do was to follow his father Jacob into the business world. He also appears to have lacked the mathematical skill to succeed in the hard sciences. Again, mathematics, the most proverbially objective and precise of all the academic disciplines, is usually a pitfall with atheist syndrome children, and Freud runs true to form. In later years, his otherwise probing mind could be thrown into absolute confusion by a railroad timetable. Freud approached medicine only through research in physiology, and despite his obvious high intelligence he took three years longer than the average student to finish medical school. One of his most impressive accomplishments in undergraduate years, incidentally, was to locate what he believed were the testes of the male eel. He had to dissect four hundred eels before he was satisfied with the results. This would seem to have been an unattractive assignment to anyone who found eels unaesthetic. Freud appears to have liked them, as he later liked cigars and asparagus.

Freud discovered a possible father-substitute during his student days in the person of Ernst Brücke, a Prussian physiologist who was teaching in Vienna in the 1870s. Brücke was an archmaterialist, like Jean Baptiste Lamarck, who had tried to devise a scheme of evolution fifty years before Darwin. Brücke's hostility to any influence of soul or spirit in science makes him sound rather like Thomas Henry Huxley. So does the fact that he came slightly unhinged at the premature death of his son in 1873. Brücke ordered that the boy's name never be mentioned again or his photograph displayed in the house. Ernest Jones reports that this cold, robot-like Prussian had a great influence on Freud. But Jones also admits that Brücke's archmaterialist theories of consciousness had to be rejected before Freud could continue with his own work and theories.

Freud was, as both his admirers and detractors have noted, intensely ambitious. He wanted to discover something of such importance that he would be world famous. Beginning in 1884, he thought he had found the key to world fame. He began his investigations into the anesthetic properties of cocaine. Freud's role here was more as publicist than a discoverer. The Indians in South America had been using coca leaves as a local anesthetic and a cure for exhaustion from overwork for centuries, and the Spaniards had brought information about the properties of coca leaves back to Europe in the sixteenth century. Freud's enthusiasm for cocaine, a derivative of coca leaves, went far beyond what one would expect from a normal, healthy mind. Freud was nearly thirty, an advanced medical student, widely read in several languages and trained in the techniques of science; but his ravings about cocaine make him sound like a teenager after his first toot. He sent cocaine to his fiance, telling her it would put color in her cheeks. He also wrote her a love note good-naturedly threatening to get loaded on cocaine and rape her. Above all, he claimed again and again that cocaine was not physically or psychologically addictive.

In the middle of all this enthusiasm for cocaine, Freud's father confided his fear that he was having eye trouble. Knowing Freud's inner feelings for his father, it's not surprising that he treated the threat of Jacob's incipient blindness with insensitive brevity. When he eventually took his father's troubles seriously, cocaine was used in the operation and a new wonder was chalked up for the wonder drug.

Freud had begun his publicity campaign and his bid to win fame through popularization of cocaine in 1884. But then by 1886, cases of cocaine addiction had begun to surface all over the German-speaking world and medical opinion began to backfire on Freud's scheming. Cocaine was addictive, and the possibilities for self-destruction by cocaine abuse were soon widely recognized. Freud's first attempt to make a world reputation ended in disgrace and in death or addiction for people who followed his advice.

Shortly thereafter, at twenty-nine, in 1885-86, he made a six-month study trip to Paris where he worked with Jean Martin Charcot, a French physician and student of hypnotism and of female hysteria.

Female hysteria — sexual obsession coupled with a powerful fear of sex, sometimes resulting in paralysis or other physical symptoms — is much less common today than it was in the late nineteenth century. The near-disappearance of female hysteria perhaps can only be explained by a vast and sweeping change in the nature of women themselves and of their role in society. When we look at the photographs of women from the Victorian era, we can hardly imagine what their lives must have been like. Even the physical details of existence have gone through an enormous transition. This was brought home to me through a friend of mine, Schuyler Grant, who played a role in the multi-award-winning films *Anne of Green Gables* and *Anne of Avonlea*, as Diana, opposite Megan Follows as Anne. Among other honors, these films won virtually every available award for accuracy in costumes. Ms. Grant said:

> At first I was really excited about the costumes and hair styles I was going to wear. But the novelty wore off very quickly. Achieving that Victorian look wasn't easy. Wearing a corset is something like being in a body cast for twelve hours. Every night I breathed a sigh of relief at the prospect of removing my gorgeous costumes and putting on some jeans and a tee-shirt. A woman who's never worn a corset doesn't know how lucky she is to be living in the twentieth century. A corset attacks and molds your spine to affect that swaybacked "womanly" posture. Unfortunately it becomes almost impossible to eat, sit, or bend over. I wore mine as loosely fitted as possible, but I still felt like I was maneuvering in a wooden box. But I suppose these were the compromises one had to make to wear the eighteen-inch waistbands of the 1800s. The reason women were so infamous for fainting spells in Victorian times was because their corsets didn't allow them to get enough oxygen to remain conscious, especially when they got excited. As a child I always dreamed of living in the 1800s, but I've outgrown it.

Women were often little more than showpieces in a man's home,
bound by society and their corsets.[3]

Corsets were, indeed, a sort of trap or cage for Victorian maidens
and matrons. It was difficult at best to regard women as authentically
human when they fainted so easily and had such trouble maneuvering.
The corset had other consequences. Because it constricted the stomach
muscles, these muscles on upper-class and middle-class Victorian women
never developed the sort of strength that they developed among uncorseted peasant women or "primitives." Childbirth became not merely ar-
duous but agonizing, because corseted women never developed the ab-
dominal strength they needed to expel the baby. Weakened by the lack
of exercise their corsets and their society imposed, they sometimes died
of heart attacks while giving birth in enormous pain. "Primitive" women,
whose bodies were strengthened by outdoor work, and other uncorseted
women sometimes gave birth in a ditch, carried the baby back home
themselves, and returned to work later the same day. At that they may
have been better off because through Freud's childhood, Victorian
"lying-in" hospitals or maternity wards were places of great danger. Puerperal infection, carried on the hands of physicians to birthing women,
often raised the mortality rate among mothers as high as 10 percent — in
some cases to 25 percent. Ignaz Semmelweis and Jakob Koletschka, two
Hungarian physicians in Budapest, had pondered this terrible death rate
among young mothers in the years just before Freud's birth. When
Koletschka, treating the dying mothers, came down with the same disease, and died of it, his friend Semmelweis theorized that an infection
was being passed back and forth between mothers and physicians. He
suggested that physicians and interns wash their hands with soap and
water between examining different patients and after autopsies. When
this was tried, the mortality rate for puerperal fever among young
mothers dropped to a fraction of 1 percent. Unfortunately, the medical
world refused to take Semmelweis seriously. The materialists needed
spontaneous generation as an antidote to belief in God. And
Semmelweis' discovery ran against belief in spontaneous generation. The
medical profession refused to accept it. For twenty years after
Koletschka's death and Semmelweis's discovery, young mothers continued to die of a disease that could have been prevented by hand-wash-
ing, because scientific atheism had no use for sanitation. Pasteur and
Lister finally convinced the world of the need for basic hygiene in
surgery in the 1870s, but by that time Semmelweis himself had died of

puerperal fever, along with thousands of women who might have been saved by soap and water.

Thus, women in the nineteenth century had every right to be afraid of sex. Not only was childbirth agonizing, but it was potentially lethal. The wonder is not that so many women were frigid, but that anyone let themselves be talked into carrying on the species. To this, too, there was a practical solution: "Nice" girls were told as little as possible about the realities of life. The feminine ideal of the Victorian and Edwardian eras was not merely the girl who'd rather die than say yes to an "indecent proposition," but the girl who wouldn't even understand what she was being asked to do.

Faced with women who had been raised in this tradition, Charcot, Freud, and Freud's older colleague Josef Breuer didn't find female hysteria to be particularly strange. The enthusiasm Freud showed for his trip to Paris may have prevented him from working out any theories on the spot, but he mentions in his rather cryptic personal writing that he saw things at the Paris morgue which society wasn't ready for.

Back in Vienna, working with Breuer, Freud began to notice a pattern in the more serious hysteria cases, a pattern he had also seen in Paris. The women who were afflicted with hysteria often charged their fathers or step-fathers with rape or attempted rape. This perversion of the normal father-daughter relationship seemed to be at the root of many of the hysteria cases. Freud was eager to make a name for himself, and possibly to make a humane contribution to medicine and psychology. So Freud worked up a paper on "The Aetiology of Hysteria" which was presented before the Society for Psychiatry and Neurology in Vienna in 1896. In this original paper, Freud took the side of his patients, the female victims of the rapes and attempted rapes who became hysterics. The Viennese medical community was appalled. The Viennese medical authorities, like most of the French ones, were not convinced. They believed that the rape stories were fantasies concocted by children for the malicious pleasure of telling lies or getting adults into trouble. Count Richard von Krafft-Ebing, head of the department of psychiatry at the University of Vienna, said that Freud's theory sounded like a fairy tale.

Freud backed off. He had already become notorious once, through his fervent publicizing of cocaine. He announced, perhaps on purely public relations grounds, that believing the women and girls had been a mistake. He postulated that, in fact, they had secretly wanted their fathers or uncles to have sex with them, and that the stories of being raped or molested were fantasies based on wish-fulfillment. Instead of being the victims, the women had become the villains.

But the idea that the women were responsible for their own hysteria through overactive imaginations and an unquenchable desire for sex was an idea that Freud's society wanted to hear.

Freud was a made man. He had found a marketable commodity, his ticket to fame and glory. He went on to construct a whole system around the idea that unfulfilled wishes became imaginary realities for women and other subhumans, even when they weren't otherwise un-balanced or schizophrenic. This is particularly important in Freud's views on religion. Hostile to religion himself because he feared Christians and hated being Jewish, Freud concocted the idea that the sort of religious experiences reported by saints and visionaries were fantasies based on wish-fulfillment. Presumably, the witnesses who also reported strange happenings, like the people who saw the candle consume itself in Ber-nadette Soubirous' hand without burning her, were also fantasizing. And so were the thousands of ordinary mortals who reported anecdotal stories about other spiritual phenomena.

Unfortunately for the "great man's" continuing reputation, Jeffrey Moussaieff Masson managed to charm his way into the Freud archives in the 1970s. Later, Masson would report in *The Assault on Truth* that he found a shocking story: Freud's original theory, that the girls really had been raped or accosted, was the reality and he knew it all along. Masson argued that Freud actually concocted the fantasy theory under social pressure to produce a theory that was pro-male and pro-authority, and antiwoman and antichild — all for the sake of popularity.

Masson also uncovered the case of Emma Eckstein. Fräulein Eck-stein, a Viennese feminist, came to Freud seeking help for feelings of weakness and what might be called women's complaints. Freud at this time was deeply attached to Dr. Wilhelm Fliess. Some of the correspon-dence Freud sent to Fliess, in fact, sounds like love letters. Freud spoke to Fliess about Emma Eckstein's case and about the fact that she con-fessed to autoerotic habits but wanted to be cured of them. Fliess calmly suggested that she could be cured by removing the turbinate bone from her nose. This operation, of course, was medical nonsense; it served no purpose at all, and was, in fact, ridiculous. Even so, Freud approved it. Fliess and Freud got into such a fever pitch of excitement about the surgical collaboration that Fliess left a long strip of gauze packing inside the incision and Fräulein Eckstein developed a serious infection and al-most died. When Freud discovered the gauze packing in the infected incision he grew faint and staggered out of the room. His friend Fliess was in medical jeopardy. "She had not lost consciousness during the massive hemorrhage," Freud wrote in a long-lost letter Masson found and translated. "When I returned to the room somewhat shaky, she greeted me with the condescending remark 'That is the stronger sex.'"[4]

Freud had barely gotten over his horror and fear when he began to rationalize and to blame Emma Eckstein, not his "dearest friend" Fliess, for the senseless operation and for the blunder that almost made it a fatal operation.

Not surprisingly, the adoring Ernest Jones doesn't deal with Emma Eckstein in any detail. Her face sustained serious damage and the operation probably cut her life short by decades.

Freud and Fliess grew apart. No one seems to know exactly what happened between them, but Freud himself admitted that he fainted during an angry confrontation. Fliess had advanced a theory to Freud that all people were actually bisexual. One wonders where he could have gotten such an idea. The two "friends" were later to attack one another in print, but Fliess's parting summation on Freud is perhaps the most quotable thing the redoutable surgeon-butcher ever said: "Freud was only a 'thought-reader' — and more — that he read his own thoughts into his patients."[5]

Freud's next beau ideal of male friendship was Carl Gustav Jung. Jung, however, was a much different article than Fliess. He seems to have had no homosexual tendencies, and long before meeting Freud he had begun to work out his own explanation for human consciousness. Jung, the son of a Swiss Protestant pastor, had begun researching spiritual phenomena while he was still in medical school. He believed that there was a spiritual component in human consciousness that materialism couldn't explain or dismiss. Jung didn't make this statement on the basis of tradition or sentimentality. He was an empiricist, a believer in experiments, to a much greater degree than Freud, who — ironically — tended to come up with theories first and then look for the evidence. The Freud-Jung friendship was probably doomed from the start, because Freud hated and feared spiritual things and Jung thought that Freud was excessively preoccupied with sex, particularly abnormal sex. Jung, however, did see some of Freud's positive achievements, and Freud seems to have wanted young Jung to be his successor as head of the psychoanalytic movement. But when Freud was confronted with Jung's spiritual beliefs — and the evidence for them — he couldn't cope. He abandoned the friendship.

Freud's clash with Jung wasn't his first encounter with evidence for the supernatural. At one point in his massive tome on Freud, Jones tells us how proud Freud was to have had several of his earlier papers read by F. W. H. Myers, the pioneer of supernatural and metaphysical research. Myers, a Cambridge classical scholar and the son of a clergyman, had begun his scientific investigation of mystical and mysterious occurrences in 1882. By the 1890s he had discovered evidence which refuted the materialist explanation that mind and brain are the same thing and pointed to the probability of life after death. To explain how people were sometimes influenced by ideas or thoughts they didn't consciously understand, Myers developed the theory of what he called subliminal consciousness. *Sub limen* in Latin means "under the threshold," and Myers meant that people often had thoughts which were below the threshold of consciousness but influenced their conscious or unconscious actions. Freud tapped this idea heavily, in fact virtually borrowed it in developing "his" theory of the "unconscious." Many Freudians don't realize that their "great man" borrowed his basic theory from a man who spent his adult life researching spiritual phenomena and came to believe firmly in life after death on the basis of scientific evidence.

Freud's resistance to the supernatural may have had something to do with this: If Freudian psychoanalysis took a turn into metaphysical research, Freud's debt to F. W. H. Myers would have been quite obvious. Myers is not as well known today as he was at the turn of the century, except to students of parapsychology. But he was a major figure in the development of psychology as well as of parapsychology. The bottom line is that Freud couldn't stand the thought of sharing the limelight.

But more probably, Freud's dislike of metaphysical research was emotional rather than practical. Christianity and Judaism are both rooted in very real supernatural and revelatory experiences. Materialism isn't. Freud had left materialism behind when he began to devise his theories about the unconscious, but he refused to admit as much to his disciples and followers. In effect then he created a sort of schizoid psychology: a human consciousness that was materialist in terms of the way Freud understood physiology, but dualist in the way Freud understood psychology. But despite this inherent contradiction, Freud clung to the notion because if he gave up materialism entirely he would be drawn irresistibly toward something very much like the traditional Judeo-Christian tradition. And this he refused to accept for purely emotional reasons that had nothing to do with observed facts.

Jung's display of spiritual belief and his unwillingness to knuckle under to Freud's emotional need to believe that sex explained everything doomed their friendship. Freud had originally chosen Jung as his successor because he didn't want the movement to be identified as essentially Jewish, another example of Freud's Jewish anti-Semitism. But such posturing was not to be. Freud's Viennese followers, jealous of Jung's influence, were resentful of Jung and the other Swiss involved in psychoanalysis. In November 1912, Freud accused Jung of not giving him credit for his theories in articles Jung had published in Switzerland. In the middle of his verbal tirade, he fainted again. It was the same hotel where he had previously fainted during his argument with Fliess. Jung picked Freud off the floor and carried him to a sofa.

"How sweet it must be to die," Freud said when he regained consciousness.[6]

Freud told Jones that he was beginning to see a pattern in all these arguments with beloved male colleagues followed by fainting spells.

"There is some piece of unruly homosexual feeling at the root of the matter," he said.[7]

Freud's next boon companion was Szandor Ferenczi, an analyst who had an intuitive skill for getting to the bottom of patients' problems. Unfortunately, Ferenczi was too intuitive. He believed in metaphysics and, to Freud, this was the first step on the road back to religious belief. Freud nudged him out of the succession and dropped him as a colleague.

Freud's Collapse: Phase Three

The wear and tear of all these emotional experiences with men seems to have made a much greater impression on Freud than his wife and his six children. Following the atheist syndrome we would expect that he would be a devoted husband and father, and this was indeed the case. His wife never really seems to have understood or appreciated his work, and the intellectually meaningful relationships of his life were mostly with other men or with other women. But he appears to have been an amiable husband and a loving father. Some people who visited the Freuds noted that his daughter Anna could be seen sitting on his lap at an age when most girls would be embarrassed to be seen doing this. But by this time his associates had been winnowed down to worshipers; the critics all had fled from his ponderous ego and irrational rages punctuated by fainting spells. Anna stayed on his lap, and later began to replace his wife as the hostess at social functions.

Freud's father was quite old when Freud first began to form impressions of him, but the psychosomatic symptoms of the atheist syndrome began on schedule.

"There were constant minor disturbances of health," Jones tells us. "His letters to his friends were full of allusions to his intestinal disorders. The disorder in question, of which chronic constipation was the most prominent symptom, was very obscure. It was at different times diagnosed as colitis, inflammation of the gall bladder, simple indigestion, or chronic appendicitis." Jones also tells us that he was "a martyr to migraines throughout his life."[8]

An observer will note that all these symptoms, and in particular the indigestion and the migraine headaches, are very similar to the ones Darwin and Huxley suffered from when they reached the age to resemble their fathers. Self-rejection set in and started to destroy the health of each man. In Freud's case, there were other, more specifically mental symptoms. Freud became obsessively afraid of death and three times predicted the date of his death in advance by recourse to numerology, a sort of occult parlor game that has no serious status with scientific investigators. After bouts of nerves and jitters Freud failed to die on schedule three times in a row. He confided to Jones that this proved there was nothing to superstition.[9]

At sixty-seven Freud contracted a disease that wasn't imaginary. He was a lifelong smoker who went through twenty fat cigars a day, and admitted that he was addicted. The result was a case of cancer of the jaw that cost him sixteen years of surgical scrapings, iodine and x-ray treatments, and a constant reminder of the presence of death. Ultimately he had to wear a prothesis to replace part of his face. The disease may have made his chronic clinical depression and nervousness comprehensible rather than deepening it. Freud's health problems antedated his cancer by many years and were undoubtedly psychosomatic.

In 1938, when the Nazis swarmed into unresisting Austria, many of the leading thinkers and intellectuals of Freud's generation committed suicide. Their era was over and they knew it. Freud, however, wanted to survive. He was working on a book which he was sure would revolutionize world thought, *Moses and Monotheism*.

The thesis of the book was that Moses was actually an Egyptian murdered by the Israelites, who then, out of guilt, constructed an elaborate story about Moses' importance. Creating such a theory out of whole cloth without evidence in ordinary times would have merely been blasphemous and silly. Freud had no fresh evidence, no evidence at all other than his own theorizing. Writing *Moses and Monotheism* in 1938, with Hitler and the Nazis howling for the exile or destruction of the European Jewish community, was in effect an act of moral and political treason. By trying to destroy Moses, Freud was subconsciously attacking his own Jewish roots. He was also offering the Nazis a potential propaganda victory of incredible magnitude. The news that the most famous Jewish writer of his era had declared Moses a fraud and the Jews a race of murderers would have been the best propaganda Hitler could have wanted.

Freud was attempting to hack away the Ten Commandments, which formed the common religious heritage of Judaism and Christianity. Throughout the Middle Ages, popes and emperors alike had refrained from the wholesale destruction of the then-helpless Jews, because medieval Christians recognized that Jews worshiped the same God and were — in medieval theology — incomplete Christians, rather than pagans like the Norse worshipers of Odin and Thor or the Slavs with their strange and now-forgotten pantheon of forest and river gods. Max I. Dimont, in *Jews, God, and History*, rightly observed that at the beginning of the Middle Ages there were many religions in Europe and by the end there were only two: Christianity and Judaism. The newly Christianized Germanic warriors had spared the Jews from forcible conversion or wholesale massacre because Moses, the law-giver, had been a Jew. Now Freud wanted him to be an Egyptian — all because Freud hated his father and his father's religion.

The potential tragedy could have been averted if any of Freud's remaining followers had had the courage to tell him that his idea was ludicrous and dangerous. None did. Religious and secular Jewish leaders got wind of what was being written and begged Freud not to publish it. But he refused to listen. At this point his insatiable ego and pathological father-hatred was more important than the survival of the four elderly sisters he had left in Vienna or the millions of Jewish Europeans who had lacked the wealth and fame needed to escape to England.

Freud published *Moses and Monotheism*. The world shrugged as it tottered on the brink of World War II. With Hitler and Stalin abroad on the earth, Freud had lost his shock value.

In September 1939, while air raid shelters were being dug in England to prepare for the battle to the death with Nazi Germany, Freud lost his vitality. He asked his personal physician for a lethal dose of morphine. At eighty-three, ravaged by cancer, Freud lapsed into silence.

"Freud died as he lived — a realist," Jones wrote.[10]

One has to wonder in retrospect what kind of "realist" would consider his personal rejection of his father's God more important than the survival of his sisters and other relatives and friends. Freud was, of course, free to believe whatever he wanted about the existence or non-existence of God. But his final exertions in the first year of Hitler's war to cap his own life with a masterpiece of anti-Semitic propaganda casts deep doubts on his "realism" — and his sanity.

PART THREE

THE SYNDROME'S CONTINUING LEGACY

SEVEN

ROBERT INGERSOLL AND CLARENCE DARROW: SCIENTIFIC ATHEISM'S AMERICAN COUSINS

The atheist syndrome did not die with the last of the Big Four. Sadly, it has been passed on from one tormented soul to another, all the way down to the present day.

In America, two of the most famous carriers of the dread malady were Robert Ingersoll and Clarence Darrow.

Robert Ingersoll was not, strictly speaking, a scientific atheist. He was by his own statements, an agnostic, not an atheist, who said that he could neither affirm nor deny the existence of some sort of divinity. Nor was he a scientist. He was a lawyer, and he contributed nothing important to the roster of scientific arguments against God or the immortal soul. Ingersoll, in fact, rather liked the idea of immortality. What he hated was organized religion.

The origin of his dislike isn't hard to fathom. Robert Ingersoll's father, John Ingersoll, was a depressed and unsuccessful Presbyterian clergyman. Robert's mother died when he was two and a half years old.

"I can remember her as she looked in death," Ingersoll wrote many years later. "That sweet, cold face has kept my heart warm through all the changing years."[1]

"John, my father, was filled with the idea that it was his duty to save his fellow men from the wrath of a God of infinite love," Ingersoll later wrote with rather ponderous irony. "He was a believer in all the consolations of Christianity, including the dogma of eternal torment. In his day this dogma was in full force. Men believed in fire and sulphur, in devils and fiends. . . . My father carried the sorrows of the world. The frightful doctrine of eternal punishment furrowed his face and made his eyes familiar with tears. This horror darkened his life. He was loving and generous in his nature, but his theology filled his sky with cloud and storm."[2]

The combination of a depressed father who wept while he threatened people with eternal damnation and a mother who died before his third birthday would have surely soured a less sensitive child than Robert Ingersoll on strict Calvinist sermons even without the third element: dire poverty. The family moved from parish to parish or school to school as his unsuccessful father preached and taught trying to support his motherless brood of five young children.

Ingersoll wrote:

When I was a boy, Sunday was considered altogether too holy to be happy in. Sunday used to commence then when the sun went down on Saturday night. . . . A darkness fell upon the house ten thousand times deeper than that of night. Nobody said a pleasant word; nobody laughed; nobody smiled. . . . On Sunday morning . . . we went to church. The minister was in a pulpit about twenty feet high with a little sounding-board above him, and he commenced at firstly and went on and on to about twenty-thirdly. Then he made a few remarks by way of application; and then took the general view of the subject; and in about two hours reached the last chapter in *Revelation*. After the sermon, he had an intermission . . . then came the catechism on the chief end of man. We sat in a row with our feet coming to about six inches of the floor. The minister asked us if we all knew that we deserved to go to hell, and we all answered 'yes.' Then he asked us if we would be willing to go to hell, if it was God's will, and every little liar shouted 'yes.' Then the same sermon was preached once more, commencing at the other end and going back. After that we started for home, sad and solemn, overpowered with the wisdom displayed in the scheme of the atonement. When we got home, if we had been good boys . . . sometimes they would take us out to the graveyard to cheer us up a little. It did cheer me. When I looked at the sunken tombs, and the leaning stones, and read the half-effaced inscriptions . . . it was a great comfort. The reflection came to my mind that the observance of the Sabbath could not last always.[3]

The sort of sulphur-spouting sermons and endless threats of endless damnation obviously weren't an appropriately balanced spiritual diet for small, sensitive children, and one really has to wonder about John Ingersoll's level of maturity in finding nothing in the Bible but the fear of eternal wrath. The total gloom of his theology, as described by his son, and his tendency to burst into tears, sound like a serious case of depression due to his wife's death and to poverty.

John Ingersoll was, by most accounts, strict without being sadistic. He was, however, a demanding teacher who didn't spare the rod. One of his favorite methods was to set an inch of lit candle before the Bible or a commentary on the Bible and to order Robert to memorize a set number of lines before the candle burned out. If the boy failed in his memorization, he would have to sit in darkness as a punishment. The idea that damnation might come in small doses would seem to be a logical consequence. Robert Ingersoll would grow up to hate the Bible for the rest of his life — and to speechify about his hatred more or less constantly.

Ingersoll himself dated his rejection of orthodox Christianity from his seventh year. A wandering Baptist preacher painted such an uncommonly vivid picture of the sufferings of the damned that Ingersoll says he told himself *It is a lie, and I hate your religion.* From that moment on, he said, "The flames of hell were quenched," and he passionately hated every orthodox creed.[4]

Ingersoll blamed part of his father's lack of material success on John Ingersoll's hatred of slavery and his honesty in condemning slave-owners. This doesn't make much sense, because the family spent most of their wandering years in New York and Ohio, both staunchly antislave states during the 1840s and 1850s, when Robert Ingersoll was growing up. In all probability, John Ingersoll just wasn't a very good preacher. Subconsciously, Robert almost certainly blamed the Almighty, or at least his father's choice of a career, for the family's poverty and constant wanderings.

After a rudimentary education, Ingersoll served for two years in the Civil War and became a brevet colonel, that is, a temporary colonel for wartime service. He served in several hard-fought battles and was once captured while fighting at the head of his troops. He left the army after his capture and exchange. He became a lawyer and built an extremely lucrative practice. His income of $100,000 a year through much of the 1880s and 1890s would be the equivalent of a million-dollar income today. His critics accused him of taking disreputable cases or defending dishonest people against the public interest, which was at least a mild inconsistency for a man who claimed that his true religion was the love of humanity. Ingersoll, however, was more consistent than some of his critics. He pointed out that he had rejected the Scriptural concept of the blessings of poverty along with his faith in the God of the Bible or of the divinity of Jesus.

Ingersoll was absolutely obsessed with the aspects of cruelty that he saw every time he looked religionward. His favorite case in point was the Spanish Inquisition, not exactly a relevant issue for Americans in the late nineteenth century, a mere three hundred years after the fact, but a very good sticking-place for a campaign against organized religion.

But his pet hatred was the Bible.

At one point, he describes how reading a list of classic authors had made him an agnostic and freed him from dependence on the Bible, not to mention a bit of an intellectual, he might have modestly added. Among those he mentions are Zeno, Cicero, Seneca, Marcus Aurelius, Galileo, Descartes, Newton, Copernicus, and Kepler. Oddly, every one of these thinkers believed in some concept of God; most of them believed in the afterlife; and Galileo, Copernicus, and Kepler were all Christians. Copernicus, in fact, was a Catholic priest. And Kepler was such a staunch Lutheran that he refused to compromise his faith even while working for the Catholic Holy Roman emperor—at some risk to his safety. It was the same Kepler whom Ingersoll extols who claimed to have discovered that the Star of Bethlehem was a convergence of the orbits of Jupiter and Saturn and would have been seen over Galilee at the time of Jesus' birth. Kepler is a very odd man to cite in an attack on Christianity. Did Ingersoll really read Kepler? If he did, did he understand that the man was a devout Christian who helped validate the New Testament?

It's also fascinating to see that when John Ingersoll was dying, his son convinced him to read not the Bible but *Phaedo*, Plato's description of the death of Socrates. *Phaedo* is a moving picture of a brave man facing death. It's also a strong argument, based both on logic and intuition, for human immortality, the human soul, free will, and the existence of a moral order in the universe. Socrates lived four hundred years before Jesus but many Christians have said that he embodied many of the Christian ethical virtues. Atheists, from Nietzsche to Bertrand Russell, have always disliked him intensely. The substitution of Socrates for Jesus indicates that Robert Ingersoll was operating under an obsessive dislike of organized Christianity, not a scientific atheism like that of Darwin or Huxley. His rejection of Christianity was clearly a bias, not a logical conclusion.

His attempts to project this bias into his judgment of art and letters led to some obvious blunders. Ingersoll greatly admired Abraham Lincoln, and in one of his pontifications he said that Lincoln was not a Christian. He was challenged on this by another Civil War veteran, General Charles H. T. Collis, who asserted that Lincoln was a Christian. Obviously, Ingersoll had such an intense bias against Christianity that he couldn't bear to believe that Lincoln was a believer.

"Lincoln was never a member of any church," Ingersoll wrote to Collis. "Mrs. Lincoln stated a few years ago that Mr. Lincoln was not a Christian. Hundreds of his acquaintances have said the same thing. Not only so, but many of them have testified that he was a Freethinker; that he denied the inspiration of the Scriptures, and that he always insisted that Christ was not the Son of God, and that the dogma of atonement was, and is, an absurdity. I will very gladly pay you a thousand dollars for your trouble to show that one statement of your letter is correct—even one."[5]

Collis replied and accused Ingersoll of trying to "proselyte" the dead president by making him appear to be an agnostic when he clearly wasn't. "That Mr. Lincoln regularly attended a Christian Church in Washington is a historical fact. Though not a 'member,' as we technically understand it, he was a constant attendant of Dr. Gurley's Presbyterian Church, near the corner of 14th Street and New York Avenue. Dr. Gurley was his pastor and was present at his deathbed. He also frequently attended Dr. Sutherland's Church. To the Methodists he said . . . 'God bless the Methodist Church, bless all the churches, and blessed by God, who in this our great trial giveth us the churches. . . . If on September 4, 1864, you had served him (Lincoln) with notice that thirty years later you would claim him as a Voltairian (that is to say, a Deist who believed in Nature's God but not in Scripture or an afterlife) because he disbelieved in the inspiration of the Bible and the divinity of Christ, he could not more emphatically have repudiated the honour than he did when he then said to the coloured men of Baltimore who presented him with a Bible: 'In regard to the Great Book, I have only to say that it is the best gift which God has given to man. All the good from the Saviour of the world is communicated in this book.'"[6]

Collis, being a gentleman, didn't add that when Mary Todd Lincoln had said her husband wasn't a Christian she was quite probably insane. Unstable at best, she had suffered what we would call a nervous breakdown after Lincoln's assassination and spent time in mental institutions, where she probably said a great many things Ingersoll could have made use of. Ingersoll doesn't name any of his "hundreds" of witnesses. But most people who knew Lincoln report that he knew large portions of the New Testament, the Psalms, and Isaiah by heart, could quote Scripture by chapter and verse, frequently prayed in public and private, and often spoke warmly of his belief in God and divine Providence. The best interpretation of Lincoln is probably that he was a believing non-denominational Christian. Calling him a "freethinker"—or in other words an atheist or agnostic—is nothing short of ridiculous and irresponsible.

Ingersoll was at his best when he had a chance to categorize Christianity as vicious and brutal. The highlight of his career came in 1885, when a traveling freethinker named Charles B. Reynolds was charged with blasphemy in Morristown, New Jersey. Ingersoll made a speech which his followers considered supremely eloquent. He defined blasphemy as "to live on the unpaid labor of other man . . . to enslave your fellow-man, to put chains on his body . . . to strike the weak and unprotected in order that you may gain the applause of the ignorant and superstitious mob . . . to persecute the intelligent few, at the command of the ignorant many . . . to pollute the souls of children with the dogma of eternal pain . . . to violate your conscience."[7] Ingersoll was also enough of a shyster to twist words. The New Jersey blasphemy statute defined blasphemy with the words "Whoever shall willfully speak against. . . ." Ingersoll presumed on the stupidity of the rural jurors by trying to claim that what the statute actually said was that for a conviction it would be necessary to prove that the defendant "made the statements attributed to him knowing that they were not true." Obviously, this isn't what the statute said. Obviously, Ingersoll knew this. So did the jury. They found Reynolds guilty.

Ingersoll paid Reynolds's fine out of his own pocket. Since the fine was $25 and Ingersoll earned more than $100,000 a year, sometimes as much as $3,500 for a single speech, it was a sweet sacrifice, especially considering the publicity he won.

Ingersoll was and still is a hero to the American atheist community, though he was technically not an atheist. His theology, in fact, seems quite confused, since he didn't believe in any form of God but considered that an afterlife was possible, if it didn't include eternal punishment, which he ruled out of order on his own authority.

His domestic life was notably happy and conventional. His wife, the former Eva Amelia Parker, was herself a second-generation freethinker, so they didn't spend much time arguing about religion. He loved good food. He loved fine wines. He loved tobacco. He loved jewelry. He spent a fortune trying to buy off the images of a youth haunted by dire poverty, constant shifts of residence, and those awful hellfire-and-damnation sermons of his father's.

Ingersoll became famous largely because he was such a flamboyant and skillful orator. He contributed nothing to the scientific theories of atheism because he didn't know anything about science. He latched onto Darwin, especially the antireligious implications of *The Descent of Man*, because it told him what he wanted to believe. But he appears never to have understood Thomas Henry Huxley's physiology, because if you accepted Huxley's physiology on face value, there was no "maybe" about immortality. To Huxley, dead was dead, and he gave reasons which seemed reasonable, even if today we can see that they were incorrect and overlooked obvious facts. Ingersoll never faced facts because he didn't know there were facts to face. He appears to have believed that he could rule out any possibility of an afterlife, happy or otherwise, by refusing to believe in it. He was, in that sense, a fitting father for organized atheism in America and a fitting paradigm for the peculiarly American version of the atheist syndrome.

The Monkey Man

American atheists have never been long on science, or even on logic. Unlike the British or Europeans, who tended to devise theories to explain the facts of existence with an antireligious bias, the American cousins of scientific atheism tended to get by on speechifying and play-acting. And the biggest name of all in American atheism, a great admirer of Robert Ingersoll's, was no slouch at play-acting and has been a hero of stage and screen ever since he faded from the scene — his own peculiar version of life after death.

Laymen who have heard of Clarence Darrow remember him in connection with the Scopes Monkey Trial in Dayton, Tennessee, in 1925. This trial, which turned into a much-touted battle of the forces of creationism versus evolution, is in turn best known by the dramatic production *Inherit the Wind*, originally a stage play and later a film (1960) and a TV movie (1988).

Darrow, ably portrayed by Spencer Tracy in the 1960 film and by Jason Robards in the TV film, comes off as a man who'd make an excellent Christian deacon if he weren't too conscientious to believe in a God he couldn't understand. This bears no relationship whatsoever to reality. Darrow in life was a consistent Darwinian, so much so that Darwin would have turned over in his grave if he'd seen what the practical application of his survival-of-the-fittest philosophy had done to common morality.

Clarence Darrow, the movie hero, is shown as brimming over with love for justice and for his fellow man. Darrow, the Chicago attorney, hated his fellow man. His view of the human race, collectively and individually, was entirely negative. He believed that life was a simple struggle for food and sex — and, of course, the money needed to procure food and sex. His ready sympathy for violent criminals stemmed from the fact that he believed that people were simply animals and that all people would be criminals if they were only bold enough. He once said, for instance, that swindling was the typical Jewish crime because Jews lacked the courage to be murderers or burglars. Among the clients he defended were big corporations which mercilessly exploited the people who worked for them, and brothels disguised as massage parlors which ruined the lives of girls and women who worked in them.

Darrow was not an original atheist. He was an imitator. His father and his mother had both been freethinkers in the homespun American mode. They were small-town people who measured the Bible against outward circumstances and decided that they couldn't believe every word of Scripture was literally true. This rather simple-minded sort of atheism, what might be called "that old-time irreligion," was the usual platform of American skeptics who came from strict sectarian backgrounds. Americans of the eighteenth century had sometimes been deists in the European mode, affirming a God of reason. In the nineteenth century, perhaps influenced by the uniquely American fascination with politics and the law, they seem to have become increasingly literal minded. Most of them saw only two choices: a faith that every word in the Bible was factually correct, or a faith that the whole thing was a forgery and a fraud. Darrow's father, originally educated as a Unitarian clergyman, went with the fraud.

Darrow's father was a carpenter who side-lined as an undertaker. He kept coffins stacked up in one corner of his workshop. He was a notably unsuccessful businessman in a young nation which worshiped success. Darrow, who actually seems to have loved his father, may have blamed the surrounding townspeople, who were mostly religious and referred to his father as an "infidel." His mother died, outside the consolation of any faith, when he was a teenager. A few years later, Darrow had scraped through to get his lawyer's papers — he crammed in a law office rather than attend a university — and set out to conquer Chicago.

Along the way, Darrow had acquired a wife, Jessie, and a son, Paul. Jessie was a shy, country-bred woman who provided him with domestic comfort on his way up. When he was forty and had reached a considerable level of earning power, he walked out on his wife and son to practice free love in the radical circles he frequented. He called this a divorce by mutual agreement in his autobiography. In point of fact, he ditched his family because he felt that marriage interfered with his sexual freedom and because he found his wife's provincialism an embarrassment among his sophisticated friends.

Darrow's friendships in radical circles were troubled by the strange fact that most of the reformers with genuinely progressive and humane programs made at least some obeisance to Christianity. Many of the people who worked in the settlement houses of this era were unconventional but committed Christians, or at least were attempting to practice a form of brotherly love rooted in Christianity. When Upton Sinclair, author of *The Jungle*, was accused of having "a Jesus complex," he replied: "The world needs a Jesus more than it needs anything else." Lincoln Steffens, another social reformer, called himself a "Christian radical," and William Stead, a writer whose life's work had been to expose and bring an end to child prostitution in England and America, was both a Christian and a metaphysicist.

Darrow couldn't fit into this environment comfortably. Respect for Jesus, even when it was sometimes willful and misguided, rubbed him the wrong way. Like Thomas Henry Huxley, he felt that Christianity was too high a price to pay for redemption from crime, prostitution, and alcoholism.

Darrow didn't object to the hypocrisy of mixing Christianity and free love. He objected to the Christianity itself. He was unable to tolerate the ambiance of brotherly love and concern for the poor and the downtrodden that he found among many of the social reformers who worked at settlement houses or supported workers' rights to better wages, shorter hours, and safer working conditions — unless these demands came with the trappings of atheism and anticlericalism, free love, and a quick recourse to violence.

Nothing showed his real feelings toward the working class better than his activities during World War I. While many radicals and Christian pacifists joined forces to oppose America's entry into a European conflict among foreign powers, Darrow invested heavily in stocks related to the war industry. The war produced windfall profits for him as it did for munitions makers and many other industrialists. When some of his radical friends accused him of indecent profiteering at the expense of working-class draftees and their widows and orphans, Darrow was indignant. The war, he said, had been a good thing for the working class. True, some of them had been killed or crippled, but the sturdy survivors could now demand higher wages because so many of their job competitors were now dead or maimed and out of the labor pool.[8]

In 1924, Richard Loeb and Nathan Leopold, two gifted and highly educated sons of Chicago millionaires, confessed to the murder of Robert Franks, a fourteen-year-old neighbor they had lured into a rented car and slaughtered with a chisel. Loeb and Leopold were avid homosexuals and the case had some perverse overtones of sexual mutilation. The cold-blooded murder of an unoffending boy was an effort to commit the perfect crime. A routine police investigation led to arrests and confessions within a week of the actual murder.

The murderers' families contacted Clarence Darrow. His admirers say that Darrow was picked because he was the greatest criminal lawyer in America. They say he was the only important lawyer with the courage to handle the case. Even Sigmund Freud turned down a chance to make a fortune psychoanalyzing the two killers when the *Chicago Tribune* offered to let him name his own price.

Darrow's detractors claimed that the Loeb and Leopold families had approached him because he had a reputation for being able to fix judges.[9]

Darrow knew that the two teenaged murderers were guilty and that their confession had been extracted without torture and was backed by circumstantial evidence. He threw them on the mercy of the court in a frantic effort to avoid the death penalty. In so doing, he made a speech for clemency which moved spectators to tears:

Babe [Nathan Leopold] took up philosophy. . . . He became enamoured of the philosophy of Nietzsche . . . a man who has probably made a greater imprint on philosophy than any other man within a hundred years, whether right or wrong. More books have been written about him than probably all the rest of the philosophers in a hundred years. More college professors have talked about him. In a way he has reached more people, and still he has been a philosopher of what we might call the intellectual cult. Nietzsche believed that some time the superman would be born, that evolution was working toward the superman. He wrote one book, *Beyond Good and Evil*, which was a criticism of all moral codes as the world understands them; a treatise holding that the intelligent man is beyond good and evil; that the laws for good and the laws for evil do not approach the superman. He wrote on the Will to Power. . . . It is not a question of how he would affect you. It is not a question of how he would affect me. The question is how he *did* affect the impressionable, visionary, dreamy mind of a boy. At seventeen, at sixteen, at eighteen, while healthy boys were playing baseball or working on the farm or doing odd jobs, he was reading Nietzsche, a boy who never should have seen it at that early age. Babe was obsessed with it. . . . Here is a boy at sixteen or seventeen becoming obsessed with these doctrines. . . . It was not a casual bit of philosophy with him; it was his life. He believed in a superman. He and Dickie Loeb were the supermen. . . .The ordinary commandments of society were not for him.[10]

In a speech that lasted more than twelve hours, Darrow put the blame for Robert Franks's murder, not on Leopold and Loeb, but on the philosophy of Nietzsche. He also made use of religious images, in a general way, to convince the judge that he himself was a soft-hearted agnostic rather than a violent atheist: "I know that all life is a series of infinite chances. . . . I have not infinite wisdom that can fathom it; neither has any other human brain. But I do know that if back of it there is a power that made it, that power alone can tell, and if there is no power, then there is an infinite chance, which man cannot solve."[11]

The uproar outside the courthouse became so furious that a policeman suffered a broken arm holding back the crowd as Darrow spoke on and on, defaming Nietzsche — who was his own favorite philosopher. He also virtually advocated censorship, just the opposite of his usual position. In the end, Leopold and Loeb received life sentences. Loeb was slashed to death in a prison razor fight twelve years later by a man he tried to sodomize.

A year later, Darrow headed for Tennessee and his most famous case. John T. Scopes, a physics teacher who had been tapped to fill in teaching biology, allowed himself to serve as defendant in a trial for violating the state's newly passed statute which made it a crime to teach evolution in a public school. Many state officials had doubted, even at the time of passage, that the law would hold up in a court test, and the American Civil Liberties Union had been itching for a chance to bring its skills to the defense of an accused teacher.

The prosecution was to be represented by William Jennings Bryan, "the silver-tongued orator." Bryan, three times an unsuccessful candidate for president of the United States, had a life-long reputation as the defender of small farmers and workers against corporate interests and banks. He was also a frequent speaker on the Bible at platform lectures, just as Darrow was a frequent lecturer on atheism, not the gentle agnosticism of his Leopold-Loeb summation, but the complete rejection of God, Jesus, and human immortality, expressed in the crudest possible terms.

Bryan obviously differed with Darrow in matters of religion. He had also differed in matters related to World War I. Darrow had cheered the conscripts on to the slaughter, as he admitted in his magnificent summation. His investments in war-related stocks he did not choose to mention. William Jennings Bryan, serving as secretary of state, had wrecked his own career trying to keep America sincerely neutral. His most trying moment came in May 1915, when the British liner *Lusitania* was torpedoed by a German U-boat off the coast of Ireland with great loss of life, including a large number of women and children and 123 American citizens. The sinking sent a cry of outrage through the United States. Hundreds of Americans enlisted in the Canadian army or the French Foreign Legion to avenge the dead of the *Lusitania*.

Bryan, however, was not eager for war. He pointed out that the Germans had begun sinking merchant ships only after the British had cordoned Germany off by naval blockade to prevent the Germans from importing food and medicine. It was also common knowledge and accepted fact that American manufacturers were producing ammunition and uniforms for British and French military use. Almost by himself, Bryan tried to avert activating hostilities between Germany and the United States and to maintain a genuine neutrality. Many of the people who had been active in social work and in bettering the lives of the working poor agreed with him.

During the diplomatic fracas that followed the sinking of the *Lusitania*, the Germans replied to American protests with a list of explanations. They said that the *Lusitania* was an auxiliary cruiser of the British navy, built for conversion to a warship; that the *Lusitania* was armed; that it carried ammunition and other war cargo; and that it was carrying Canadian troops to Britain at the time it was torpedoed.

A German national named Gustav Stahl also told the U.S. state department and the *New York Times* that he had seen guns being loaded onto the *Lusitania* before the ship's final voyage. Stahl was arrested for perjury after a certain customs inspector named Dudley Field Malone reported that, based on his personal search, the Lusitania had been unarmed. Stahl was imprisoned. Bryan kept asking other U. S. officials to at least make a fair investigation of the German charges, but they didn't. On June 8, 1915, he resigned as secretary of state, hoping that his action would lead to an impartial examination of the Lusitania incident.

The facts didn't come out completely until the 1970s after divers reached the hulk of the Lusitania and after classified documents were released to historians. The divers found that the ship had been hit by one torpedo, not two, as the war-hungry press had charged. The "second torpedo" explosion had been a massive internal explosion of ammunition carried in the hull. The Lusitania was so gutted by the ammunition explosion that the great liner sank in eighteen minutes, not enough time to use many of the lifeboats. The cargo manifests, which had been falsified by Dudley Field Malone at the time of the 1915 furor, actually showed that the Lusitania had carried over a thousand cases of three-inch shrapnel shells, filled four shells to each case, and two hundred fifty cases to each lot. That means at least fifty-one tons of shells. The ship also carried almost five million rounds of British rifle ammunition, made by Remington Small Arms Company and addressed to the Royal Arsenal at Woolwich. The rifle ammunition weighed nearly two hundred tons.[12] The forward end of the Lusitania was a floating ammunition dump, but this was unknown to the Americans who took passage on what they thought was an unarmed liner. The Germans, however, had published warnings in newspapers that passengers who took ship for England on British vessels did so at their own risk. However, passengers were assured by Cunard Line officials at the gangplank that there was no risk.

William Jennings Bryan, the man who tried to maintain a sincere neutrality, and Dudley Field Malone, the customs inspector who had falsified the manifesto and faked the inspection which helped involve America in World War I, were to meet again at the Scopes Monkey Trial. Malone was Clarence Darrow's top legal assistant. Malone is usually described as "a Catholic" to stress how much Darrow respected the rights of all men to follow their own consciences and objected not to religion, but to religious bigots. In fact, Malone was an excommunicated Catholic.

The media image of the Monkey Trial of 1925 is that the main issues were fairness, honesty, and free speech. The main issue in point of fact was William Jennings Bryan's defense of populism versus Clarence Darrow's hatred of Christianity. When Bryan supported the right of religious institutions to maintain an interest in the public school curriculum, he specifically included Catholics and Jews as well as Protestants whose views were more liberal than his own. Darrow, on the other hand, made no bones about his hatred of all religious teachings. Several relatively impartial observers noted that Darrow's "village atheism" was perhaps more provincially old-fashioned and narrow than Bryan's backwoods fundamentalism. Darrow literally seems to have believed that he could repeal the existence of God if he found a few apparent contradictions of fact in Scripture. In the end, Darrow exhausted the aging and diabetic Bryan with merciless cross-examination, though the brilliant Bryan got in a few good licks of his own, which were not generally reported, since the influential newspapers were all pro-Darrow. Darrow's leading journalistic supporter, incidentally, was H. L. Mencken, the Baltimore editor who absolutely doted on Nietzsche.

In the end, John T. Scopes was convicted and fined one hundred dollars. The defense appealed. Bryan, the pacifist and the defender of the poor and the farmers, had won his day in court. Mencken and the journalistic "smart set" reviled him as a bigot and an idiot. Darrow, the defender of brothel keepers and millionaire child-murderers, had lost his day in court. The "smart set" made him into a hero of tolerance and free speech.

Five days after the trial in the awesome heat of a Tennessee summer, William Jennings Bryan ate an enormous meal and lay down for a nap. He passed away quietly in his sleep.

When they told Clarence Darrow that the man he had subjected to brutal examination had died of a broken heart, he replied, "Broken heart nothing; he died of a broken belly."[13]

The Scopes Monkey Trial marked the apogee of Darrow's fame. He handled other cases, and he roamed the country delivering platform lectures on the glories of atheism. At seventy-five, he wrote his autobiography. The book portrays a life that sounds like one unending case of clinical depression. "I am inclined to believe that the most satisfactory part of life is spent in sleep, when one is utterly oblivious to existence," Darrow said. And a few lines later, "I am satisfied that no one with a moderate amount of intelligence can tolerate life, if he looks it square in the face."[14]

But his attempt at a noble pessimism wasn't strong enough, in the end, to stand up to the terror of death that had haunted him since his boyhood around the coffins in his father's workshop. In his seventies, the lifelong atheist made a pathetic pilgrimage to spiritualistic and occultic mediums "in most American cities and many in Europe."[15]

He never achieved any conviction. The same morbid and depressed personality which had hated the Christian notion of the soul and the afterlife prevented him from finding any consolation in the confusing and rarified atmosphere of the occult. He was past eighty when he died, but even a friendly biographer described his last months as "pitiful and ugly."[16]

Darrow was all but deified by the entertainment industry, which has sentimentalized him beyond recognition. Before senility set in, he would have laughed at the way he was portrayed in *Inherit the Wind*, which was written almost twenty years after his death. To give the man his due, he had no use for pretension or sham—except in the courtroom. His writings reveal him as a consistent, greedy amoralist with a powerful death wish for most of his life. His last-gasp ventures into the occult, in fact, may have been a nervous attempt to prove to his own satisfaction that there wasn't an afterlife.

Darrow's old opponent, William Jennings Bryan, met his own death with confidence in an eternity of glory. It was the world he was leaving, not the one he believed he was about to depart for, that worried Bryan. "Our purpose and our only purpose," Bryan had said, "is to vindicate the right of parents to guard the religion of their children against efforts made in the name of science to undermine faith in supernatural religion. There is no attack on free speech, or freedom of the press, or freedom of thought, or freedom of knowledge, but surely parents have the right to guard the religious welfare of their children."[17]

Christianity, Bryan said, was the only safeguard of morality, and without that sort of ethical belief system any outrage was possible.

Even as he spoke, the situation in Europe had begun to confirm his opinion.

EIGHT

ADOLF HITLER: NEO-DARWINISM AND GENOCIDE

T he rattle-trap agnosticism of a Robert Ingersoll or the lurid livid
atheism of a Clarence Darrow would have been dismissed with a
good-natured sneer in Germany. Few German thinkers of the mid-nineteenth century would have any patience with the notion that there was
no God, even though the nation was hardly a bastion of Christian orthodoxy. For more than a hundred years, German thinkers had been
devising profound and often confusing systems of belief based on logic,
on intuition, and on arguments so involved that philosophy had become
a major national industry, like toy-making. Immanuel Kant, Wilhelm
von Leibnitz, and many other influential German thinkers had dropped
out of formal Christianity but come back to belief in God and in human
immortality for reasons they themselves believed as compelling as Scripture. Hegel, the reigning German philosopher of the later nineteenth
century, was a church-going Lutheran who saw no conflict between the
basic creed of Christianity and his belief in the creative evolution of
human and political institutions as ordained by an intelligent
Providence. When the materialist philosopher Ludwig Feuerbach
propounded a system which accepted God but denied human immortality, he had an enormous amount of trouble finding a printer who
would even publish it. Feuerbach, who was to exercise an enormous influence on the Marxists, is said to have been the man who coined the
catch-phrase *Man ist was er isst* (One is what he eats). Even Feuerbach,
originally trained as a theologian, denied that he was an atheist. German

philosophy had to wait for the paretic ravings of Nietzsche before it produced a single important atheist.

The freedom to speculate, coupled with a profound belief in God and a deep interest in spiritual matters, had, in fact, produced a climate of great religious tolerance in Prussia, the Protestant kingdom which was to unify modern Germany in 1871. The two founders of the distinctly Prussian school of German literature were two of the great names in the history of religious liberty: Ephraim Gotthold Lessing, a believing Christian, and Moses Mendelssohn, a believing Jew. Mendelssohn's great work was *Phaedo*, named for the last dialogue of Socrates. He combined Jewish, Christian, and classical sources to provide arguments in favor of the existence of God and the immortality of the soul that were eagerly received in the eighteenth-century Europe bored with deism and as yet unimpressed by atheism. Mendelssohn's *Phaedo* was a best seller in several European languages. Lessing's great work was *Nathan the Wise*, a drama in which a wise old Jewish merchant-scholar helps Christians and Moslems learn peaceful co-existence and mutual respect during the Crusades. Nathan the Wise, asked to say which of the three faiths of Judaism, Christianity, or Islam is the true one, proposes the solution of the three rings. Imagine, he says, three beautiful rings, each made with an equal weight of the same pure gold. Each ring was crafted in the shape most pleasing to its owner. Only the owners could say which ring was best, though each preferred his own. *Nathan the Wise* became a classic of German literature — until the Hitler era.

Starting in the 1830s with Feuerbach's disbelief in human immortality, a small group of German thinkers began to advocate a purely materialistic view of man. This was the faction of Freud's physiology teacher, Ernst Brücke. The other members were Hermann Helmholtz, Carl Ludwig, and Emil Du Bois-Reymond. These men, all of them born around the second decade of the nineteenth century and influential after the 1860s, organized what was called Helmholtz's School of Medicine. Their creed was: "No other forces than the common physical-chemical ones are active within the organism. In those cases which cannot at the time be explained by these forces one has either to find the specific way or form of their action by means of the physical-mathematical method or to assume new forces equal in dignity to the physical-chemical forces inherent in matter, reducible to the force of attraction and repulsion."[1]

This was, in essence, the creed of materialism. Mind and brain were the same thing, or, more correctly, mind was a simple function of brain.

When Helmholtz himself was confronted with evidence for spiritual realities, he acted as if he'd be morally outraged by the very idea. No amount of evidence, he said, would ever convince him that such things existed.

When Helmholtz's School of Medicine first heard of Darwin's theory of evolution by natural selection, a mutual admiration society quickly achieved critical mass. Ernst Haeckel, a German biologist, became Darwin's point man in Germany, and Huxley, who read German as his second language, kept up an enthusiastic correspondence with Haeckel. To read their letters is to realize that these men had all embarked on what Huxley was frank enough to describe as a "Crusade against Christianity."

The German who was to take the Crusade against Christianity to its ultimate conclusion, however, was not an educated gentleman like Helmholtz or Haeckel. In fact, he wasn't even a German technically. He was an Austrian of rather tangled ancestry, born seven years almost to the day after Darwin died and in the same year that Nietzsche finally went incontestably mad.

Too much, perhaps, has been written about Adolf Hitler. Robert G. L. Waite, one of the leading academic authorities, counted fifty thousand serious books on Hitler up to 1975, and dozens more have come out since. With horrible irony, the only person to rival Jesus as the subject of biographies has been the man whom many Christians have described — understandably — as "the antichrist."

Most of the works on Hitler describe him as a psychopath. A few of the works though, including some by responsible academic historians, describe him as a traditional German statesman who got into a particularly bad situation and let things get out of hand. This is a very curious idea that has of late gained more and more credence. In the aftermath of the Hitler era and the Holocaust, it seems inviting to use phrases like "the historic German tradition of anti-Semitism." But it's also simplistic and essentially dishonest. In the year Hitler was born, Germany itself, ruled by the Hohenzollern royal family of Prussia, was scarcely more anti-Semitic than England, and far less so than Russia, or, for that matter, France, where the term "anti-Semite" had first appeared in a newspaper article. In the Middle Ages, the Jews had been exiled from England, from France, and — in 1492 — from Spain. But under the civil codes enacted and enforced by the medieval German emperors, "Jews not bearing arms" (not living as robbers) enjoyed the same legal protection as Catholic priests and monks. Forcible conversion was forbidden "by reason of humanity," because some of the potential converts might die under torture. In the language of carved stone, the cathedral statue representing the Jews was more often than not a beautiful woman with a blindfold around her eyes — an authentic human, separated from the Christian world only by the refusal to accept Jesus as the Savior. Various German medieval emperors, from Otto II in the tenth century to Frederick II in the thirteenth century had close Jewish advisers. So did many later rulers. The fact that Yiddish, the language of Jews living in Russia and Poland, is essentially a Germanic language with some Russian and Hebrew words intermingled in the vocabulary indicates which medieval culture the Jews themselves preferred.

In the eighteenth and early nineteenth centuries, Prussia, in particular, was noted for the good relations between Christians and Jews. The Prussian kings made good use of Jewish expertise in trade and finance to build up a primitive rural economy into a powerhouse of Europe. The Mendelssohn family was a case in point: Moses Mendelssohn was one of the founders of Prussian literature; his son Abraham managed and developed the Mendelssohn Bank, one of the biggest in Central Europe; and his grandson Felix was one of the great composers of early nineteenth-century Europe and a friend of both the Prussian and British royal families. Prussian military medals cast from the bronze of captured French cannons and struck in 1814 and 1815 to commemorate the victories of Leipzig and Waterloo display the six-pointed Star of David, which is also, of course, the Star of Bethlehem. And Bismarck, the statesman who unified modern Germany, had a Jewish banker, a Jewish physician, and two Jewish writers among his roster of personal friends and advisers.

The person who knows the horror of World War II, the millions of dead, the death camps, and any part of the awful story of Hitler's attempt to destroy the Jews of Europe can only be puzzled by this strange background to the worst anti-Semitic outrage in modern times. Many names have been cited beside that of Hitler to explain the Holocaust.

Oddly enough, Charles Darwin's is almost never among them.

Two aspects of Hitler's life really have to be considered at this point. The first aspect is the way in which something resembling the atheist syndrome shaped Hitler's own savagely distorted personality. The second is the way in which Darwin's and Huxley's picture of man's place in the universe prepared the way for the Holocaust.

Hitler's Childhood: Phase One

Hitler's past contains a number of mysteries. His father, Alois Hitler, was born out of wedlock to a peasant serving maid Maria Anna Schicklgruber, in 1837. No one is sure who Adolf Hitler's real paternal grandfather was. Hans Frank, an early Nazi and future war criminal, reported shortly after his conversion to Catholicism and immediately before his hanging for atrocities in Poland that he had conducted an investigation in 1930 at Hitler's request. Frank claimed — in the shadow of the gallows — that there was some evidence that Hitler's actual grandfather was the nineteen-year-old son of a Jewish family which paid Maria Anna Schicklgruber support money after the birth of Alois Hitler until Alois was a teenager. Other historians have claimed that there is no evidence that such a family ever existed. The future Alois Hitler remained Alois Schicklgruber until Maria Anna Schicklgruber married a vagabond named Georg Hitler, and Georg acknowledged Alois Hitler as his son.

Alois Hitler was not a conventional Victorian father. He appears to have enjoyed three women more or less at the same time, and ultimately to have married each of them in turn. He began life as an illegitimate son of a servant girl, but worked his way up through the lower ranks of Austrian customs officials. His first wife, fourteen years older than he was and described as homely, brought him a solid dowry. While still married, Alois took into his home a restaurant cook and enjoyed her as well. She became his official mistress while the first wife was ailing. Meanwhile, Alois' niece, Klara Pölzl, arrived to help out with the cooking and appears to have been appropriated for Alois's bed as well as his kitchen. The official mistress objected and Klara left to find other work in Vienna. The first wife died and Alois married the mistress, who by now had given him two illegitimate children. Shortly, her health also began to fail and Klara Pölzl came back into the household, the kitchen, and the bed. After the second wife died, Alois Hitler sought and obtained a papal dispensation to marry Klara, who was his niece. His grounds for seeking the dispensation were that she might never again have a chance to make such a good marriage. At the wedding, the groom was forty-eight and the bride was twenty-five and four months pregnant.

Hitler, of course, mentioned none of this in *Mein Kampf*, his official biography. He asserted respect for his father and enormous affection for his mother. The second assertion is clearly true. He carried his mother's photograph with him everywhere, sought out paintings that looked like her, and in general behaved like someone who had an incest fixation à la Sigmund Freud.

The assertion that he loved his father is somewhat more dubious. Robert G. I. Waite wrote a massive and fascinating book, *The Psychopathic God: Adolf Hitler,* in which he discusses factual and inferred evidence for father-hatred in Hitler and its effect in warping his personality. Among the stories Waite cites are:

- Hitler told one of his secretaries that his father once beat him 230 strokes while his mother cringed outside the bedroom door, afraid to interfere.
- Hitler's father used to whistle for him exactly as he whistled for a dog.
- Hitler's father loved smoking long Austrian pipes. Hitler not only didn't smoke, but once he achieved power he wouldn't allow anyone else to smoke in his presence.
- Hitler once implied — though he did not clearly state — that he saw his mother and father having sex, and appears never to have forgiven his father for "assaulting" his mother — or his mother for so obviously enjoying the assault.

There were other traumas worth noting in Hitler's childhood. His younger brother, Edmund, originally resented as a rival, appears to have become a welcome playmate to Hitler later. Edmund died when he was six and Adolf was eleven. Their father was having some kind of feud with the village priest. Alois Hitler didn't go to Edmund's funeral and didn't allow his wife to go. Hitler attended his little brother's funeral by himself.

Throughout the Hitler family, there are clear patterns of second-degree incest — marriages between cousins or uncle and niece — and a number of people who are either mildly deformed or mildly feeble-minded. Four of Klara Hitler's children died before reaching their teens. The only survivor, other than Adolf, was his younger sister, Paula, described by American Intelligence officers who interviewed her after World War II as passive, shy, and mildly retarded. Judging his family by the very eugenic standards that he embraced, the Hitler gene-pool was unimpressive to say the least. There are no brilliant physicians or scientists to counterbalance the insane people, as there were in Darwin's or Huxley's families; no scholars as there were in the lines of Nietzsche or Freud; nor even failed clergymen as in the immediate families of Robert Ingersoll or

Clarence Darrow. Hitler's known ancestors included peasants, servants, and vagabonds — a great many vagabonds.

Trying to play the role of iron-willed bureaucrat when he came from a line of tramps and philanderers may have imposed a heavy strain on Alois Hitler. In any case, he was no bargain as a father as far as Hitler was concerned. Alois staunchly opposed Hitler's desire to become a painter. Hitler, in turn, refused to even consider following his father into the civil service. He appears to have thwarted his father's plans by deliberately contriving to fail in school. His grades in primary school were excellent. But then his disagreement with his father, as recorded in *Mein Kampf*, sent them plummeting.

Alois Hitler was a rather crude article. He doesn't seem to have been endowed with much wit, grace, or charm. His ability to juggle three women who were either much richer or much younger than he was probably had a lot to do with supreme masculine self-confidence and a knack for what might be called "rough sex." Adolf Hitler never actually identified with his father in this regard. His first "love affair" was to be a four-year, long-distance platonic crush on a girl named Stefanie, whom he never so much as spoke to. Robert Waite says that Hitler's first serious love affair was with a sixteen-year-old girl — when Hitler was thirty-seven. All his biographers agree that the real love of his life was Geli Raubal, his niece and a granddaughter of Alois Hitler by his second wife. Geli Raubal shot herself after a violent quarrel when she was twenty-three and Hitler past forty. In fact, of the seven women known to have been physically or emotionally intimate with Hitler, six attempted suicide and three were successful. His favorite style of lovemaking is said to have involved disgusting masochistic practices on his own part which the women found repulsive and distressing. The fact that he was reluctant to marry or to produce children in or out of wedlock was well known. His official staff urged him to marry. He joked that it would cost him five million female votes. But he also admitted that he was afraid his children might be subnormal mentally or physically.

Hitler's failures and quirks as a lover may have stemmed from a comparative inferiority in the face of his father's rough-and-tumble ways with women. In the end Hitler tried to reject his father in any number of ways. Alois wanted him to be a solid civil servant. Adolf wanted to be an artist. Alois loved Austria and took great pride in his Austrian title and the uniform of his office. Hitler hated multilingual Austria-Hungary. He yearned for union with Germany. Perhaps it's no coincidence that his mother, with her prim features and luminous blue eyes, looked much more German than his father.

Two facts are confirmed by almost all biographers. The happiest year of Hitler's childhood was the year that his father left him home with his mother and the other children to work at a distant customs post. The happiest years of his adolescence, and in fact of his entire life, came after his father's sudden death from a stroke in 1903. Now he had his mother's attentions more or less to himself.

Hitler's indecisiveness about a career, his inability to concentrate, and his early loss of religious faith are all typical of the atheist syndrome. He was deeply shaken by his mother's death from cancer when he was eighteen. Earlier, he had failed to gain admission to the Viennese Academy either as an artist or an architect. Now he moved back to Vienna and found odd jobs and — though he doesn't mention this — lived on his father's pension funds and money inherited from his mother. Most recent biographers believe that the dire poverty he described in *Mein Kampf* and in his subsequent conversations was a fabrication to win sympathy and to portray himself as a man of the people from humble surroundings.

Hitler's Flight: Phase Two

After many years of failure to make a name as an artist in Vienna, Hitler crossed the border into Germany and lived in Munich, capital of the south German state of Bavaria. But he was an artistic failure there as well. The Austrian authorities attempted to call him home for military service early in 1914, and he responded with a letter of such cringing servility that it sounds as if he were still afraid of his bureaucrat father a decade after Alois's death.

When World War I broke out, Hitler's escape phase began. He had avoided service in the Austro-Hungarian army by fair means and foul. He volunteered to serve in the German army even though he was still an Austrian citizen. The war, which ruined so many other lives, was the making of young Hitler. He was decorated five times, and won the Iron Cross, second class, in 1914, and the Iron Cross, first class, in 1918. Even his paintings improved. His officers regarded him as a reliable soldier, though he was never promoted above the rank of *Gefreite* (senior private). Friends and enemies later referred to Hitler as a corporal, perhaps to compare him to Napoleon Bonaparte, sentimentally called the Little Corporal in the years after his death. Napoleon, however, was never a corporal. He attended a cadet school reserved for the sons of the nobility and became a junior lieutenant at the age of fifteen. Hitler never became a corporal either, he remained a senior private.

Perhaps the crowning irony of his career is that the officer who recommended him for the Iron Cross was Lieutenant Hugo Gutmann, a Jew. Hitler professed to regard all Jews as shirkers and malcontents during the war, but this was a fabrication of a mind already twisted by a bizarre childhood. There were over a hundred thousand Jewish soldiers in Kaiser Wilhelm's German army, and they were decorated, promoted, wounded, or killed in roughly the same proportional numbers as other Germans. The problem of Jewish loyalty to the kaiser's Germany existed largely in Hitler's own mind.

The collapse of Kaiser Wilhelm's army and government left Hitler without a spiritual homeland. He hated his father's Austria-Hungary, where revolutionaries had also driven the last Habsburg emperor into exile. He hated the Weimar Republic, which grew up in the wake of the kaiser's defeat. And out of that hate, he built what he hoped would be the Third Reich.

The first two Reichs (*Reich* in German means "kingdom" or "realm") were distinctly Christian. The First Reich had been founded by Charlemagne, crowned Holy Roman Emperor by the pope in A.D. 800 Charlemagne, in fact, had completed the Christianization of the last heathen Germanic tribes with immense bloodshed on both sides shortly before his coronation. After one battle with the Saxons, he beheaded 4,200 prisoners who had gone back on their oath to him and resumed pagan religious practices after having accepted baptism.

A hundred years later, with Charlemagne's dynasty breaking down, a Christianized Saxon chieftain named Otto and his son, Henry the Fowler, restored the vital force of the distinctly German part of Charlemagne's old empire. Henry's grandson, Otto II, began the policy of friendship between the imperial government and the Jews after a Jewish vassal saved his life during a battle in Italy. The battle cry of the First Reich, when fighting in the Crusades against Moslems or against Slavic pagans, had been *Sieg und Heil!* ("Victory and salvation!"). The expressed idea was that the Germanic warriors were fighting for Christianity: salvation for their pagan enemies once the enemies were conquered; salvation for themselves if they were killed in battle on the Lord's behalf.

Modern liberals may find this a naive or even barbaric aspiration, but the warriors of the First Reich at least regarded their enemies as having souls worth saving. Massacres took place, but they rarely included women and children. In most cases, defeated males were also spared. And since Christians disliked holding other Christians as slaves, they were generally freed within the same generation as their capture.

The original "Prussians," in fact, were a Slavic tribe who lived near the Baltic and were conquered by Germans from western Germany. Later additions to the Prussian nation included Dutch and Flemish peasants from still farther west; thousands of French Huguenots, who were splendid soldiers and immensely industrious businessmen; and later still, Irish and Scottish soldiers imported by the Prussian kings of the early eighteenth century as mercenary troops for their professional armies of well-drilled regulars.

Hitler's incredible energy in inventing lies somehow portrayed this blend of nationalities into a homogeneous German race in danger of pollution by menacing Jews and Slavs. Oddly enough, this idea took its strongest hold in Bavaria, where many Germans have dark eyes and curly or wavy brown hair. When Arthur de Gobineau, the French count who was the grandfather of Nazi-style racism, was drawing up a map to show where the racially superior "Aryans" might be found, he left Bavaria out. But the Bavarians supported Hitler so the Bavarians were Aryans. During World War II, the Japanese were also declared Aryans.

Hitler needed the Aryan myth because he had decided, as early as the early 1920s, to make the Jews the scapegoats for Germany's defeat and for all the troubles of an overindustrialized and underemployed society in the aftermath of a major military defeat. Jews had been used as scapegoats and stock villains before. After the Franco-Prussian War of 1870-71, anti-Semitism had sprung up in defeated France. Hitler's anti-Semitism was different, though, because he based it clearly on Darwinian principles.

Before Hitler, anti-Semites had attacked Jews verbally or physically because of their religious differences from Christians. Hitler's anti-Semitism identified the Jews as a race. This identification of course has no basis in science, because modern Jews are composed of several different national and racial stocks. To talk about the Jewish "race" is as absurd as talking about the Catholic "race" or the American "race." Hitler's writings on race, like his anti-Semitism, were picked up during his down-and-out years in Vienna and are a mixture of occultic pseudoscience and Viennese gutter politics. The Darwinian strain of his thinking, however, is perhaps the most dangerous element of all—and the only one with a link to a reputable scientist.

Darwin believed, and Huxley wrote, that "man is a brute." The clear message of *The Descent of Man* and of Huxley's physiology is that man is an animal — better yet, a sort of machine which functions on a physiochemical basis, without a soul, or spirit, or will, or conscience. This man-as-machine is ruled by two passions: food and sex. Food accounts for the survival of the individual. Sex accounts for the survival of the species. Darwin and Huxley also believed that the Jewish and Christian Scriptures were pointless forgeries with no basis in historical or spiritual reality. They may themselves have been model Victorians, faithful to their wives, though the weakness and nausea engendered by their chronic clinical depression would probably have ruled out the amatory exploits of an Alois Hitler. But in what they believed, they were absolutely clear-cut spiritual ancestors of Hitler and the Holocaust.

Hitler was obsessed with an idea we first found in Nietzsche, the deliberate breeding of a superior race. He was also obsessed with the Nietzschean idea that the "race" was breeding itself down rather than up. Since his own family included many examples of second-degree incest and several people who were deformed or feeble-minded, we can readily see where these ideas came from.

"In general, Nature herself usually makes certain corrective decisions with regard to the racial purity of earthly creatures," he wrote in *Mein Kampf.* "She has little love for bastards. . . . Not only is the value of the originally highest element of the cross-breeding taken from them, but with their lack of blood unity they lack also unity of will-power and determination to live. . . . Taken together, this means not only a certain inferiority of the racially divided being compared with the racially unified one, but in practice also the possibility of a more rapid decline. *In innumerable cases where the race holds up, the bastard breaks down*" (italics mine).[2]

In language clearly influenced by Darwin and also by Nietzsche, Hitler then proposes a solution. The breeding habits of Aryans must be restricted to prevent intermarriage or other relations with "bastards" or "inferiors." Hitler's description of Africans as "half-apes" echoes the words and manifest feelings of Darwin and Huxley toward nonwhites. His hatred of Jews mimics some of the things that Nietzsche had to say in *The Antichrist*. Nietzsche and Hitler both imagined a mortal Jesus who opposed the hypocrites and clergymen of his day, though Hitler also imagines that Jesus was an Aryan, following some of the ravings of a crank philosopher named Houston Stewart Chamberlain.[3]

Nietzsche claimed that Jesus was the only real Christian, that Christianity died on the cross at Calvary, and that Saint Paul set out to corrupt the Graeco-Roman world with his own malicious version of Christianity. Hitler appears to have believed that Jesus never rose and that Christianity was a sort of Jewish conspiracy. This "discovery" enabled Hitler to talk out of both sides of his mouth. To his early followers, mostly working-class defectors from leftist organizations, he could mouth anticlerical and even anti-Christian slogans. To the right-wingers whom he had to court to obtain money and the support of the German army, he could pose as a defender of Christianity against the Jews and the Communists. Double-think paved the way to double-talk. It's impossible for a sincere Biblical Christian to be a consistent anti-Semite, since the New Testament is clearly based on the Old Testament. But Hitler made it look easy, with a little help from Darwin's theories and Nietzsche's philosophy.

Having rejected Christianity for themselves, Hitler and the Nazis began efforts to undermine whatever elements of Christian culture were left in Germany. They benefited, in a way, from the tendency of prewar German philosophers to equate God with the German state as God's handiwork on earth. The defeat of World War I shook this belief to its roots and caused an increase in secularism and a dabbling in the occult and esoteric Eastern religions, both popular in Germany during the nineteenth century. In the chaotic but energetic years of the Weimar Republic, occultism, nudism, and vegetarianism all abounded. So did cocaine abuse, free love, homosexuality, and political extremism of both the left and right. The Germany of the kaisers, officially Christian and ruled by believing Christian monarchs, had survived for forty-seven years without a single political assassination. During the first four years of the Weimar Republic, there were almost four hundred. When the Nazis came to power through the back door in 1933, manipulating their way to power through intrigue after losing the most critical election, they vowed to put a stop to the climate of random violence. And in a sense they kept their word. With Christianity replaced by the pseudoscientific theories of Darwin and Huxley and the mad philosophy of Nietzsche, the violence ceased to be random. It became official policy.

The first effects of political Darwinism began through the medical profession. German medicine since the days of Robert Koch, Rudolf Virchow, and Paul Ehrlich, younger contemporaries of Louis Pasteur, had justifiably enjoyed an enormous reputation. During World War I, French soldiers had often deliberately left their seriously wounded comrades behind because they knew that the French wounded would get better treatment from German front-line doctors than from their own. French medics were frequently beaten up by French infantrymen during localized mutinies in 1917. The philosophy of Helmholtz and Brücke, however, had long been percolating in the ranks of German physicians: Helmholtz and Brücke had believed that the human body was a physiochemical apparatus and that the soul was an illusion, just as Huxley had. Doctors and medical students were so thoroughly trained in mechanistic thought patterns that their antisoul view of human nature cast a sort of sepulchral gloom over their minds. "Living people are dangerous and stink," German medical students were taught. "Dead people merely stink."

The mechanistic outlook of the German medical profession itself was held in check during the days of the German Empire by official Christianity and a general climate of propriety, in some cases of gingerbread sentimentality. It probably required a strong Christian outlook by society to counterbalance the idea of all too many German physicians that life itself was a form of pathology, which is a part and parcel of scientific atheism.

When Hitler came to power, Germany was no longer under the control of a culture or a government that took Christianity seriously.

Hitler had begun to write about selective breeding of human beings as early as 1923. Ten years later, and less than a year after he came to power, the Nazis put a law on the books demanding the castration of genetically defective males. This law was intended not for Jews, but for "Aryans." From 1933 through the end of the war in 1945, thousands of young German men with relatively mild birth defects were legally castrated by members of the medical profession. Many of these young men had defects so minor that they could have served as workers or even as soldiers, and in many cases the defects were not even hereditary.

The Nazis subsequently enacted laws to prevent the intermarriage of Jews and gentiles, the so-called Nuremberg Laws, and began further legislation to deprive Jews of their civil rights. These campaigns aroused some minor opposition from the German people, but there were no seismic protests. Bismarck and Kaiser Wilhelm had tacitly encouraged Germans who weren't happy in Germany to seek their happiness elsewhere. Millions of Germans had emigrated, particularly to the United States and to Canada. People of German ancestry, in fact, made up the second largest ethnic component of the United States and the third largest in Canada. The tendency to vote with one's feet meant that people who might have become protesters in other countries became former residents in Germany. Those who stayed behind tended to be complacent, or perhaps frightened.

To silence the few people who did object to the mandatory castrations and the racial laws, the Nazi film industry turned out documentaries to be shown before or between feature films in German theaters explaining Nazi racial theory.

The Nazi racial theory was called "new-Darwinism. "

The films explained that proper breeding produced beautiful creatures: sleek and glossy thoroughbred stallions, burly beef cattle, and blond athletes of both sexes. All life was a struggle to feed and to breed. The law of life was that the strong overpowered and devoured the weak. Or, as Huxley so aptly put it, "man is a brute."[4]

The films also depicted the dangers of nonselective breeding. Jews, the films proclaimed, bred like rats. This was dramatized by photographs of weary-looking elderly Jews juxtaposed with rats scampering around. Clearly, the film implied, something would have to be done about this. But the films weren't ready to say just what—yet.

By the beginning of 1939, neo-Darwinism was ready for its next application. Psychiatrists from all over Germany and German-occupied Austria convened in Berlin for a conference in which the medical professionals supported a program to weed out and kill all the patients of German and Austrian mental hospitals who could not be expected to recover. Psychiatrists all over Germany and Austria, including some of the world leaders of psychiatric research, took part in evaluating harmless senile or retarded people and sentencing them to death. To the degree that it was discussed at all, the program was depicted as a large-scale mercy killing of people who were severely retarded or wildly schizophrenic. In fact, it was ultimately expanded to take in mildly retarded people, war amputees, epileptics, deaf-mutes, children with minor defects, and even normal children who had educational problems. Adults were usually gassed. Children were often given overdoses of sedatives, or, in the case of passive retarded children, simply allowed to starve. The psychiatrists not only evaluated the mental patients but checked their mouths for gold teeth, to be removed after the patients' deaths. The number of each patient's gold teeth was stamped on his chest so that no teeth were missed. In some cases the brains were also removed for further research.

Fredric Werthan, M.D., who wrote a chilling chapter on the Nazi euthanasia program in his book *A Sign for Cain*, pointed out that one of the psychiatric hospitals involved in the euthanasia programs was at Wurzberg. Wertham noted that Wurzberg had been offering kindly and humane treatment to mental patients since the late 1500s, only to begin murdering them in 1940. He might have added that in the 1500s Wurzberg's operating philosophy was based on Christianity. In 1940 it was based on neo-Darwinism. "Souls" were now machines. And defective machines could be broken up for scrap.

There were a few objectors. Two German psychiatrists of genuine courage, Dr. Gottfried Ewald and Dr. Theo Lang, flatly refused to take any part in the euthanasia program, and Lang actually protested to Nazi officials. Both men survived the war unscathed. Two Christian clergymen, Pastor Fritz von Bodelschwingh and Father Clemens von Galen, Catholic Bishop of Munster, also protested to Nazi officials, without results. Father Galen, who had successfully blocked Nazi attempts to remove the crucifixes from the schools in his district, risked his freedom — and perhaps his life — by actually preaching a sermon against the euthanasia program. "These unfortunate patients must die because according to the judgment of some doctor or the expert opinion of some commission they have become 'unworthy to live' and because according to these experts they belong to the category of 'unproductive' citizens. Who, then, from now on could have confidence in a physician?"[5]

Other churchmen did what they felt they could to show opposition to the program. Most psychiatrists, however, thought it was a good idea. Dr. Ernst Ruedin, professor of psychiatry at the University of Munich, warned his younger colleagues about the dangers of "excessive compassion and love of one's neighbor characteristic of the past centuries." The centuries, that is, before Darwin.

The first two years of the euthanasia program had deliberately exempted Jewish patients from the benefits of death. The program was touted as "heroic," and Nazi rhetoric held that Jews were incapable of "heroism." In 1942, however, the Jewish patients were hurriedly rounded up and killed as quickly as possible. By this time the mass murder of Jews had also become official policy.

The Nazis had originally tried to find some sort of pretext for killing people. The mental patients were killed because they were "useless eaters, unworthy of life." The Nazis had to take their supposedly tainted genes out of the gene-pool, in order to properly build the race of supermen Nietzsche had prophesied. Young men of Christian pacifist religious groups like the Hutterites and the Moravians were classified as traitors and beheaded for refusing to serve in the armed forces. When the Nazis invaded Russia in the summer of 1941, large numbers of Jews in the sectors immediately behind the front lines were rounded up and massacred. The pretext was that these Jews represented a Marxist fifth column and were a menace to security. Since most of the people murdered were women and children and men too old or sickly to bear arms, it was a very shabby pretext. But it served to cover almost a million murders.

By the beginning of 1942, the Nazis had come into possession of several million Jews in countries they had conquered or otherwise occupied. At a conference in Wannsee, a suburb of Berlin, Reinhard Heydrich, second in command of the Nazi S.S., explained what was to be done with the remaining Jews. "The Jews should be sent to the Eastern territories as laborers, the sexes being separated. They should be employed in building roads as they move eastward, and no doubt a large part of them will be eliminated by natural diminution. The survivors, the hardiest among them, must be given an appropriate treatment, because they represent a natural selection, and if they were allowed to go free, they would be the seedbed for a new efflorescence of Jewry. Witness the examples of history. In the course of the final solution, Europe will be raked over from west to east. The Jews thus evacuated will be transported by train to temporary ghettos, and from these ghettos they will be dispatched farther and farther east."[6]

Note two phrases: *appropriate treatment*, like *special treatment*, is a Nazi euphemism for deliberate execution, as opposed to death by overwork or neglect. The term *natural selection*, of course, and the idea that the survivors might live to breed a sturdier race, is right out of Darwin.

Heydrich had outlined what would later be called the Holocaust. Jewish civilians from all over Europe were rounded up and shipped to concentration camps in Poland, where those deemed incapable of useful work were usually executed on arrival. The stronger victims were worked to death. It was calculated that an otherwise healthy man would last about eight months under conditions of overwork and poor nutrition if he wasn't carried off by an epidemic. Laborers who wore out were sometimes finished off by lethal injections, a technique pioneered during the "mercy killings" of "defective" Aryans in the German and Austrian hospitals. No exact figures exist for the number of innocent people who died in this way, but the postwar figure of four and a half million is probably about right.[7]

To the millions of murdered Jews, the hundreds of thousands of murdered mental patients and infirm elderly people, and the thousands of Christian pacifists from minority sects, Nazi racial ideology added one more huge group of victims: Soviet and Polish prisoners of war.

Hitler and his relatives in the Waldviertel section of Austria hated the Czechs, their Slavic neighbors. This is ironic because most of them were undoubtedly of similar ancestry to their Czech neighbors, but it probably explains the desperate need Hitler had to constantly assert how German he was. He hated anything foreign. The school subject in which he received the worst grades was always French, and he was virtually the only European statesman of his era who didn't know a single foreign language. The "foreign" Slavs, in Hitler's view, were a primitive people who would be dominated by somebody—either the Jews, by which he meant the Communists, or by the Germans. In *Mein Kampf*, he argued that the future of the Germans was to seize the lands to the east for settlement by sturdy German farmers. The fact that these lands were already occupied by sturdy Russian and Polish farmers called for more "special action."

By official orders from Hitler's headquarters, the Germans were to treat first the Poles and then the Russians with unrelenting harshness. These orders, and the general climate of the war on the Russian front, led to carnage such as the world has never seen before or since. Three million Russian prisoners are said to have died in Nazi custody, by shooting, by freezing, or by starvation and unsanitary conditions in prisoner-of-war compounds. Camps were usually nothing more than barbed-wire corrals where the Russians were deprived of their fur hats and heavy overcoats by half-frozen Germans who forgot to bring their own overcoats to Russia. Communist party officials, Jews, and in some cases exotic-looking Asiatics from eastern Russia were sometimes shot on the spot when they gave themselves up. Other prisoners, including civilian women, were deported to Germany to work in factories or on farms. The total number of Soviets killed by battle or massacre is said to have exceeded twenty million.

Hitler's Collapse: Phase Three

Hitler's policy of ruthless racism proved to be the most self-defeating of all his decisions. Millions of Soviet citizens had developed such a hatred for the cruelty of Stalin that they welcomed the invading Germans with open arms or threw away their guns without fighting—until they found out that they'd been slated for mass murder or more slavery by yet another maniac, this one a foreigner to boot. The heroic Soviet resistance stemmed from the fact that Hitler's Darwinian theories convinced him to treat the Russians as brutes rather than as human beings. Where individual German commanders ignored Nazi racial policy and cultivated the anti-Stalinist hatred of Russian prisoners-of-war, they were able to form anti-Stalinist Russian battalions of the German army which fought as courageously as many German units. Using Russians to fight Stalin could have won Hitler the war on the Russian front. His racial bigotry, rooted in Darwinian theories of natural selection and Nietzsche's ravings about the superman, made this impossible. The million-plus Russians who fought in German uniform could have been augmented by millions of others, if Hitler hadn't ordered his commanders to murder them.

At war's end, the Russians entered Berlin. Hitler had spent the years since the 1930s suffering from stomach problems and chronic depression. Since Darwin's days, however, there had been major advances in pharmacy. Hitler sustained himself with an incredible welter of drugs and delusions in his bunker while children in their early teens and senior citizens fought the Soviets for possession of Berlin. Finally in the end, he shot himself.

The Russians also captured the Nietzsche archives in Weimar on their final sweep from the east. There Nietzsche's sister Elisabeth, widowed about the time he went mad, had spent the years between 1889 and her own death in 1935 turning "the mad philosopher" into the favorite touchstone of the Third Reich's intellectuals. Elisabeth's cousin, Major Max Oehler, was the custodian. When the first Russian officers arrived, they were polite and curious. They read German, like most educated Russians, and they spent some time going over the "great man's" collected works. Unlike armchair experts in the United States, the Russian officers had no trouble at all seeing the relationship between Nietzsche's ravings and the starved and bullet-riddled bodies they'd been climbing over on their thousand-mile road from the outskirts of Moscow to Berlin and Weimar. They told Major Oehler to get his clothes together and come to Russia for "forced labor," which meant the same thing to the Russians that it did to the Nazi Germans. Major Oehlers told him that he was too sick to go. They shrugged, threw him down the cellar stairs, and locked the door. He starved to death in the cellar, the last casualty of the several million victims of Nietzsche's superman theory.[8]

The Russians didn't have any use for Nietzsche. But in Russia, Darwin's works went right on killing people.

NINE

SCIENTIFIC ATHEISM FROM MARX TO STALIN

The Darwinian point-man in the social sciences and politics was Herbert Spencer. Spencer, born in 1820, was the son of a failed Methodist clergyman. He looked at the evidence for evolution by natural selection and propounded a philosophy called social Darwinism.

Social Darwinism was the polite English version of what the rude Nazis were later to call neo-Darwinism. The principal difference is that Nazi neo-Darwinism tried to give Darwinian natural selection a helping hand with the novel and unnatural tactics of forced castration for defective "Aryans" and mass murder for healthy "non-Aryans."

Social Darwinism, on the other hand, was based on noninterference with the survival of the fittest. Spencer didn't actually suggest that the strong should kill the weak. He argued that the strong should merely let the weak die of natural causes without helping them to survive if they got into trouble. To Spencer, the strong were the upper-class and middle-class Victorians who lived on inherited money. The weak were the laborers who toiled in the factories and shipyards. These people—the working class in general, and the working poor in particular—must be inherently inferior, Spencer said, since they'd never been able to amass enough money or to acquire enough education to climb into the Victorian middle class. Society owed them nothing. In fact, Spencer said, society owed itself the protection of making sure that the working poor received no asssistance from a misguided government or public charities to make their lives easier. If the poor survived in their poverty, Spencer argued, they'd only breed faster and create more useless people like themselves: numbskulls who couldn't read Latin or Greek.

We have to pinch ourselves to remember that Herbert Spencer was not a lower-class Nazi thug fulminating against Polish or Russian peasants. He was an Englishman talking about his fellow Englishmen. Anyone who believes that Nazi-style neo-Darwinism with its gassing and starvation of harmless mental patients and innocent Jewish children couldn't have happened anywhere else is confronted with Herbert Spencer and the fact that his social Darwinism was a major influence on staid British politicians who opposed more humane conditions for their own working class. In the early days of the Industrial Revolution, when the railroads and factories first began to change the face of Europe, British workers were famous for their immense capacity for hard work and their willingness to tackle any job. A few decades of social Darwinism and the sort of neglect that social Darwinism preached to their upper-class and middle-class employers undermined their enthusiasm. Social Darwinism reduced their numbers both through premature death and through emigration to the United States, Canada, and Australia. The "natural selection" that developed under social Darwinism wasn't at all what Spencer had in mind. The best natural workers naturally selected to leave England. And the ones who stayed developed an ingrained suspicion of their so-called "betters" that has characterized management-labor relations in England ever since. Spencer's attempt to substitute the Darwinian notion of survival of the fittest for the Christian-feudal notion that an employer is directly responsible for the welfare of his employees severely damaged the British ability to compete with imperial Germany, where the workers enjoyed far more social protection than they did in England. This helped lead, at least indirectly, to the First World War. It also helped lead to the pathetic state of the British economy in the years after World War II. Hostility between labor and management grew up directly out of social Darwinism. The theory was that the workers were "brutes." The reality was that they were authentic humans, with a stronger sense of right and wrong than the bosses who exploited them, and a distinctly British knack for confusing and sabotaging the employers who sneered at them.

Spencer fits into the atheist syndrome in more than his contempt for humanity. It should be no surprise that for the second half of his life he was a semi-invalid due to headaches, nausea, chronic weakness, and digestive complaints — the same symptoms as Darwin and Huxley and Nietzsche and Freud. The irony may have been lost on Spencer, but if he'd tried to hold down the same sort of twelve-hour job as one of the factory workers he despised as "inferior," he probably would have been fired in a matter of days or dead of overwork in a few months.

Karl Marx

The problem of the factories of the Industrial Revolution and the laborers who worked in them came to the attention of thinkers less smug and more daring than Herbert Spencer with his self-serving creed of social Darwinism. The history of Europe might have been very different if these men too hadn't jumped on the Darwinian bandwagon. Much misery could have been averted if some of Europe's most important political thinkers hadn't integrated scientific atheism into their plans for social and economic reform.

Karl Marx is without a doubt the most influential political atheist of all time. Because Marx espoused atheism in his attempt to destroy capitalism, half the world today is officially committed to atheism as a political philosophy. Atheism is, or was, the "state religion" of the Soviet Union under Lenin and Stalin and of China under Mao Tse-tung.

Karl Marx, however, did not suffer from the atheist syndrome. Marx never hated his father, and in fact he had every reason to love him. Because of this lack of father-hatred in Marx, the atheism that goes hand-in-glove with Marxist political thought is a glaring inconsistency. Many critics have remarked that Marxism is in fact a religion and that in the purest form, as propounded by Karl Marx himself, Marxism depends on divine Providence much to the same degree that Islam or Taoism do. Bertrand Russell, who was a consistent atheist, said that "Marx professed himself an Atheist but retained a Cosmic Optimism which only Theism could justify." In other words, Marxism without God doesn't compute. The reason for this can be seen if—as Marx did to the dialectics of Hegel—we turn the atheist syndrome on its head.

Karl Marx is sometimes billed as a Great Man of Judaism. The Nazis, in fact, used Marx's Jewish ancestry to "sell" anti-Semitism to the Germans and eastern Europeans who lived in the shadow of invasion or revolution from the Soviet Union. The trick worked all too well in terms of promoting anti-Semitism. Historically it was just another shabby pretext. Marx was baptised as a Lutheran at the age of six, and was a Protestant as long as he retained any belief in God. His own writings, and his personal correspondence in particular, are full of anti-Semitic slurs.

He was born in 1818 in Trier, the oldest city in Germany and a former capital of the late Roman Empire many centuries before. His father, Heinrich Marx, was an influential attorney and the son of an important rabbi. Heinrich himself had been a practicing Jew as a child but had grown away from ritual Judaism as a young man. When the French occupied the Catholic Rhineland, they removed the restrictions which had been placed on Jews some centuries before. Heinrich Marx was able to build a substantial law practice working with government agencies. After 1815, the section of the Rhineland which included Trier was awarded to Prussia, and the largely Catholic population came under the control of a country where the state religion was Protestant. Prussia had emancipated Prussian Jews from legal restrictions at the same time that the Prussians abolished serfdom, in 1813. There remained only two restrictions: Jews could not become officers in the regular army, and they had to be individually approved to practice law. Heinrich Marx had no trouble receiving an individual approval to continue his law practice. But the insecurity of the situation didn't appeal to him. When his son Karl was six, he took the boy to a Lutheran Church and father and son were baptized. Heinrich Marx himself believed in God, but he was essentially a deist who believed in a God of logic rather than a God of revelation. Karl, his son, was never exposed to any conflict between Judaism and Christianity. He attended a Lutheran elementary school where he learned a good deal about Scripture in a congenial atmosphere.

The Marx family became friendly with another Protestant family of Prussian bureaucrats stationed in Trier. Baron Ludwig von Westphalen, a Prussian nobleman whose mother's Scottish relatives were descended from the Earls of Argyll, became a firm friend of the whole Marx family and was especially fond of young Karl, a bright boy whose stocky build and swarthy complexion led family members to call him the "Moor." Baron von Westphalen was a man of broad liberal principles. His first wife having died, he had married Caroline Heubel, the daughter of a horse trainer, and produced a second set of children. The oldest girl of the second set was Jenny, the future Mrs. Karl Marx.

Karl Marx was a boy who had just about everything handed to him. His father and his father's best friend, Baron von Westphalen, were men of money, power, intellect, and influence. From his teens, it was assumed that he would marry Jenny von Westphalen, sometimes described as the prettiest girl in Trier and a genuine aristocrat, at least on her father's side of the family. And his intelligence and the good influences of his family enabled him to make a fine academic record. During his first year at the University of Bonn he spent a great deal of time drinking and roistering, was once thrown in jail overnight for disturbing the peace, and fought in a student duel in which he was slightly wounded by a sword cut over his right eye. Like any upper-class Prussian, he wore the scar proudly for the rest of his life. It should be pointed out that neither the drinking, the jail, nor especially the duel was typical of what a serious Jewish father would have expected of his son. Marx also piled up heavy debts, which his father duly paid, not without some complaints. Shortly after a conference, Karl Marx transferred to the University of Berlin, which had a somewhat more serious atmosphere than Bonn or the other drinking-and-dueling universities of the Rhineland.

It was at the University of Berlin that Marx made two decisions. After an exposure to the philosophy of Epicurus and the materialism of Ludwig Feuerbach, he abandoned his belief in religion. He also decided that he no longer wanted to be a lawyer like his father. What Karl Marx really wanted to be was a poet.

The 1830s in Germany were the years of Heinrich Heine. Like Marx, Heinrich Heine was born to a Jewish family in the Rhineland and, like Heinrich Marx, he submitted to baptism so that he could practice law without impediments. Heine, however, didn't want to practice law and hated the world of business and commerce. After a tragic love affair with a cousin whose family wouldn't allow her to marry him, he began to write poetry which quickly built up a tremendous following. A political liberal, a Romantic, and something of a cynic, Heine had the same sort of instant success in Germany that Byron had in England. He was a cult hero to the younger generation of Germans too young to have fought against Napoleon and bored with the "philistine" middle-class society that cared only about money and propriety. Heine was a rebel and a malcontent, but he was a genuine poet and after the death of Goethe in 1832, perhaps the best German poet then living. His works translate badly, but in the original German they have an immediate power, particularly on young people, and they make wonderful lyrics for songs.

Karl Marx decided that he wanted to be another Heinrich Heine. His only problem was that he didn't have any talent. Marx's mind was very good at handling academic disciplines, but when it came to inspiration he was utterly dull. He couldn't write poetry. The critics told him so, and eventually—after a long struggle—he came to admit it to himself. It was the first time he'd ever failed at anything, and neither his family nor the ever-reliable Westphalens could help him.

Friedrich Engels

While Marx was making his vain attempts to become another Hein-rich Heine, another young Prussian was in Berlin doing his year of military service as an artilleryman. Friedrich Engels, born two years after Marx, in 1820, also came from the Prussian Rhineland, but his family was very different from the liberal and tolerant Marx-and-von-West-phalen coterie. Friedrich Engels, Sr., was a hard-driving capitalist and a Christian pietist. Critics have called Friedrich, Sr., a "fanatic." Friedrich, Jr., appears to have had the same kind of negative childhood experience with Christianity that influenced Thomas Henry Huxley or Robert In-gersoll to distance themselves from religion at the earliest possible age. His strict and overbearing father prejudiced Engels against formal religion with the usual atheist syndrome methods. Friedrich responded in kind. He was obviously brilliant but achieved mediocre grades and left the *gymnasium* (or high school) in Elberfeld without finishing. His father then put him to work in the administration of the family's weaving and cloth business. Engels called it "a dog's life." His bright, imaginative mind rejected the tedium of ledgers and files. He also sympathized with the workers at his family's factories, partly out of a genuine humanity and also, one suspects, partly as a way of acting out his rejection of a father he disliked and feared. It is with Engels, the former fundamen-talist Christian, rather than Marx, the formerly Jewish child who loved his father and his father-in-law, that the atheist syndrome first enters the history of communism.

Engels's escape phase came about through the good graces of the Prussian army. Once they finished their basic training, Prussian soldiers of this era enjoyed a certain degree of freedom and considerable social prestige.

Engels used his time in Berlin to investigate the university and the ideas that were simmering there. Ludwig Feuerbach's materialism (*Man ist was er isst!*) struck an immediate responsive chord with the young man who rejected his father's formal religion.

Engels tried some free-lance journalism and found that he enjoyed it but couldn't make a living. By 1842, he was on his way to England to work for his father's company. He studied British philosophy and economics, meanwhile working as a capitalist and hating every minute of it.

The later 1840s found both Marx and Engels on the move. Marx was unable to secure a teaching post at the Prussian universities, and

Engels was unable to stomach any more capitalism with his father's companies. Both of them lived on family funds and journalism as they roamed around Europe, studying the working class and pondering ways to change society. Both men worked for leftist newspapers and came to sympathize with the very genuine hardships of workers in the early days of the Industrial Revolution. Overworked and underpaid, the industrial laborers of Europe, and particularly of France, began to talk about a new revolution.

Communism

By 1848, Marx and Engels had become friends and collaborators working on leftist newspapers. In Brussels, Belgium, the two German journalists put together a pamphlet they called *The Communist Manifesto*. Karl Marx has traditionally been credited as the author, but some authorities believe it was actually written by Friedrich Engels with Marx's advice.

Drawing heavily on the work of contemporary and earlier thinkers, *The Communist Manifesto* attempts to explain all of history as a struggle for property between social classes. Since Marx and Engels were materialists influenced by Feuerbach, they ignored the influence of religion almost completely, a naive mistake and one that has been rejected by most serious historians of more recent times. They also ignored race, technology, and anything else not connected with working-class productivity. Marx and Engels aserted that the "bourgeoisie" (middle-class investment capitalists) had engineered previous revolutions to overthrow the aristocracy. They said the next revolution would be a revolution of the "proletariat" (industrial workers). This coming revolution was treated as an inevitable event, brought on by the course of history as the workers got poorer and poorer and had less and less to lose. When the Communists won their inevitable revolution, Marx and Engels said, they would abolish private property and middle-class marriages, in which, they charge, the wife is actually a form of property of the husband.

"The distinguishing feature of Communism is not the abolition of property generally, but the abolition of bourgeois property," *The Communist Manifesto* says. "But modern bourgeois private property is the final and most complete expression of the system of producing and appropriating products, that is based on class antagonism, on the exploitation of the many by the few." In this sense, the theory of the Communists may be summed up in a single sentence: Abolition of private property.[1]

The Communists would also abolish nations and make the whole world into one great society, without private property or formal marriages. Other changes Marx and Engels suggested include:

1. Abolition of property in land and application of all rents of land to public purposes.
2. A heavy progressive or graduated income tax.
3. Abolition of all right of inheritance.
4. Confiscation of the property of all emigrants or rebels.
5. Centralization of credit in the hands of the state, by means of a national bank with state capital and an exclusive monopoly.
6. Centralization of the means of communication and transport in the hands of the state.
7. Extension of factories and instruments of production owned by the state, the bringing into cultivation of waste lands, and the improvement of the soil generally in accordance with a common plan.
8. Equal liability of all to labor. Establishment of industrial armies, especially for agriculture.
9. Combination of agriculture with manufacturing industries; gradual abolition of the distinction between town and country, by a more equable distribution of population over the country.
10. Free education for all children in public schools. Abolition of children's factory labor in its present form.

"When, in the course of development," they wrote, "class distinctions have disappeared, and all production has been concentrated in the hands of a vast association of the whole nation, the public power will lose its political character. Political power, properly so called, is merely the organized power of one class for suppressing another. If the proletariat during its contest with the bourgeoisie is compelled, by the forces of circumstances, to organize itself as a class; if, by means of a revolution, it makes itself the ruling class, and, as such, sweeps away by force the old conditions of production, then it will, along with these conditions, have swept away the conditions for the existence of class antagonisms, and of classes generally, and will therefore have abolished its own supremacy as a class. In place of the old bourgeois society, with its classes and class antagonisms, we shall have an association in which the free development of each is the condition for the free development of all."[2]

These ideas, written in 1848, are communism as Marx and Engels actually intended it. Later elaborations made the ideas even more clear. "To each according to his need — from each according to his ability" summed up the idea of day-to-day economics. The world of the future, the classless society that Marx and Engels hoped for, would be "a worker's paradise."

Marx is credited with having said that "religion is the opiate of the people." A consistent Darwinian atheist would have to say, however, that Marxism is the mescaline or LSD of the people. There is no reason why, in a godless universe, the workings of blind cosmic chance should cooperate to produce a worker's paradise. And the Darwinian idea of natural selection and survival of the fittest, if they are believed, find their logical culmination in Nietzsche and in Herbert Spencer, not in Marx and Engels.

It's pretty clear what happened here. Marx, baptized and raised as a Christian from the age of six, and Engels, the son of a fanatically Christian pietist, produced an unconscious and twisted plagiarism of the New Testament and passed it off as a revolutionary doctrine of philosophy.

What must be understood is that Marx's perverse plagiarism wasn't simply a blasphemous parody. The man was absolutely serious in subconsciously identifying himself as the nineteenth-century messiah of the working class. Mikhail Bakunin, the Russian anarchist who knew Marx personally, and disliked him intensely, remarked more than once that Marx tended to talk as if he believed he were Jehovah. Even Bertrand Russell, writing in the 1940s, puts the Marxist "worker's paradise" in the same category as the Second Coming of Christ. Russell was an atheist and didn't expect to see either event. But Marx, having rejected Christ, appears to have proposed himself as a substitute.

The Communist Manifesto was published in the same year that the revolutions of 1848 broke out all across Europe. The revolutions of 1848, however, were not communist revolutions. The Forty-Eighters, as they were called, were a mixed bag of believers in democracy and in constitutional monarchy. Richard Wagner was a revolutionary in 1848. So was Carl Schurz, a German university student who later fled to the United States where he battled against slavery in the American Civil War and, as secretary of the interior, championed decent treatment for American Indians. Giuseppe Garibaldi and his band of freedom fighters fought to restore the Roman Republic in Italy.

Marx managed to keep out of the line of fire in 1848. Engels, on the other hand, was under fire in four separate engagements before the forces of the Prussian king routed the liberals in the Rhineland. Marx and Engels both fled back to England.

Marx and Engels spent the rest of their lives trying to get a wider public to take them seriously. They were largely unsuccessful in this. Engels — back working for his father again — supported Marx's whole family and his common-law wife, an Irish girl named Mary Burns. When Mary died, Engels lived with her sister Lydia, known as Lizzy. "She came of real Irish proletarian stock, and the passionate feeling for her class, which was instinctive with her, was worth more to me than all the blue-stockinged elegance of 'educated' and 'sensitive' bourgeois girls," Engels wrote.[3] He was so "proud" of her that he kept one household for her and another for his bourgeois British business associates. The former Jenny von Westphalen, having conveniently forgotten that her own mother had been the daughter of a horse trainer, snubbed both Burns girls on all possible occasions.

Marx and his wife had seven children. Four died in childhood and of the three girls that grew to womanhood two were ultimately destined to commit suicide. That wasn't a terribly good record of successful parenting, even in the nineteenth century. The overwhelming impression is that Marx was interested almost entirely in himself and Mrs. Marx agreed with him. The children fended for themselves, or didn't. This is the exact opposite of what we would expect from a sufferer of the atheist syndrome. In the atheist syndrome, the son-victim overcompensates for the harshness of his own childhood by being especially concerned and devoted as a father, as Darwin and Huxley were, and as Freud was if we overlook the unsavory possibilities of his fondness for incest theories. Marx seems to have regarded his children as excess baggage until they grew old enough to begin parroting his theories.

Engels achieved his lifelong goal in 1869. After a life of misery as a bourgeois businessman, he finally squirreled away enough money to invest in bonds which, through interest payments, would support him and his friends the Marxes, a fascinating insight into how dedicated he was to his own theories about the evils of investment capital and interest. "I shall never forget the triumphant 'For the last time' which he shouted as he drew on his top-boots in the morning to make his last journey to business," Marx's daughter Eleanor wrote of Engels' departure from active capitalism. "Some hours later, when we were standing at the door waiting for him, we saw him coming across the little field opposite his home. He was flourishing his walking stick in the air and singing, and laughing all over his face."

Two years later, Marx and Engels got another chance to grab for the gold ring of fame. Working-class Parisians, embittered by the loss of the Franco-Prussian War to Germany and at the lackluster performance of the rest of France, refused to surrender their rifles and cannons to their own national government. This was the Paris Commune: a doomed, courageous, and extremely bloody uprising by laborers and some professional revolutionaries in defense of their own neighborhood and against government forces they suspected of wanting to restore a monarchy to France. Unfortunately, the Paris mood was bitterly anticlerical. They first arrested and then executed the Archbishop of Paris, Monsignor Darboy, along with several priests and regular army officers and many policemen. When the French regular forces, most of them devoutly Catholic, recaptured part of the city and discovered the archbishop's body, they began a full-scale massacre. As many as twenty thousand French revolutionaries were shot by their own countrymen and thousands of others were savagely beaten and then dispatched for forced labor in the tropical colonies.

The Communards of Paris were not Marxists. Few had ever heard of Marx. Their politics ranged from liberal-democratic to anarchist. During their brief heyday in control of Paris, the Communards attempted to stamp out prostitution, but made no effort to nationalize the Bank of France, which would have caused their enemies considerable embarrassment. Their revolution was more an explosion of injured pride and resentment against the idea of a monarchy than it was an attempt to bring about a Marxist "worker's paradise." Their inspiration came from the French Revolution of 1789. Marx, however, had the opportunism and bad taste to turn the twenty thousand dead of the Paris Commune into a platform for his own ideas, which still weren't being taken seriously. Once again, he was largely ignored.

Marx lacked two of the hallmarks of the atheist syndrome. He didn't hate his father, and he was a poor father himself. He also devised a system which was supposed to be atheistic, but actually supposed that the cosmos is controlled by a benign Providence — possibly with Marx himself as the messiah. One can argue about whether his later years were a punishment for this titanic blasphemy or whether Marx was filled with rage because nobody took his ideas seriously, thus sending his own body a self-destruct message. It's a fact, however, that the second half of his life was a hell of ailments which were largely psychosomatic: liver troubles, sore boils, and persistent headaches and indigestion. He couldn't sleep without drugs and for the last years of his life he was almost incapable of literary work. He died sitting in his armchair in 1883.

Engels, on the other hand, was a bon vivant. He loved food, wine, and witty company, and his health up to the last few months before his death from cancer in 1895 was rather good. He had himself cremated and his ashes were strewn around his favorite seaside resort. Most of the world would have soon forgotten these two bourgeois revolutionaries, who lived on stock dividends while they plotted the destruction of free enterprise. But other events soon intervened.

The dates, of course, speak for themselves. Marx and Engels put *The Communist Manifesto* down on paper in 1848. Darwin and Wallace didn't go into print with the theory of evolution by natural selection until ten years later. Once Darwin's ideas started to percolate through Europe, the Marxists seized on them eagerly as a sort of antidote to organized religion. Marxism and Darwinism have little in common other than a common and inconsistent profession of atheism. Animals don't "work" without instinct, which Darwin never successfully explained. And Marxism doesn't "work" without some sort of deity to make sure that the "worker's paradise" comes to pass on Earth. But because Darwin provided a "scientific" reason to reject belief in traditional Christianity, the Marxists adopted evolution as if they'd invented it. And Darwin, in the last years of his life, talked to some Marxists and nodded in approval as they explained they didn't believe in God. What the former candidate for ordination in the Church of England thought of the "worker's paradise" and its strange resemblance to the Biblical Book of Revelation is anybody's guess.

The fusion of Darwin and Marx would wait for the next generation.

Social reform began to come to the countries of Western Europe in a way Marx and Engels hadn't expected. After the Franco-Prussian War of 1870-71, there would be no large-scale war between European powers for more than forty years. But Europe became an armed camp. France instituted wholesale military conscription. At one point, Frenchmen could be drafted for as much as five years' active service. Germany maintained conscription as a defense against vengeful France. The other nations of the continent all built conscript armies. The large number of armed men available to revolutionaries at any given time may have convinced the various European governments to extend the right to vote to their citizen soldiers. In monarchies, of course, the king continued as a hereditary figurehead, often of some considerable power. But adult males could vote for representatives in parliaments or elect local officials. In Germany, where the Social Democrats and other workingmen's political parties began to have an influence, the government of Otto von Bismarck took the initiative and developed systems of pensions and hospitalization to protect disabled or elderly working people from starvation and serious poverty. Bismarck did this, in large part, to undercut the political power of left-wing political parties. But the effect was to make Germany more industrially efficient than nations which practiced "untrammeled free enterprise" and left disabled or elderly workers to depend on charity or to starve.

Lenin

The great exception to the liberalizing trend of Europe was Russia. Industrialization in Russia brought greater misery to the common people than they had endured under serfdom, which had been abolished in 1861. Landless serfs became landless laborers. The Russian Orthodox Church, though it produced many men of genuine faith, was crassly involved in the persecution of other denominations and faiths. Polish Catholics and the Christian minority sects which sprang up in Russia from time to time were rigorously oppressed. It was a crime, for instance, for a Catholic priest to engage in any discussion with a member of the Russian Orthodox Church which might lead to conversion to Catholicism. The worst sufferers of all were the Moslems and Jews. Orthodox Russians treated the millions of Moslems in southern Russia like dirt. The Moslems responded by calling all Russians "pigs" because they ate pork, which is unclean to Moslems and Jews. And Jews who lived in rural areas of Russia often lived in literal fear for their lives from mobs who burst into Jewish villages or shops, looting, raping, and frequently killing.

On this medieval setting of religious persecution and worsening economic conditions, the Marxist idea of a "worker's paradise" took on a strange plausibility. Russia in the nineteenth century, like Palestine in the first century, was very clearly approaching the end of an age. Even Marx's infantile egotism in declaring himself the messiah seemed less bizarre in a country where holy men walked hundreds of miles barefoot with chains wrapped around their legs seeking penance or revelation. The religious aspects of Marxism were also acceptable because they ignored the visible symbols of the traditional religions. Drop-outs from

Christianity and from Judaism who hated the old order could join hands to bring about a new order without the stigma of having deserted their ancestral faiths that would have arisen from an outright religious conversion.

Above all, Marxism was billed as "scientific." The Marxists had considered themselves as much scientists as philosophers. They had adopted Darwin as a fixture of their new worldview because he was an atheist and because his theory of evolution by natural selection, taken at face value, helped to undermine the Judeo-Christian view of man. The early Marxists seem never to have understood that there was no place for a friendly Providence bringing about the "worker's paradise" in Darwin's depressed and depressing view of the world.

The man who brought communism to Russia was born in 1870 to a respectable middle-class family. His father, Ilya Nikolayevich Ulyanov, had been raised to the lowest rank of the Russian aristocracy as a reward for service to the state. Ilya Ulyanov was a Chuvash, a member of one of the small obscure tribes which had lived in backwater areas of Russia for centuries. An exotic-looking people with reddish hair and yellow skin, Chuvashes were natural pacifists, fonder of work than of warfare. They enjoyed keeping bees, which was the source of the name *Ulyanov*, which means "beekeeper." Ilya, an extremely intelligent young man, had obtained an excellent education through the charitable efforts of the Romanov dynasty and had become first a schoolteacher, then an inspector of schools, working to help educate his own people and rural Russians in general. He was a gentle man with sad eyes and a great penchant for work. He founded more than five hundred schools for peasant children. He was also sincerely religious and a member of the Russian Orthodox Church. Ilya's wife, Maria, was half German and half Swedish. They were devoted to one another and to their children, who all adored their kindly father. Their lives were comfortable, never affluent, but above all warmed by affection and enjoyment of nature and one another's company. Ilya was an educator and bureaucrat of amazing diligence. At home he liked to make things grow, and the ripening of the cherries from his little orchard was always a cause for celebration among the children, who left them untouched until his birthday, July 20, which was marked with a real miniature festival.

Unfortunately, the gentle Ilya, a man who really deserved better, appears to have gotten a bad shuffle in some sort of power play in the tsarist Russian educational system. An extension of his tenure in office was canceled with only one year's grace, rather than the five years' extended tenure he had expected. This bureaucratic blip threw the little family into turmoil. Ilya was not a businessman, and his plans for his sons' university educations and the support of his family had been dependent on a continued full salary. With no outward rage, but with immense sadness, he slumped into a deep depression, punctuated by brief, harmless bouts of insanity. Within a year of the bad news, he gave his family a strange, soulful look — they said he looked as if he were saying goodbye to life — took to his bed, and died. "I was sixteen when I gave up religion," his son Vladimir later wrote.[4] Vladimir gave up his previously unquestioned faith beside his father's deathbed in 1886. To his cold, analytical mind, the gentle and lovable Ilya had lived a truly Christian life and had been repaid by bureaucratic betrayal and premature death. His sixteen-year-old son wouldn't make what he viewed as the same mistake.

A year later in 1887, Vladimir Ulyanov suffered a second shock. His older brother and idol, the handsome Alexander Ulyanov, was arrested with a group of conspirators who admitted to plotting the assassination of Tsar Alexander III. Some of the other conspirators weakened or gave devious answers. Alexander, undoubtedly embittered by his father's bureaucratic betrayal and subsequent death, went out of his way to claim responsibility for the clumsy bomb plot. He was hanged a little more than a year after his father's death, facing the noose with calm courage.

Among Alexander's books, Vladimir found *Das Kapital* by Karl Marx. Probably for the first time he began to shift his attention from classical and Russian literature to Marxist theory and scientific atheism. His struggle to bring communism to Russia would take another thirty years, most of them spent in exile in Western Europe. When he returned to Russia, paid handsomely in gold by the German general staff to start a revolution and take Russia out of World War I, he would be known not as Vladimir Ulyanov but as Lenin.

Before the deaths of his father and his brother, Lenin's family life had been, if anything, abnormally benign. Whatever strictness he may have encountered in the Russian Orthodox Church was probably tempered by his father's instinctive natural Christianity. The wellspring of his religious revolt came not from a father's brutality, but from the betrayal of his father and the hanging of his brother by a tsarist government intimately bound up with the Russian Orthodox Church. After these two traumas, there were others. He left the university after only three months because of negative grading due to his dead brother's notoriety. His common-law wife, Nadezhda Krupskaya, was also the child of an honest bureaucrat from the lower aristocracy who had suffered disfavor in a tsarist power shuffle. The "scientific" doctrines of the two bourgeois Germans, Marx and Engels, provided fuel for Lenin and Krupskaya, two Russian elitists. Lenin and Krupskaya shared a desire to help the poor and oppressed. They also shared a tribal passion for familial and personal revenge against a system that had betrayed both their fathers. The gentle Ilya certainly wouldn't have approved.

Charles Darwin also played a part in Lenin's worldview. The only piece of art work in Lenin's office was a kitsch statue of an ape sitting on a heap of books—including *Origin of Species*—and contemplating a human skull. This rather vulgar artifact, a comment in clay on Darwin's view of man, remained in Lenin's view as he worked at his desk, approving plans or signing death warrants as he deemed necessary. The ape and the skull were to Lenin what a gilded icon might have been to his father. The ape and the skull were a symbol of his faith, the Darwinian faith that man is a brute, the world is a jungle, and individual lives are irrelevant. Lenin was probably not an instinctively vicious man, though he certainly ordered a great many vicious measures. Perhaps the ape and the skull were invoked to remind him that, in the world according to Darwin, man's brutality to man is inevitable. In his struggle to bring about the "worker's paradise" through "scientific" means, he ordered a great many deaths. The ape and the skull may have helped him stifle whatever kindly or humane impulses were left over from a wholesome childhood.

Joseph Stalin

Lenin's successor in control of the world's largest country needed no help in overcoming any latent feelings of mercy or remorse. Josef Stalin was perhaps the most perfect and most horrible example of a victim of the atheist syndrome in the political sphere. Only Hitler could be considered a serious competitor.

Like Hitler, Stalin may have been in doubt as to his immediate ancestry. During the height of the Stalinist terror, a persistent legend among inmates of the slave labor camps maintained that Stalin's biological father had been Nikolai Przhevalsky, a Russian explorer. The story is that Przhevalsky had seduced Stalin's mother, Ekaterina Geladze, and then paid Stalin's surrogate father, Vissarion Dzugashvili, to make an honest woman of her and to give the baby a home. If the story is true,

Przhevalsky should have saved his money. The child of Ekaterina and "whoever" grew up in a hellish atmosphere.

Vissarion Dzugashvili, a failed businessman, worked as a shoemaker around the city of Tiflis, in Georgia, a once-independent country then located in the southernmost portion of tsarist Russia. He was a Georgian peasant, and spoke the national language, which is very different from Russian. Georgia was once part of the Greco-Roman and Byzantine world, with a civilization much older than that of the Russians to the north. Ekaterina was an Ossetian, a member of a mountain tribe from the nearby Caucasus Mountains. Ossetians — tall, fair-haired, pale-skinned, somewhat primitive by either Georgian or Russian standards — had been tribal warriors until fairly recent times.

The marriage of Vissarion and Ekaterina was marked by a great deal of wife-beating and child-beating, poverty, drunkenness, and squalor. Stalin's official remembrances report that his father was a brutal drunk who beat him hard and often, but that his mother was gentle, kindly, and protective. People who knew the family, however, report that both parents used to beat Stalin. His father was a chronic alcoholic and bully, and his mother was embarrassed by his physical appearance. Small and ungainly — his maximum height was to be five-feet-four — young Stalin appears to have been born with two toes of his left foot stuck together. Since poor children like Stalin often played barefoot in the summer, this must have marked him as a bit of a freak. His face was pitted with smallpox scars, and his left elbow was permanently stiffened by un-treated blood poisoning during his traumatic childhood. By the age of nine, young Dzugashvili's fear of his violent father was tempered with a good deal of contempt. He began to defend himself from his father's beatings by pulling a knife on him when Vissarion got out of line. This may or may not have convinced Vissarion to take his drunken brutality elsewhere, and may have led to his downfall. Somebody else pulled a knife on Vissarion Dzugashvili and Stalin lost his father at the age of nine to a stab wound inflicted in a drunken knife fight. His wife and only son didn't miss him.

Ekaterina seems to have destined her son for the Russian Orthodox priesthood because she didn't think he was much good for anything else. Even good Christians — and Ekaterina was a life-long believer — regarded the priesthood as a safe meal ticket. Orthodox priests who didn't aspire to become bishops were free to marry, and seminaries provided poor boys with a free education. Stalin became a seminarian in Tiflis. The other boys there bullied him, but he developed a toughness of spirit that caused some of them to admire him. During schoolyard games, he once jumped on another boy's back and rode around the courtyard shouting "*Ya stal! Ya stal!*" (I am steel! I am steel!). This was to be his future name: Stalin, man of steel. While he was at the seminary, however, he adopted the first of his assumed names. He called himself Koba, after the hero of his favorite novel, a romantic tale of blood-and-thunder banditry in which Georgian heroes battle the Russian oppressors. The name of his favorite novel was *The Parricide*, meaning "the man who kills his father."

Dzugashvili — or Koba, as he was now known to his friends at the seminary — had no reason to doubt the traditional beliefs of the Russian Orthodox Church for the first few years of his religious education. At one point, he and some of his friends witnessed a multiple hanging, in which some local bandits joked with the spectators before being strung up and left to dangle as an object lesson. The boy seminarians got into a discussion about whether the hanged bandits would have to suffer in the next world. Young Koba stoutly maintained that their deaths had expiated their sins and that they would enter paradise. At this point in his life, the church may have been a welcome substitute for a normal home life. Corporal punishment was never used at the Tiflis seminary, though the teachers sometimes spied on the students and pored over their belongings looking for subversive literature. Compared to his childhood, the seminary was a rest home. Some of his classmates even remember Koba as being devout.

Unfortunately, one piece of subversive literature that got past the priests was to have a powerful impact on the teenaged Koba. The pamphlet, printed by the Social Revolutionaries, attacked the Russian Orthodox Church as smug and corrupt and mentioned Darwin's theory of evolution by natural selection to "prove" that man was a mere animal and not a being created by God. The Darwinian view of life as brutal and savage struck a responsive chord in Koba. It was his childhood writ large over the world of nature. He became an avid Darwinian, abandoned the faith in God, and began to tell his fellow seminarians that people were descended from apes and not from Adam.

Koba concealed his loss of faith from the priests, if not from his classmates, but he never became a priest himself. He left the seminary before graduating to become a more or less full-time revolutionary. From Darwin he found his way to Marx and then to Lenin and other enemies of the tsarist government.

Koba was a much cruder article than Lenin. He was at home among thugs and street people rather than intellectuals who were themselves of bourgeois or even of aristocratic origins. Lenin supposedly elevated Koba to the upper levels of revolutionary activities because so many of the people around Lenin were gentry. The revolutionaries needed at least one man of peasant or worker origins to make a show of being men of the people. Koba, seminary background aside, was squalid enough for anybody's taste. The story of how he clawed his way to power, eventually succeeding Lenin and perhaps contributing to his death after a series of paralytic strokes, would take a book in itself. And the list of atrocities that he, redubbed as Stalin, was to commit as head of the Union of Soviet Socialist Republics would fill a number of books. His brutal childhood and the worldview he acquired in that childhood, reinforced by reading Darwin, convinced him that mercy and forebearance were weak and stupid. He killed with a coldness that even Hitler might have envied — and in even greater numbers than Hitler did.

I once interviewed the Russian dissident Alexander Ginsburg, who had recently been "exiled" to the United States after many years in Soviet prisons and labor camps. Ginsburg was speaking, through an interpreter, at an Amnesty International meeting. Most of the people in the audience were people I knew by sight from local political and social activities, and they were mostly humanists or members of ultraliberal congregations. They were rather surprised to find out that Ginsburg was an Orthodox Christian. Some of them had thought he was a Jewish dissident. In fact, Ginsburg had adopted the name from his mother's side of the family to protest Soviet anti-Semitism. The humanists and liberals were also surprised to hear Ginsburg's ringing defense of Christianity as the only spiritual force powerful enough to stand up to Soviet intimidation. Alexander Solzhenitsyn, once the hero of the American liberal press, had sparked a wave of liberal horror a few months before when he said essentially the same thing. Christianity was a message that a great many of those humanists weren't ready for, or interested in.

For two hours, these well-meaning people, most of whom had never been before a judge for anything more serious than a traffic ticket, tried to convince a man who had spent half his life in dungeons or doing hard labor that he didn't know what he was talking about when he said Christianity was necessary for the survival of human dignity and freedom. Ginsburg, on the other hand, was appalled by the naiveté of his audience. Someone had given him access to a bowl of sangria, which he thought was fruit punch, and he needed most of it to get through the question-and-answer period without blowing his stack. I'll never forget the expression on his face when some earnest woman asked him why "education" hadn't improved the lot of the Russian people by eliminating superstition and prejudice. It was a pat question, stuck in, obviously, to tout her own very important role as an educator. Ginsburg all but lost control. A look of terror mixed with utter contempt flashed across his face—"My God! Are these people really this naive?"—and he threw back an answer in a voice that was almost a shriek.

"Education, of the kind you mean, is not possible in the Soviet Union! You are speaking of a government which, since the revolution, has murdered sixty million of its own citizens! The country is only now returning to a semblance of being alive!"

She obviously couldn't understand what he was trying to say.

Ginsburg had been a journalist for the few adult years he hadn't spent in prison, and after the meeting we spoke privately about the figure of sixty million dead. This figure, he said, included the dead of the Russian civil war that followed the Russian revolution, of the revolution itself, and of the purges that had begun under Lenin but flared to staggering proportions under Stalin.

The figure of sixty million dead Russians did not include the twenty million dead the Russians lost in World War II. Stalin must bear at least some share of the responsibility for the war. His pact with Hitler led directly to the joint Nazi-Soviet invasion of Poland, which led Britain and France to declare war on Hitler, though not on Stalin. This means that Stalin was responsible for about eighty million violent deaths. In tandem with Hitler, his sometime ally and fellow Darwinian, he can be linked to about one hundred million violent deaths. Secular humanists who liked to cite religious intolerance as the major cause of man's inhumanity to man might want to stop and ponder that figure.

Stalin killed people for two principal reasons: because they were personal threats to him, or because they were threats to progress—which in Marxist-Darwinian terms meant some sort of evolution to an earthly paradise of a type never yet shown to exist. The personal motive explains the murder of most of his old friends and former revolutionary comrades, who were killed, one by one or in small groups because Stalin was afraid they might try to replace him. Another group to suffer was senior military officers. In 1938, Stalin purged the entire staff of the Red army. Three of the top five marshals of the Soviet Union, three of the four full generals, 136 out of 199 divisional commanders and about one lower-grade officer in 4 were shot, with or without trial. The most capable and competent officers were the first to die.

When Nazi Germany attacked the Soviet Union in 1941, the purge-weakened Red army collapsed like a house of cards. The Germans destroyed six thousand tanks in one vast battle. They advanced to the gates of Moscow and Leningrad before mud and snow slowed up their badly supplied armies. But Hitler had paused for a senseless and vicious vendetta of his own against Yugoslavia and Greece that consumed six weeks of the time he could have used for the 1941 invasion of Russia. He could have almost certainly captured both Moscow and Leningrad, and won the war on the Eastern front, if he hadn't indulged his personal penchant for vengeance by rescheduling the attack so he could "punish" the Yugoslavs and Greeks for resisting his friend Mussolini.

The second and largest category of Stalin's victims were those who threatened not him, but the Marxist-Darwinian timetable of social progress. Marx and Lenin had written that agriculture should be run like industry. Stalin ordered vast collective farmers to replace the small individual farms that dotted the Russian countryside. The first wave of collectivization was resisted by peasants who slaughtered their horses and cattle rather than handing them over to city-bred bureaucrats. Five million peasants died, mostly by firing squad. A second wave of collectivization, primarily in the Ukraine, killed another five million peasants, mostly by starvation, in the late 1930s. Hundreds of thousands of other Soviet citizens were deported to do forced labor in Siberia at projects which were deemed necessary for the good of the state. Most of these died also, due to primitive conditions and the brutality of supervisors, who were often paroled criminals. Like Hitler — and like Clarence Darrow — Stalin had a fondness for criminals. They made good administrators in his kind of government.

Some of Stalin's biological categories for extermination make little sense. As late as the 1930s, there survived in the Ukraine about two hundred bardic singers. These elderly men, many of them blind, were balladeers who sang traditional songs about warriors and dragons, witches and maidens and goblins. They were the last remnant in Europe of the skalds of Scandanavia, the bards of Anglo-Saxon or Germanic lore, or the ancient minstrels of Ireland. Stalin invited the two hundred old men to a conference on folk arts. Then he had them all murdered.

Other mass executions showed a genuine extension of Darwinism into politics. Reinhard Heydrich, Hitler's delegate to mastermind the final solution to the Jewish problem, had stated clearly that special care must be taken to kill the Jews who didn't die of overwork, because these would be the healthiest and capable of reproducing the strongest descendants. Stalin anticipated the principle that Heydrich articulated. When Hitler and Stalin divided Poland between them in 1939, the Soviets captured fifteen thousand Polish regular and reserve army officers. These officers represented not only the old Polish aristocracy but most of the engineers, attorneys, professors, and school teachers of military age, the people who would be needed to rebuild a strong and modern Poland after the war. The fifteen thousand Polish officers disappeared from history in April 1940, while they were in Soviet custody. Three years later, German army engineers uncovered a mass grave of four thousand corpses in Polish uniforms at the Katyn Forest, near Smolensk in western Russia. The Germans claimed that the Polish officers had been murdered by the Stalinist Russians. For once, they were telling the truth. Stalin had decreed the death of the entire Polish intelligentsia to prevent the resurgence of Poland as an independent nation.

Brutality like this, particularly in the Ukraine and in the Caucasus, temporarily backfired. German invaders arrived at Ukrainian and Caucasian villages to find the peasants and townspeople cheering them as liberators, offering bread and salt as the traditional gifts to a conqueror, and volunteering to serve as soldiers or informers for the Germans against the Soviets. After the massacres of collectivization through the late 1920s and all of the 1930s, a huge number of Soviet citizens concluded that Hitler couldn't possibly be as bad as Stalin. The roundup and massacre of Jewish civilians conducted by special units of the Nazi S.S. shortly thereafter convinced some Russians to change their minds. But in the Ukraine — which unfortunately had a long tradition of anti-Semitism far older than Hitler's neo-Darwinian variety of racism — even massacres of Jews couldn't dissuade Ukrainians who had seen their relatives and neighbors starve in Stalin's planned famine from preferring the Nazis. When the hard-pressed Nazis offered to accept fifteen thousand Ukrainians in a combat division of the Waffen-S.S., they were swamped with forty-five thousand volunteers. Some of the Ukrainians, once they had weapons, refused to accept orders from the Germans. They fought anyone who wasn't Ukrainian: Soviets, Germans, and hapless Jews. Stalin's insanity had bred a counterinsanity which combined desperate patriotism with a blind passion against the guilty and the innocent alike. In isolated areas of the Ukraine, anti-Stalinist partisans were still attacking Soviet forces years after World War II had ended everywhere else.

The shadow war in Russia grew out of Stalin's Marxist Darwinism and out of Hitler's neo-Darwinism. By treating the peasant landowners and the Soviet minorities as so many beasts for the slaughter, Stalin provided Hitler with millions of willing or more-or-less willing collaborators. By treating the Russian and Soviet minority defectors as subhumans to be subjugated by Aryans, Hitler prevented his generals from making the best possible use of the Russian defectors. Many Russians would have served the Germans willingly on the promise of an independent Russia without Stalin and the Stalinists. Instead they sat on the sidelines or returned to the Marxist fold when they realized that the best the Russian people could expect from Hitler's neo-Darwinian racists was a postwar return to serfdom. Incredibly enough, some of the Soviet minorities hated Stalin so much that even serfdom under Germans seemed a blessed relief. Many German divisions had special assault battalions made up of Russian defectors. Alexander Solzhenitsyn, an artillery officer in the Soviet Red army, said that the Red army men all knew they were facing fellow Russians who fought as ferociously as any Waffen-S.S. fanatic.

Needless to say, the Russians in German uniform were shot on sight if they fell back into Soviet hands. At the end of the war, many of them had escaped to Western Europe. Stalin engineered a deal with the western Allies to return all Soviet prisoners. Some of the Russians in German uniform committed suicide when they heard where they were going. Others were numbly resigned to their fate. In many cases, the Stalinists showed their contempt for the British authorities who were handing back the Russian prisoners for "re-education" by executing them within earshot of the British officers, who were supposed to think that the defectors would get a fair trial.

While disposing of the Russians who had fought for the Germans, Stalin also disposed of the Russians who hadn't fought for the Germans. Some Russians had elected to refuse service with the Nazis. Others had simply been rounded up as slaves and sent west to toil on farms and factories for German overseers. These hapless returnees, several million of them, were also executed or sent to hard labor in Siberia, a death sentence in slow motion. Their only crime was to have seen that Western nations had a higher standard of living than the Soviet Union.

Toward the end of Stalin's reign of terror, he fixed on a new target: Jewish doctors. He somehow conceived the fantasy that various important Soviets had been murdered by Jewish doctors. It's not impossible that he ordered their deaths himself and then lost count. When Stalin died, the usual propaganda preparations were being made for a campaign against Jews which would certainly have been worse than anything seen under the tsars. No one can be sure that he wasn't murdered by his own leery underlings. No one could have deserved it more.

During his lifetime, Stalin had convinced many Western observers that he was a basically normal man, perhaps a little rough due to his circumstances, but not really all that bad. Prominent atheists and leftists from England were particularly susceptible to the idea that the man Franklin D. Roosevelt called "Uncle Joe Stalin" was a progressive democratic leader. "I have never met a man more candid, fair, and honest,"[5] H. G. Wells wrote in 1934, after Stalin's peacetime collectivization had already killed several million people. A few years later, George Bernard Shaw, another English critic of Christianity, met Stalin and described him as "charmingly good-humored — no malice in him. . . . You have only to meet the Russian bogeys face to face to find out they are harmless and beneficient spirits."[6]

Once Stalin's death and the quick removal of some of his toadies by vengeful or frightened Soviets made free speech slightly more safe, a different picture began to emerge. Stalin portrayed himself as devoted to his mother. In private he referred to her as "that old whore." His first wife had died while he was a fugitive from the tsarist police, leaving him a son named Jacob. Stalin treated Jacob so badly that Jacob tried to shoot himself. He later recovered. Stalin's second wife, who disagreed with some of his mass-murder policies, fled a party after he gave her a vicious tongue-lashing in front of the guests. The next day she was found dead with a bullet through her heart. No one to this day knows whether she killed herself or whether she was killed by his orders. During World War II, the hapless Jacob Stalin was captured by the Germans. He was kept in a special prison. Hitler offered to exchange Jacob for Field Marshal Friedrich von Paulus, who had surrendered the Nazi Sixth Army at Stalingrad against Hitler's orders. Stalin refused to trade. At this point, according to some sources, Hitler offered to trade Jacob for one of his own distant relatives, an enlisted man of no great importance who was related to Geli Raubal. Still no deal. Stalin didn't think his own son was worth a single German enlisted man. When Jacob learned of his father's decision, he committed suicide.

Stalin's daughter Svetlana had been spared the worst of his sarcasm during her childhood, but when she fell in love with a Jewish filmmaker, Stalin slapped her around and virtually disowned her. He later approved her marriage with a shrug and a few coarse epithets. She left for exile in the West. His savage treatment of his own family was only a miniature reflection of the way he treated the entire world—with complete distrust and complete indifference to life and death.

Stalin's contributions to science have been largely overlooked by students of his mass murders. But he made use of two scientists whose frame of reference matched his worldview. It had been through Darwin's writings that Stalin first deviated from Christianity to atheism. Now, as ruler of the Soviet Union, Stalin was to out-Darwin Darwin by subsidizing a revival of the popularity of Darwin's predecessor, Jean Baptiste Lamarck. The archmaterialist Lamarck had proposed a theory of evolution in 1800, before Darwin was born, as an antidote to belief in God. Lamarck's theory tried to explain the fact that life has developed from lower to higher forms by the ability to pass on acquired traits. There was no evidence in favor of this theory in Lamarck's time or at any time afterward. He devised it because he needed it as a weapon against religion. But in Stalin's time, an ambitious biologist named Trofim Lysenko tried to supply new evidence for Lamarck. He faked the results of experiments to show that acquired traits could be passed on by heredity. Stalin and the Stalinists seized on this. The inheritance of acquired traits fit into Marx's picture of the benign but godless providence which would produce the "worker's paradise." Lysenko was not only honored as a great scientist, but given a virtual license to persecute other biologists who didn't agree with him. Strange and disastrous things happened when the Soviets tried to develop new and more productive strains of wheat and other crops based on Lamarck's theories. But of course that didn't make the theories wrong. The theories had to be right—because Stalin said so.

The second Stalinist contribution to science was the revival of spontaneous generation in a new form called abiogenesis. Stalin undoubtedly remembered that the Bible described God as creating heaven and earth. Since he had rejected God, he had to explain how life came to exist without God's help. He found his answer in the work of a Russian scientist named Alexander Oparin. Oparin invented a highly refined version of abiogenesis. He asserted that life simply arose by accident from primary inorganic chemicals in prehistoric seas which began to duplicate themselves and grew ever more complex. He never explained why the same chemicals could not or would not duplicate the fact in a laboratory. Perhaps they were shy.

Oparin's "discovery" made him a hero of Soviet science. His idea today has been borrowed by Carl Sagan, among others, to explain how life arose on earth. The fact that it works without God makes it so attractive that many scientists are willing to overlook the fact that it is in fact entirely untenable.

After sixty million murders it seems rather strange to talk about the arts. But it's obvious that, among other things, Stalin aborted the development of Russian literature. The later nineteenth century had produced Leo Tolstoi and Feodor Dostoevski, two of the giants of world literature and two men of powerful Christian spirituality as well as of enormous literary talent. The era of Lenin and Stalin split Russian literature into two politically oriented categories: propaganda and protest. Stalinist propaganda is so craven and so obviously motivated by stark terror that it can only be read with a sort of cruel amusement today. The poets of protest can be seen, however, as an affirmation that Stalin would never have learned from reading Darwin and Huxley. Man is not a brute. A spirit within man exists which — at least in the best and strongest souls — can't be crushed even by sixty million murders. Huxley's epiphenomenalism can't explain men like Alexander Ginsburg and Alexander Solzhenitsyn. To understand them, one must understand Christianity not as a sterile doctrine but as a spiritual reality.

Camus and Sartre

Unfortunately, the impact of scientific atheism with a pro-Communist bias wasn't limited to the hapless Soviet Union. No one who attended college in the United States in the 1950s and 1960s could escape the influence of Jean Paul Sartre and Albert Camus, two French atheists who wielded a tremendous influence over American intellectuals in the mid-twentieth century. Campuses were rife with existentialism, the belief that it was necessary to make choices and to give life a meaning based on one's own decisions. This doesn't seem like a very original idea. But the 1950s and 1960s saw a vast number of Americans entering colleges and universities as the first members of their families ever to go beyond high school. Ideas had a certain power to intoxicate when they were treated as original by professors who should have known better. The idea that man is free to "wing it" and make his own rules in the absence of God or Scriptural laws had been around for hundreds of years. Dostoevski, a Christian, expressed it as a genuine danger in The Brothers Karamazov a century before Sartre and Camus were the rage on campus. Dostoevski also warned that any social system which tried to create a paradise on earth that wasn't based on Christian principles and ethics would create a catastrophe instead. It's rather a pity that college students read so much Camus and Sartre and so little Dostoevski.

The tremendous vogue of the two French existentialists introduced a whole new generation to atheism as a personal philosophy. Sartre and Camus were not scientists and added only rhyme, not reason, to the atheist litany of antireligious dogma. They accepted the nonexistence of God and of the immortal soul as dogma handed down from previous generations — or perhaps simply decided that they didn't believe in God because they didn't feel like it. It's interesting to note that Jean Paul Sartre and Albert Camus both lost their fathers when they were two years old. Like Nietzsche, the first continental philosopher to be an atheist, they grew up without male parenting. Their works also contain frequent references to digestive problems: the psychosomatic footprints of the atheist syndrome. Sartre's first novel, in fact, was called *Nausea*. Camus's most famous novel, *LÉtranger* (the Stranger) describes the misadventures of a man who is incapable of feeling grief or love, or of taking any control of his own destiny. These incapacities are among the most common symptoms of chronic clinical depression. It's rather amazing, considering the penchant that college sophomores have for psychologizing everybody half to death, that nobody ever put two and two together and realized that the absence of fathers, the stomach problems, and the *anomie* — as the atmosphere of futility and despair Camus and Sartre conjured up came to be called — were causes and symptoms rather than intellectual choices.

The liberal churches didn't seem to understand it either. In a frantic effort to stay current and fashionable, some ultraliberal theologians backed so far away from Christian tradition and belief in the reality of God, Jesus, and the supernatural that they became little more than atheists themselves. Finally, at the height of the campus craze for Camus and Sartre, somebody gave the deed a name and proclaimed, speaking as a theologian and not a scientist, "God is dead."

It has been argued that this callow blasphemy was uttered to try to force people out of smug conventional religion and to challenge them to Christian social commitment. The challenge backfired. Young people with spiritual interests and social concerns heard the Nietzschean quote coming from "Christian" theologians and decided that liberal Christianity no longer believed in itself or had anything left to offer believers. The brief heyday of the God-is-dead theologians was the middle of the 1960s. By the end of the 1960s, hundreds of thousands of the brightest and most spiritually aware young people from liberal Christian backgrounds were streaming into Buddhist, Hindu, and Islamic-based movements or into spiritualism, occultism, and belief systems inspired by American Indian religions. By the 1970s, a few began to return to Christianity through the "Jesus movement" which skipped over the endless wordgames of traditional theology in favor of immediate spiritual experiences, spiritual experiences which were very real to the people who had them, but were certainly not what the God-is-dead theologians had expected to generate.

Marxism is not dead either. Eventually Camus had the courage to be a consistent atheist and admitted that the "worker's paradise" was probably in the same league as the Easter Bunny and the Tooth Fairy in terms of plausibility. Sartre never forgave him for this deviation from Marxist orthodoxy. Jean Paul remained a Stalinist for most of his literary career, which lasted a lot longer in democratic France than it would have in the Stalinist Soviet Union he professed to admire. Even the small deviations from the party line that Sartre allowed himself would have had lethal consequences under the government he most admired. The kind of "free will" that Sartre and Camus urged their readers to follow in making their own rebellion and their own values was, of course, totally inconsistent with mechanistic atheism. And only the Judeo-Christian-based democratic society Sartre despised allows that kind of public inconsistency to escape terminal punctuation—with a bullet.

T E N

FREEING THE FUTURE

W hen the smoke cleared after World War II and the dead were buried, it became clear to most thinking people that scientific atheism had failed in its major premise: that the elimination of religious beliefs would enable people to live together in peace and harmony. World War II was definitely not a religious war—unless one considers the clash between Nazi-style neo-Darwinism and Soviet-style Marxist-Darwinism to be a battle between two distinct religious sects. Nor could it be said that Christianity provided much motivation for the belligerence of the western Allies. They fought Hitler because they had no choice.

Hitler and Stalin between them murdered more innocent victims than had died in all the religious wars in mankind's history. They murdered these victims not with the misguided intentions of saving their souls or punishing their sins, but because they were competitors for food and obstacles to "evolutionary progress." Many humanitarians, Christian, Jewish, or agnostic, have understood the relationship between Nietzsche's ideas and Hitler's mass murder teams and crematoria. Few have traced the linkage back one step further to Darwin, the "scientist" who directly inspired Nietzsche's superman theory and the Nazi corollary that some people were subhuman. The evidence was all there—the term neo-Darwinism was openly used to describe Nazi racial theories. The expression "natural selection," as applied to human beings, turns up at the Wannsee Conference in the prime document of the Holocaust. Perhaps Darwin escaped blame because he was English, while Nietzsche, though he expressed his dislike for "Teutons and other buffalos" more than once, was born in Germany. But Houston Stewart Chamberlain and Count Arthur de Gobineau are often cited as proto-Nazi philosophers, and they were not Germans.

We can see the events of Hitler's Germany and of Stalin's Russia as a meaningless collection of atrocities which took place because Germans and Russians are terrible people, not like us at all. Or we can realize that imposing the life-is-pathology theories of Huxley and Darwin, of clinical depression masquerading as science, played a critical role in the age of atrocities. And we can take warning. People have to learn to stop thinking of other people as machines and learn to think of them as men and women possessed of souls. The truth seems to be, in fact, that the human soul really is more powerful than electrochemical functions of the brain. If we think of ourselves as a little lower than the angels (Psalm 8), we may become better than we ever dreamed possible. And if we think of ourselves as brutes, we have the capacity to become worse than any animal. That was the real lesson of Hitler and Stalin.

Starting in the middle of the nineteenth century, a handful of influential scientists claimed to have discovered facts that made God and the immortal soul "unscientific." They did not, in fact, discover all these ideas. They invented many of them, because they had a strong negative bias toward any concept of God or of human spirituality.

We can understand the atheist syndrome as hostility toward hard fathers and a brutal pattern of childhood that turned into hostility toward God and toward belief in immortality. We can then understand why they made these glaring mistakes: why Darwin ignored human intuition and animal instinct to make living creatures more mechanistic than they were and are, and why he seriously miscalculated the timetable of evolution to allow the development of species to take place by blind chance; why Huxley invented a theory of consciousness so obviously inadequate to deal with observed facts even in his own era; why all of them, and Freud especially, refused to consider spiritual phenomena as factual despite a large amount of available data; and why nonscientists like Nietzsche, Ingersoll, and Darrow, to list only a few, were to seize so eagerly on the antireligious opinions of Darwin and Huxley and to try to turn the subjective bias, caused by chronic clinical depression and accompanied by serious psychosomatic illness, into a philosophy for a new age.

Scientific atheism is by no means scientific. Where their research infringed on the realm of the human soul or spirit, or for that matter on the whole realm of philosophy or theology, Darwin and Huxley and Freud were mad scientists, just as Nietzsche was a mad philosopher. They projected their biases into their work so intensely that the work itself was contaminated.

The nineteenth-century's hidebound conviction that spontaneous generation must take place slowed the development of antiseptic surgery. The psychologists and psychiatrists and medical professions who cling to Huxley's materialism in explaining the function of the mind and the relation of the mind and the body may well be thwarting new discoveries in psychology and in the healing arts as a whole.

The political impact of scientific atheism is perhaps still more obvious. Its chief exponents were Hitler and Stalin. History has judged the results. We should rise up individually and collectively and tear the laurels from the shrines of the men who tried to "kill" God because they hated and feared their fathers. History doesn't need another one hundred million deaths to prove that scientific atheism is a form of mental illness. Scientific atheism is an idea whose time has gone. Once its dead hand is pried away from science, from politics, and from humanity, we can all become more free, more happy, and more authentically human.

And the grace of God can have its reign in our culture once again.

END NOTES

CHAPTER 2: THE ROOTS OF A MADNESS

1. Herodotus, *The Persian Wars*.
2. *League of the Iroquois* by Morgan, among many other books, mentions this.

CHAPTER 3: CHARLES DARWIN: HIS ORIGIN AND DESCENT

1. Charles Darwin, *The Autobiography of Charles Darwin 1809-1882* (New York, Harcourt Brace and Company, 1958), pp. 223-224.
2. Ibid., p. 224.
3. Ibid., pp. 33-34.
4. Ibid., p. 22.
5. Ibid., p. 241.
6. Ibid., p. 24.
7. Ibid., p. 242.
8. Ibid., p. 242.
9. Ibid., p. 242.
10. Ibid., p. 44.
11. Ibid., p. 48.
12. Ibid., p. 57.
13. Ibid., p. 63.
14. Ibid., pp. 64-65.
15. Christopher Rallings, ed., *The Voyage of Charles Darwin* (New York: Mayflower Books, 1979), p. 155.
16. Robert Jastrow, *God and the Astronomers* (New York: W. W. Norton, 1978), p. 116.
17. D. I. Winner, M.D., *Louis Pasteur and Microbiology* (London: Wayland, 1974), p. 24.
18. Sir William Thomson, later Lord Kelvin, advanced the idea of an inadequate amount of time to explain evolution by natural selection while Darwin was still active, in 1869. But the Darwinians refused to take his argument seriously.
19. Charles Darwin, *Origin of Species* (Encyclopedia Britannica Great Books Edition), p. 119. (Note: So many editions of *Origin of Species* have been published that I chose the Encyclopedia Britannica Great Books edition so that anyone who wishes to verify my quotes may have ready access to a commonly available version.)
20. Charles Darwin, *The Voyage of the Beagle* (New York: Harper & Row, 1959), p. 141. (Notes by Millicent Selsam. Ms. Selsam is a Darwin admirer, but her notes

in this edition are important to the understanding of Darwin's mistakes and misunderstandings in evaluating "primitive" man.)

21. Charles Darwin, *Origin of Species*, (Encyclopedia Britannica Great Books Edition), p. 134.
22. Darwin, *Autobiography*, p. 138.
23. Ibid., p. 139.
24. Charles Darwin, *The Descent of Man* (Encyclopedia Britannica Great Books Edition), p. 597. (Note: As with *Origin of Species*, this edition, originally published in 1871, is available in the same volume and was chosen for convenience of reference.)
25. Charles Darwin, *Autobiography*, p. 236 (notes).
26. Charles Darwin, *The Descent of Man*, p. 597.
27. Ibid., p. 597.
28. Charles Darwin, *Autobiography*, pp. 85-96.
29. Ibid., pp. 85-96.
30. Ibid., pp. 85-96.
31. Ibid., pp. 85-96.

CHAPTER 4: THOMAS HENRY HUXLEY: THE FIRST AGNOSTIC

1. Ronald W. Clark, *The Huxleys*, (London/New York: McGraw-Hill, 1968), pp. 8-9.
2. Ibid., pp. 9-10.
3. Houston Peterson, *Huxley: Prophet of Science* (London: Longmans, Green and Co., 1932), pp. 7-8.
4. Clark, *Huxleys*.
5. Clark, *Huxleys*.
6. Clark, *Huxleys*, pp. 10-11.
7. Ibid., p. 12.
8. Ibid., p. 42.
9. Ibid., p. 58.
10. Ibid., p. 59.
11. Peterson, *Huxley: Prophet of Science*, p. 199 (notes).
12. Ibid., p. 199.
13. Ibid., p. 159.
14. Ibid., pp. 192-193.

CHAPTER 5: FRIEDRICH NIETZSCHE: SUPERMAN AND SYPHILITIC

1. Friedrich Nietzsche, *Thus Spake Zarathustra*, trans. Thomas Common (New York: Modern Library, 1950), p. 6.
2. Ibid., pp. 68-70.
3. Friedrich Nietzsche, *The Philosophy of Nietzsche* (New York: Modern Library Giant, 1927, 1954), p. x.
4. Nietzsche, *Thus Spake Zarathustra*, pp. xix-xx.
5. In German *begeisten* has the same semantic impact.
6. H. F. Peters, *Zarathustra's Sister: The Case of Elisabeth and Friedrich Nietzsche* (New York: Crown Publishers, 1977), p. 5.
7. Freud, among others, understood this etiology in a general way, though characteristically he never applied it to himself.

8. Friedrich Nietzsche and Richard Wagner, *The Nietzsche-Wagner Correspondence*, ed. by Elisabeth Förster-Nietzsche, introduction by H. L. Mencken, trans. by Caroline V. Kerr (New York: Liveright, 1921), p. 309.

9. Ibid., p. 66.

10. Ibid., p. xii.

11. Peters, *Zarathustra's Sister*, p. 49.

12. Mongrel values. *Chandala* is a Sanskrit word which refers to children born of breeding between castes or from incest. Nietzsche here uses it to refer to early Christians.

13. Mongrel values.

14. Friedrich Nietzsche, *The Twilight of the Idols* in *The Portable Nietzsche*, trans. by Walter Kaufmann (New York: Viking Press, 1954), pp. 504-505. (Once again, this particular edition was chosen because it was readily available to anyone who wishes to verify the quotes in context.)

15. Nietzsche, *The Antichrist* in *The Portable Nietzsche* (New York: Viking Press, 1954), p. 593.

16. Ibid., p. 625.

17. Ibid.

18. Friedrich Nietzsche, *Ecce Homo* in *The Philosophy of Nietzsche* (New York: Modern Library Giant, 1927, 1954), p. 814.

19. Nietzsche, *Nietzsche Contra Wagner* in *The Portable Nietzsche* (New York: Viking Press, 1954), p. 676.

CHAPTER 6: SIGMUND FREUD: PSYCHOPATHOLOGY IN EVERYDAY LIFE

1. Ernest Jones, *The Life and Work of Sigmund Freud* (New York: Basic Books, 1961), p. 17. (Note: The one-volume edition has been selected because it is more generally available to students and laymen than the three-volume original.)

2. Ibid., p. 19.

3. Schuyler Grant—personal letter to the author.

4. Jeffrey Moussaieff Masson, *The Assault on Truth: Freud's Suppression of the Seduction Theory* (New York: Farrar, Strauss, and Giroux, 1984), p. 64.

5. Jones, *The Life and Work of Sigmund Freud*, p. 204.

6. Jones, *The Life and Work of Sigmund Freud*, p. 206.

7. Ibid., p. 20.

8. Ibid., p. 363.

9. Ibid., p. 363.

10. Ibid., p. 530.

CHAPTER 7: ROBERT INGERSOLL AND CLARENCE DARROW: SCIENTIFIC ATHEISM'S AMERICAN COUSINS

1. Eva Ingersoll Wakefield, *The Life and Letters of Robert Ingersoll* (London: C. A. Watts & Co., 1952), p. 3.

2. Ibid., p. 2.

3. Ibid., p. 7.

4. Ibid., p. 6.

5. Ibid., p. 150.

6. Ibid., pp. 151-152.

7. Ibid., p. 36.

8. Kevin Tierney, *Darrow, a Biography* (New York: Thomas Y. Crowell, Pub., 1979), pp. 287-294.

9. Ibid., p. 328.

10. Clarence Darrow, *Attorney for the Damned*, ed. and with notes by Arthur Weinberg; Foreword by Justice William O. Douglas (New York: Simon & Schuster, 1957), pp. 70-72.

11. Ibid., p. 74.

12. Colin Simpson, *The Lusitania* (Boston: Little, Brown and Company, 1972), pp. 105-106.

13. Lawrence Levine, *Defender of the Faith: William Jennings Bryan, the Last Decade 1915-1925* (New York: Oxford University Press, 1965), p. 357.

14. Clarence Darrow, *The Story of My Life* (New York: Scribner, 1932), p. 36.

15. Tierney, *Darrow*, p. 438.

16. Ibid., p. 438.

17. Levine, *Defender of the Faith*, p. 341.

CHAPTER 8: ADOLF HITLER: NEO-DARWINISM AND GENOCIDE

1. Ernest Jones, *The Life and Work of Sigmund Freud*, (New York: Basic Books, 1961), p. 31.

2. Adolf Hitler, *Mein Kampf*, trans. by Ralph Manheim; original German first edition published in 1925 (Boston: Little, Brown, and Co., 1942), p. 400.

3. Chamberlain, son of a British admiralty and political family, used a certain penchant for scholarship and irresponsible guesswork to "prove" that Jesus' father was a Roman soldier. He based this on a libel circulated by anti-Christians in Roman imperial times. For more details, read *The Bible As History* by Werner Keller.

4. Scenes are reproduced in the "Holocaust" segment of BBC's "World at War" documentary series and in *The Sorrow and the Pity* by Marcel Orphuls.

5. Fredric Werthan, M. D., *A Sign for Cain* (New York: MacMillan, 1966), p. 186.

6. Robert Payne, *The Life and Death of Adolf Hitler* (New York: Praeger Publishers, 1973), p. 466.

7. This figure does not include the victims of mobile extermination teams in 1941-1942. The total figure is estimated at 5.8 million.

8. In *Zarathustra's Sister* by Peters.

CHAPTER 9: SCIENTIFIC ATHEISM FROM MARX TO STALIN

1. Karl Marx and Friedrich Engels, *The Communist Manifesto*, trans. by Samuel Moore; first published in Belgium in 1848 (Chicago: Henry Regnery Company, 1954), pp. 40-41.

2. Ibid., pp. 55-57.

3. Saul K. Padover, "Engels, Friedrich," article in *McGraw-Hill Encyclopedia of World Biography* (New York: McGraw-Hill, 1973), p. 580.

4. Robert Payne, *The Life and Death of Lenin* (New York: Simon & Schuster, 1964), p. 62.

5. Adam B. Ulam, *Stalin: The Man and His Era* (New York: Viking Press, 1973), p. 359.

6. Jules Archer, *Man of Steel: Joseph Stalin* (New York: Julian Messner, 1965), p. 99.

SELECT BIBLIOGRAPHY

CHARLES DARWIN: HIS
ORIGIN AND DESCENT

Bailey, Edward. *Charles Lyle.* New York: Doubleday, 1963.

Brent, Peter. *Charles Darwin: A Man of Enlarged Curiosity.* New York: Harper & Row, 1981.

Darwin, Charles. *The Autobiography of Charles Darwin 1809-1882.* New York: Harcourt Brace, 1958. (With original omissions restored. Edited with appendix and notes by his granddaughter Nora Barlow.)

Darwin, Charles. *The Descent of Man.* Encyclopedia Britannica Great Books Series. (Original published in London, 1871.)

Darwin, Charles. *The Origin of Species.* Encyclopedia Britannica Great Books Series. (Original published in London, 1859.)

Darwin, Charles. *The Voyage of Charles Darwin.* New York: Mayflower Books, 1979. (Autobiographical writings selected and arranged by Christopher Rallings.)

Darwin, Charles. *The Voyage of the* Beagle. New York: Harper & Row, 1959. (Edited and with chapter notes by Millicent E. Selsam.)

De Camp, L. Sprague, and De Camp, Catherine Crook. *Darwin and His Great Discovery.* New York: Macmillan, 1972.

Dubos, René. *Pasteur and Modern Science.* New York: Doubleday Anchor Books, 1960.

Gallant, Roy A. *Charles Darwin: The Making of a Scientist.* New York: Doubleday, 1972.

Gregor, Authur S. *Charles Darwin.* New York: Dutton, 1966.

Jastrow, Robert. *God and the Astronomers.* New York: W. W. Norton, 1978.

Moorehead, Alan. *Darwin and the* Beagle. New York: Harper & Row, 1969.

Winner, D. I. *Louis Pasteur and Microbiology.* London: Wayland, 1974.

THOMAS HENRY HUXLEY:
THE FIRST AGNOSTIC

Bedford, Sybille. *Aldous Huxley: A Biography.* New York: Harper & Row, 1974.

Bibby, Cyril. *Scientist Extraordinary: T. H. Huxley.* New York: Pergamon Press, 1972.

Bibby, Cyril. *T. H. Huxley: Scientist, Humanist and Educator.* New York: Horizon Press, 1960.

Clark, Ronald W. *The Huxleys.* New York: McGraw-Hill, 1968.

Huxley, Thomas Henry. *On a Piece of Chalk.* New York: Scribner, 1967. (Re-issue with an introduction by Loren Eiseley.)

Peterson, Houston. *Huxley: Prophet of Science.* London: Longmans, Green & Co., 1932.

FRIEDRICH NIETZSCHE:
SUPERMAN AND SYPHILITIC

Nietzsche, Friedrich. *The Philosophy of Nietzsche.* New York: The Modern Library, 1927. (Introduction by Willard Huntington Wright.)

Nietzsche, Friedrich. *The Portable Nietzsche.* New York: Viking Press, 1954.

Nietzsche, Friedrich. *Thus Spake Zarathustra.* New York: The Modern Library, 1950. (Translated by Thomas Common.)

Nietzsche, Friedrich & Wagner, Richard. *The Nietzsche-Wagner Correspondence.* New York: Liveright, 1921. (Edited by Elizabeth Förster-

Nietzsche with an introduction by H. L. Mencken, translated by Caroline V. Kerr.)

Peters, H. F. *Zarathustra's Sister: The Case of Elisabeth and Friedrich Nietzsche.* New York: Crown Publishers, 1977.

SIGMUND FREUD: PSYCHOPATHOLOGY IN EVERYDAY LIFE

Fisher, Seymour, and Greenberg, Roger P. *The Scientific Credibility of Freud's Theories and Therapy.* New York: Basic Books, 1977.

Freud, Sigmund. *The Interpretation of Dreams.* New York: Modern Library, 1950. (Translated by A. A. Brill.)

Freud, Sigmund. *Psychopathology in Everyday Life.* New York: Modern Library, 1938. (Translated by A. A. Brill.)

Jones, Ernest. *The Life and Work of Sigmund Freud.* New York: Basic Books, 1961.

Koestler, Arthur. *The Roots of Coincidence: An Excursion into Parapsychology.* New York: Random House, 1972.

Masson, Jeffrey Moussaieff. *The Assault on Truth: Freud's Suppression of the Seduction Theory.* New York: Farrar, Strauss and Giroux, 1984.

Masson, Jeffrey Moussaieff. *The Complete Letters of Sigmund Freud to Wilhelm Fliess, 1887-1904.* New York: Harvard University Press, 1985.

ROBERT INGERSOLL AND CLARENCE DARROW: SCIENTIFIC ATHEISM'S AMERICAN COUSINS

Bailey, Thomas A., and Ryan, Paul B. *The* Lusitania *Disaster.* New York: The Free Press, 1975.

Coletta, Paolo E. *William Jennings Bryan, 1909-1915.* Omaha: The University of Nebraska Press, 1969.

Darrow, Clarence. *Attorney for the Damned.* New York: Simon & Schuster, 1957.

Darrow, Clarence. *The Story of My Life.* New York: Scribner, 1932.

Levine, Lawrence. *Defender of the Faith: William Jennings Bryan, the Last Decade: 1915-1925.* New York: Oxford University Press, 1965.

Simpson, Colin. *The* Lusitania. Boston: Little, Brown, and Co., 1972.

Tierney, Kevin. *Darrow: A Biography.* New York: Thomas Y. Crowell, 1979.

Wakefield, Eva Ingersoll. *The Life and Letters of Robert G. Ingersoll.* London: C. A. Watts & Co., 1952.

Wilson, Charles Morrow. *The Commoner: William Jennings Bryan.* Garden City, NY: Doubleday, 1970.

ADOLF HITLER:
NEO-DARWINISM AND GENOCIDE

Crankshaw, Edward. *Bismarck.* New York: Viking Press, 1981.

Dimont, Max I. *Jews, God, and History.* New York: Simon & Schuster, 1962.

Harding, James. *The Astonishing Adventures of General Boulanger.* New York: Scribner, 1971.

Heston, Leonard L., M.D., and Heston, Renate, R.N. *The Medical Casebook of Adolf Hitler.* New York: Stein & Day, 1979.

Hitler, Adolf. *Mein Kampf.* Boston: Houghton Mifflin Company, 1942. (Translated by Ralph Manheim: German-language original published in 1925.)

Jones, Ernest. *The Life and Work of Sigmund Freud.* New York: Basic Books, 1961.

Keller, Werner. *The Bible as History.* New York: William Morrow, 1956. (Translated by William Neil.)

Payne, Robert. *The Life and Death of Adolf Hitler.* New York: Praeger Publishers, 1973.

Pool, James, and Pool, Suzanne. *Who Financed Hitler: The Secret Funding of Hitler's Rise to Power, 1919-1933.* New York: Dial Press, 1978.

Shirer, William L. *The Rise and Fall of the Third Reich.* New York: Simon & Schuster, 1960.

Stern, Fritz. *Gold and Iron: Bismarck, Bleichroder and the Building of the German Empire*. New York: Random House, 1977.

Waite, Robert G. L. *The Psychopathic God: Adolf Hitler*. New York: Basic Books, 1977.

Wertham, Fredric. *A Sign for Cain*. New York: Macmillan, 1966.

SCIENTIFIC ATHEISM FROM MARX TO STALIN

Archer, Jules. *Man of Steel: Joseph Stalin*. New York: Julian Messner, 1965.

De Jonge, Alex. *Stalin and the Shaping of the Soviet Union*. New York: William Morrow, 1986.

Horne, Alistair. *The Fall of Paris: The Siege and the Commune, 1870-71*. New York: St. Martin's Press, 1965.

Levine, I. E. *Lenin: The Man Who Made a Revolution*. New York: Simon & Schuster, 1969.

Marx, Karl and Engels, Friedrich. *The Communist Manifesto*. Chicago: Henry Regnery Company, 1954. (Translated by Samuel Moore.)

McLellan, David. *Karl Marx: His Life and Thought*. New York: Harper & Row, 1973.

Tolstoy, Nikolai. *The Secret Betrayal, 1944-1947*. New York: Scribner, 1977.

Ulam, Adam B. *Stalin: The Man and His Era*. New York: Viking Press, 1973.

ABOUT THE AUTHOR

John Koster is the author of five non-fiction books and more than one hundred articles in such magazines as *American Heritage, Oceans,* and *Civil War Times Illustrated.* He is a contributing editor to *World Book Encyclopedia* in Chicago and *Tree of Knowledge* in Britain.

A journalist for almost twenty years, he has been a reporter on daily newspapers and the editor or publisher of several suburban weekly newspapers. His news articles and features have been syndicated by AP, UPI, and NANA. Koster is the winner of the 1974 New Jersey SDX Award for Highway Safety reporting and has been nominated for the NJPA Award, the Ernie Pyle Award, and the National Historical Society Writer's Award.

He reads seven languages, including French, German, and Biblical Greek.

Koster lives with his wife and two children in Glen Rock, New Jersey, where he is Disaster Control Communications Coordinator and a relief Sunday school teacher at the Glen Rock Community Church, an affiliate of the Reformed Church in America.

COLOPHON

The typeface for the text of this book is *Goudy Old Style*. It's creator, Frederic W. Goudy, was commissioned by American Type Founders Company to design a new Roman type face. Completed in 1915 and named Goudy Old Style, it was an instant bestseller. However, its designer had sold the design outright to the foundry, so when it became evident that additional versions would be needed to complete the family, the work was done by the foundry's own designer, Morris Benton. From the original design came seven additional weights and variants, all of which sold in great quantity. However, Goudy himself received no additional compensation for them. He later recounted a visit to the foundry with a group of printers, during which the guide stopped at one of the busy casting machines and stated, "Here's where Goudy goes down to posterity, while American Type Founders Company goes down to prosperity."

Substantive Editing by George Grant

Copy Editing by Alice Ewing

Cover design by Kent Puckett Associates, Atlanta, Georgia

Page composition was done using Xerox Ventura Publisher

Pages were output on a Printware 720 IQ laser printer

Printed and bound by Maple-Vail Book Manufacturing Group, Manchester, Pennsylvania

Cover printing by Weber Graphics, Chicago, Illinois